AF600675

RECEIVING THE BIBLE IN FAITH

RECEIVING THE BIBLE IN FAITH

HISTORICAL AND THEOLOGICAL EXEGESIS

DAVID M. WILLIAMS

THE CATHOLIC UNIVERSITY
OF AMERICA PRESS
WASHINGTON, D.C.

The paper used in this publication meets the minimum requirements of American National Standards for Information Science—Permanence of Paper for Printed Library materials, ANSI Z39.48-1984.

∞

LIBRARY OF CONGRESS CATALOGING-IN-PUBLICATION DATA
Williams, David M., 1966–
Receiving the Bible in faith : historical and theological exegesis / David M. Williams.
p. cm.
Includes bibliographical references and index.
ISBN 0-8132-1375-4 (cloth : alk. paper)
ISBN-13: 978-0-8132-1375-0 (cloth: alk. paper)
1. Bible—Criticism, interpretation, etc.—History. 2. Biblical scholars. 3. Bible. N.T.—Relation to the Old Testament. I. Title.
BS500.W548 2004
220.6′01—dc22
2003016054

To my teachers both inside and outside the classroom:

Those who are wise shall shine like the brightness of the sky, and those who lead many to righteousness, like the stars forever and ever.

—Daniel 12:3

CONTENTS

ACKNOWLEDGMENTS

"No man is an island," we read, and the proverb is equally true of books. Though the words as well as any flaws and oversights are my own, thanks are due to all those whose help has made this volume possible. The text began as a Boston College doctoral thesis, partially funded by a grant from Boston College's Institute of Medieval Philosophy and Theology, and written for Fr. Matthew Lamb and Prof. Pheme Perkins, together with Fr. Brian Daley SJ. Without their teaching and encouragement it would never have been finished, much less revised and submitted to the press. Throughout the process, Michael Gorman contributed his practical advice and critical insight. As the manuscript was being revised, the editors of *Fides Quaerens Intellectum* accepted a version of the fourth chapter as an article ("After the Hermeneutic Circle: The later Segundo and the Bible," *Fides Quaerens Intellectum* 2 [2002]: 91–112) and so gave me additional reason to forge ahead. From our first contact, David McGonagle, Gregory LaNave, and Susan Needham of The Catholic University of America Press have been knowledgeable and understanding guides for someone embarked on an initial voyage through the shoals of preparing a manuscript for publication.

For the last few years I have been on the faculty of Belmont Abbey College, where this project was completed, and where I continue daily to be reminded that we humans are incarnate beings dependent upon one another. Settling in as one of the faculty and developing a full slate of courses while yet finding time and energy to write was difficult, even with encouragement from the rest of the campus community. Without their help, it would have been impossible. I am particularly grateful to Nathalie Coté for her friendship and collegial advice, which often served as a key impetus to continue writing, and to the Benedictine community of Belmont Abbey for their hospitality and example.

INTRODUCTION

Christians have always regarded the Bible as the Word of God in a unique sense. Without forgetting the human character of the biblical witness, Christians make a strong affirmation that God has spoken in and through these texts. The holy books have proven central to Christian life in a variety of times and places; a renewed appropriation of biblical themes is at work in nearly every reforming or creative movement. We find a recent example of this phenomenon in the resurgence of Roman Catholic biblical studies since Vatican II.[1]

This singular place accorded to Scripture has caused the relationship between the text and present circumstances to be a frequent topic of reflection. One can trace through the patristic period the development of a common perspective that would set the terms of discourse until the beginning of the modern age. Its roots can be discerned within the New Testament itself, as the biblical writers dealt with the Scriptures of Israel which were the only Bible known to the first Christian generations. The nascent community had a vital interest in showing that acceptance of a crucified man as Lord and Messiah fulfilled biblical hopes without inverting them. Two fundamental beliefs regarding the modes of divine revelation had to be reconciled: "God spoke to our ancestors in many and various ways by the prophets" as presented in Scripture and "in these last days he has spoken to us by a Son" (Heb 1.1,2). There are differing explanations for the way these beliefs fit together, but there is no doubt that they do so. Before long, dividing these elements becomes equivalent to the rejection of Christianity itself.[2] Another related issue lies in the scandal of histori-

1. Summarized by Enzo Bianchi, "The Centrality of the Word of God," in *The Reception of Vatican II,* ed. Giuseppe Alberigo, Jean-Pierre Jossua, and Joseph A. Komonchak, trans. Matthew J. O'Connell (Washington, D.C.: Catholic University of America Press, 1987), 115–36.

2. As one can observe in Irenaeus's defense of the OT against Valentinian gnosticism and Marcion; cf. *Adversus Haereses* IV.5,33 in particular.

cal particularity, more simply put as the relative obscurity and insignificance of the events that the NT presents as mediators of universal salvation. Traces of this difficulty appear as far back as the parable of the mustard seed, and in other passages such as Acts 26.26, with Paul's assertion that "these things were not done in a corner." As the Christian mission spread into the urban culture of the empire, the scandal worked against not only the gospel *kerygma* itself but also its foundation in the life and history of Israel.

Despite these problems, reception of Scripture (augmented by inclusion of the NT writings) as the Word of God remained unchallenged in the main stream of Christian development. One finds it incorporated into the conciliar creeds, albeit indirectly, in such phrases as "in fulfillment of the Scriptures," and "spoken through the prophets." The difficulties were met with a sophisticated doctrine of multiple senses or levels of meaning in the Bible. The letter of a passage would be its literal or apparent meaning, bearing a higher or spiritual meaning hidden within it. Often there were further levels to the spiritual meaning, which could be applied to different aspects of Christian existence. The city of Jerusalem served as a classic example; depending on the situation of the exegete and the text at hand, the city might represent the metropolis of Judea, the Church, the inmost citadel of an individual's soul, or the heavenly city of God. The validity of these differing but related senses was guaranteed by God's unique activity in the creation, transmission, and ongoing reading of the biblical texts.[3]

Modern biblical studies offered a radically different way of engaging with the scriptural writings, often characterized as "historical criticism." Initiated by Spinoza's *Theologico-Political Treatise* in the late seventeenth century, the new method became prevalent over the course of the next two and a half centuries. The most significant

3. For a basic summary see Raymond E. Brown and Sandra M. Schneiders, "Hermeneutics," in *The New Jerome Biblical Commentary,* ed. Raymond E. Brown, Joseph A. Fitzmyer, and Roland E. Murphy (Englewood Cliffs, N.J.: Prentice-Hall, 1990), 1153–55, together with Raymond Collins, "Inspiration," in *New Jerome,* 1024–28. Manlio Simonetti, *Biblical Interpretation in the Early Church,* ed. Anders Bergquist and Markus Bockmuehl, trans. John A. Hughes (Edinburgh: T and T Clark, 1994), offers a more integrated presentation.

change it presented was an abandonment of the Christian attitude in favor of a strictly historical paradigm; the Bible was regarded as no different from any other book. As a consequence, this approach "studies the biblical text in the same fashion as it would study any other ancient text and comments upon it as an expression of human discourse." Concern for the history that generated the writings and the circumstances of their reception grounds the historical character, while the use of "scientific criteria that seek to be as objective as possible" ensures a critical or neutral position (deliberately prescinding from ecclesial faith) in dealing with documents invested with such authority. The fundamental aim here is to understand the Bible, or more precisely, the texts of which it is composed as they stand together with the historical situation from which they grew and in which they were heard.[4]

It is far from hyperbolic to say that more is known about the biblical times, persons, and environment today than ever before, and historical-critical scholarship must take credit for this achievement. Yet just as its effort began to bear fruit, over a century ago, Nietzsche pointed out some questionable aspects of the modern orientation toward history. The ideals of historical scholarship as formulated in the nineteenth century were objectivity, disinterest, and detachment. The good historian was to be a pure mirror, devoid of personal involvement and receptive to whatever the critically judged data would show. Nietzsche condemned these ideals as destructive of the entire historical enterprise, for when pursued in this fashion, history "injures every living thing and finally destroys it."[5] That is to say, the data of the past become void of meaning due to an inability to dis-

4. "Historical criticism" is a somewhat hazy term. For present purposes, it will be used interchangeably with such phrases as "historical-critical method" and "modern biblical studies." The citations in this paragraph are taken from Pontifical Biblical Commission, *The Interpretation of the Bible in the Church* (Boston: St. Paul Books and Media, 1993), I.A.1. I regret that the valuable study by Peter S. Williamson, *Catholic Principles for Interpreting Scripture: A study of the Pontifical Biblical Commission's* The Interpretation of the Bible in the Church (Rome: Editrice Pontificio Istituto Biblico, 2001), came into my hands only as the manuscript was in the last stages of revision.

5. Friedrich Nietzsche, *On the Advantage and Disadvantage of History for Life*, trans. Peter Preuss (Indianapolis: Hackett, 1980), 10.

cern what is significant for our historical context. The historical events lose all relevance, despite the abundance of information. This stress upon historical work also affects the ability to engage the contemporary situation. Keen awareness of the variety of human history can make it difficult to deal seriously with affairs at hand, for even matters of pressing concern begin to blur together: "things were different in all ages, it does not matter how you are."[6] The study of history, when carried to the full extent of its inner logic, undermined its own foundations.

This Nietzschean critique aimed at historical studies in general, but it bears even more strongly when focused upon biblical scholarship. There the emphasis on history disrupts the unity of the Bible, assembled as it was over the course of a thousand years, and the individual books or portions of books are parceled out among the circumstances of their original composition. The more accurately those circumstances are recovered, the more closely the biblical text is bound to them and the more distant it becomes from the present situation. When carried to an extreme, this tendency can make the Bible a book bound with many seals whose voice or more properly voices are addressed to Israel in the eighth century or Galilee in the first—anywhere except the situation of those who are reading it now. An inability to draw present meaning from the data of history, however, can have an even stronger effect. It is hardly novel to say that Christianity is a historical religion inseparably tied to the narrative of a particular people and their God, summed up in the career of one unique individual in a small part of the Roman Empire. But if the *gesta Dei (in et per Iudaeos)* are made irrelevant for later understanding, a religion founded upon them must also lose its meaning or be transformed into an assemblage of non-historic truths.[7]

This brief review of changing approaches to the Bible leaves sever-

6. Nietzsche, *Advantage and Disadvantage*, 41.

7. A remark of Adolf Harnack's illustrates this point by saying "that the Gospel is in nowise a positive religion like the rest; that it contains no statutory or particularistic elements; *that it is, therefore, religion itself* [emphasis his]," in *What Is Christianity?* trans. T. B. Saunders (Philadelphia: Fortress Press, 1986), 63. Nietzsche would have been interested to see this great historian using his skill to show that the message of Christianity has no essential connection with history.

al difficulties in its wake. To begin with, it is clear that one cannot simply maintain the pre-critical view of the biblical writings and their origin without making a radical sacrifice of the intellect. Two and a half centuries of historical-critical study have revealed too much about the times, circumstances, and composition of the Bible. Yet a purely historical orientation falls into the dangers Nietzsche identified while also, in its determination to read the Bible in the same way as any other book, rejecting a central affirmation of the Christian religion. The aim of this project is to investigate these problems within the context of Christian practice and belief. The inquiry is in some part historical, in order to set the stage with the theological perspectives that continue to influence discussion, but modern figures and systematic concerns draw the greater share of attention.

Before setting out, however, a decent respect for the expectations of the reader requires a few words on our lack of engagement with contemporary literary hermeneutics. Literary or narrative approaches to Scripture, often following in the footsteps of continental philosophers such as Ricoeur and Gadamer, have become more and more popular as ways to get beyond the isolating effects of historical study, where "methodologically justified progress from the text into the present of lived experience seemed impossible." Without abandoning the need for historical-critical research, these hermeneutical strategies seek out transformative interpretations where the biblical witness can function as a "locus and mediation of revelatory encounter with God."[8] Neither the initial impetus nor the goal are foreign to the aims of this study, and one can scarcely deny that literary readings have done much to illuminate dimensions of the Bible that elude a

8. Both citations are from Sandra Schneiders, *The Revelatory Text: Interpreting the New Testament as Sacred Scripture,* 2nd ed. (Collegeville, Minn.: Liturgical, 1999) 2, 4; this is an influential text that has much to offer, and serves as a good representative of the literary/narrative line of biblical interpretation. Setting the goal of interpretation as revelatory encounter with God is particularly important, for often one finds that approaches to the Bible as literature à la Northrop Frye deal with it solely as literature and avoid engaging theological claims. In the words of George Steiner (review of *The Literary Guide to the Bible* by Robert Alter and Frank Kermode, *New Yorker* (January 11 1988): 97), however illuminating an interpretation of a given text, a separation of that sort is "radically factitious. It cannot work."

strictly historical approach. Nothing said here is meant to disparage the contributions of contemporary hermeneutics and narrative interpretations. Yet the point of departure here is different, and leads to a major reservation regarding the theological sufficiency of literary/hermeneutical modes of reading.

Rather than general hermeneutics or pragmatic dissatisfaction with historical interpretations, we begin from tensions between the core Christian affirmations of Scripture as the Word of God in some unique sense and the affirmations of modern historical studies. Because my training focused for the most part on historical/ systematic theology, it seemed reasonable to let theological factors set the parameters of this investigation just as they do for any discussion of the Bible as Scripture. Among these parameters one finds a firm attachment to recovery of authorial intention as a major interpretive goal. To take but one example, there is a consistent understanding, which runs throughout the last sixty years of Catholic teaching, that the communicative intention of the author grounds the literal sense of Scripture and that this literal sense must be the foundation of exegesis. Approaches derived from continental hermeneutics, whose proponents can dismiss the mere notion of authorial intention as "not only impossible in fact but undesirable in principle," tend to find themselves in some difficulty with this idea of literal sense.[9] When one also considers that some analytic philosophers of religion as well as theologians in the tradition of Bernard Lonergan defend the legitimacy of authorial intention as an interpretive concern, and that postmodern theories of interpretation play little role in any of the figures examined here, devoting significant attention to contemporary philosophical hermeneutics as applied to Scripture does not seem necessary.[10] Yet in the interests of clarity the concluding chapter will

9. Cf. Williamson, *Catholic Principles*, 164–67, for a review of the notion of "literal sense," and its link to the importance of authors, as presented in the PBC statement. The quotation is drawn from Schneiders, *Revelatory Text*, 163, who finds authorial intent undesirable due to its constricting effects on the Bible's polyvalent meaning and attempts to substitute an "ideal meaning of the text, that is, what it actually says about its immanent referent" (161).

10. The best representative of the analytic tradition on this question would be the work of Nicholas Wolterstorff, *Divine Discourse: Philosophical Reflections on the Claim That God Speaks* (Cambridge: Cambridge University Press, 1995), with par-

offer a brief argument in favor of authors and their intentions, cast in terms drawn from Lonergan, and related subjects may be found in other chapters.

The investigation proper begins with a comparative exposition of classic and modern approaches to biblical study; Origen and Thomas Aquinas serve as exemplars of the former, while Benedict Spinoza and Ernst Troeltsch present the theoretic underpinnings of the latter. Once this background has been established, we turn to modern encounters with the two perspectives. The figures chosen operate out of differing backgrounds but share a common element: an acknowledgement of the utility and results of modern biblical scholarship combined with reception of the Bible in faith. Part of that faith is the conviction that the words of Scripture are also the word of God, or at least linked with it, in a way that nothing else is. Maintaining at once both classical and modern affirmations in this way forces a deeper consideration of the issues involved. The first writer to be examined, Raymond Brown, exemplifies what one could call the main line of Catholic exegesis in North America. In addition to substantial exegetical work, he spent significant time reflecting upon the status of modern biblical studies within the Church. Brevard Childs approaches these questions of interpretation as a Protestant exegete of the OT (almost a mirror image of Brown), and with a substantially more negative view of present exegetical work. For him, the primary focus of exegesis must be reoriented toward the canonical texts and the processes of canonization that shaped them. The next two figures are neither North American nor drawn from the guild of biblical scholarship, with one from Latin America and one from a prior generation in Europe. Of the many individuals whose labors have gone

---

ticular reference to his discussions of Ricoeur and Derrida. More recent (albeit with significant difficulties regarding authorial intention) is Jorge J. E. Gracia, *How Can We Know What God Means?: The Interpretation of Revelation* (New York: Palgrave Macmillan, 2001). It is to be regretted that the focus of this study on a given set of figures precluded significant exploration of analytic philosophy of language and religion. Given the relative lack of analytic influence upon Catholic theology in the United States, it is a potentially fruitful area of research now mined mainly by evangelical theologians; cf. Kevin J. Vanhoozer, *Is There a Meaning in This Text?: The Bible, the Reader, and the Morality of Literary Knowledge* (Grand Rapids: Zondervan, 1998).

into the enterprise of liberation theology, Juan Luis Segundo presents the most detailed consideration of the biblical presuppositions and exegetical tendencies informing that movement. In his work there is a strong conviction of the present significance of the Bible, as read from the perspective of the oppressed poor and shown to be critical of existing tradition. The last person examined, although not precisely contemporary with the others, remains vital to an ongoing discussion. Henri de Lubac and those associated with him in the movement of *ressourcement* took their bearings from a reappropriation of the Church Fathers; while not rejecting modern scholarship in toto, he believed that the historical-critical emphasis needed to be joined with a renewed and purified form of spiritual understanding modeled upon patristic exegesis. The current existence of "a small but swelling stream of conferences, scholarly books, and doctoral dissertations" focused upon patristic readings of Scripture is a testament less to prescience on de Lubac's part than to the lasting impact of his work.[11]

A set of common questions structures the consideration of these four writers, with a chapter devoted to each of them, in order to maintain focus and also to help keep this project within manageable bounds. We begin with their analysis of the present condition of biblical studies and the particular concerns sparked by it. With that context established, their understanding of the relationship between the biblical texts as human documents with particular histories and their ongoing function in the life of the Church is analyzed and evaluated. The final chapter attempts to bring together the positive gains made by each one into a larger synthesis where theological and historical affirmations regarding the nature of the Bible may not only coexist but cooperate with one another.

11. Brian E. Daley, "Is Patristic Exegesis Still Usable?: Reflections on Early Christian Interpretation of the Psalms," *Communio* 29 (2002): 184. Robert Louis Wilken ("In Defense of Allegory," *Modern Theology* 14 [1998]: 197–212) puts the argument for reconsidering older modes of reading well, and is himself in the forefront of the stream Daley mentions. One also finds biblical scholars such as Luke Timothy Johnson turning more and more in that direction; cf. his contributions to Luke Timothy Johnson and William S. Kurz, *The Future of Catholic Biblical Scholarship* (Grand Rapids: Eerdmans, 2002).

CHAPTER ONE

CLASSICAL AND MODERN EXEGESIS

While it is easy to speak of comparing classical and modern exegesis, actually performing such a task is far more problematic. The range of authors involved in mastering even one element of the comparison would be far beyond the limits of time and space that can be allotted to any one work. The only serviceable plan is to choose a few authors whose thought is both sufficiently influential and representative for them to serve as emblems of the broader situation. Further, since our primary interest lies in the ways the chosen modern authors have dealt with their status as heirs of both exegetical traditions and not in the past bearers of those traditions per se, the range of texts must also be restricted. Nonetheless, it is still possible to gain an understanding of the two traditions' basic contours that is accurate as well as useful.

Origen and Thomas Aquinas will stand as exemplars of the classic exegetical tradition. Each in his own way sets the tone for subsequent development, particularly Origen due to his position as one of the first Christians to engage in detailed biblical commentary. Aquinas, on the other hand, is heir to both a millennium of Christian thought and a renewed engagement with the literal sense of the Bible that had been going forward for several generations. While his primary concerns as a thinker did not lie with these topics—he was more concerned with matters of metaphysics and theological anthropology—no one whose main professional title was *magister in sacra pagina* could fail to reflect upon the proper reading of Scriptures.[1]

1. Furthermore, while they are read less often today than his other works, Thomas engaged in significant commentaries on Paul, John, and Matthew. The standard treatment of his life and activities is Jean-Pierre Torrell, *Saint Thomas*

Although there are some noteworthy differences between these two, as will be noted later, a deeper unity remains that allows them to be taken together.

The choice of at least one representative of modern principles can safely be called automatic. Despite occasional lobbying for others, no serious case can be made for anyone other than Benedict Spinoza as the pioneer of historical-critical exegesis.[2] His *Theologico-Political Treatise* sets out the crucial strands that serve to constitute the new approach, despite later adjustments or modifications. Echoing his mundane work as a lens-grinder, Spinoza ultimately succeeded in an attempt to recast the lenses of the mind with which people view Scriptures. Some difficulty arises in choosing the second member of this diptych; different options are certainly possible. Yet for present purposes, Ernst Troeltsch in his essay on "Historical and Dogmatic Method in Theology" seems to capture perfectly the characteristic emphases of the developed modern approach. In addition, it is only shortly after the publication of this essay (1898) that sustained doubts and objections begin to be raised regarding some key principles of the historical-critical method.[3] By taking this work as the final

Aquinas: The Person and His Work, trans. Robert Royal (Washington, D.C.: Catholic University of America Press, 1996); see 54–75 for a discussion of the first period as a Paris master. The older account of James Weisheipl, *Friar Thomas D'Aquino: His Life, Thought, and Works* (Washington, D.C.: Catholic University of America Press, 1983), also remains useful.

2. See Robert M. Grant with David Tracy, *A Short History of the Interpretation of the Bible* (Philadelphia: Fortress Press, 1984), 105–8, for a short discussion of Spinoza's role; at more length, Roy A. Harrisville and Walter Sundberg, *The Bible in Modern Culture: Baruch Spinoza to Brevard Childs,* 2nd ed. (Grand Rapids: Eerdmans, 2002), 30–45. There is a tendency to cite the Oratorian Richard Simon, as the first to publish "a series of books in which he applied critical method to the Bible" (Edgar Krenz, *The Historical-Critical Method* [Philadelphia: Fortress Press, 1975], 15). However, unlike Spinoza, Simon was without heirs or influence for hundreds of years.

3. Begin to be raised, that is, from circles familiar with historical criticism and intimately involved with the theology of the day as opposed to many elements within the Christian community that simply rejected it root and branch. Though Nietzsche's essay *On the Advantage and Disadvantage of History* had been published earlier, it is only later that its critique begins to be heard. There are also the reservations of Karl Barth and others, as expressed most prominently in the prefaces to Barth's Romans commentary (1st and 2nd editions).

element in our comparison, we can be more sure of encountering modern principles in a relatively pure and integral way.

After this review, the chapter concludes by setting out the most salient characteristics of the two approaches. While today neither tradition is without its advocates, who quite often see no need for any serious modifications, the present enterprise is predicated on the insufficiency of either classical or modern exegesis when taken alone. Assessment of their diverse strengths and weaknesses is essential as the subsequent chapters analyze various attempts at correction or even new syntheses.

ORIGEN

Origen's clearest statement of his exegetical stance appears in *De principiis,* which current scholarship largely accepts as a defense of his theology and exegesis written in response to objections raised against his Genesis commentary. The first three chapters of book IV contain a detailed explanation of scriptural interpretation, which we will examine before closing with a summary of his central principles.[4]

Unique status of Scripture

Before discussing the proper way of interpreting Scripture, one must first establish its importance. No one bothers to seek the proper way of interpreting a complex text without first being convinced that it deserves such attention, and so Origen attempts to claim the reader's interest by looking to the Bible's impact upon the world.

He makes a blunt contrast between philosophy and Christianity when it comes to the question of efficacy. A host of philosophers presume to have found the truth, yet none can succeed in persuading "even one" nation to follow their ways. Many did not even make an effort to win such large bodies of people. The Christian teaching, on the other hand, has persuaded a great number of people from every

4. The translation for *De principiis* IV.1–3 is taken from *Origen: An Exhortation to Martyrdom, Prayer, and Selected Works,* trans. Rowan Greer (New York: Paulist Press, 1979), 171–216. See Pierre Nautin, *Origène* (Paris: Beauchesne, 1977), 370, for circumstances of composition. In-text citations with Roman numeral refer to *De principiis,* without Roman numeral refer to chapter and section of *De principiis* IV.

nation, even though they are faced with persecution and death for abandoning their prior ways. This would be surprising in itself, but when one realizes that the teachers of this faith "are neither very capable nor very many" it becomes clear that this growth is not due to any human achievement (1.2). As a further proof of this, Origen brings in various biblical prophecies that he understands to predict and confirm this success.

The question of prophecy leads him to touch upon the applicability of Old Testament prophecies to Jesus. As he knows, the Jews deny that any prophecies refer to Jesus and look instead for another. Several texts are given to contradict this position, with the emphasis being on the sad state of the Jewish nation. The blessing given in Genesis 49.10 (LXX), that "princes shall not depart from Judah nor leaders from his loins, until the one comes for whom it is kept safe, and until the expectation of the Gentiles comes," is the foundation of the response. Clearly, with the fall of Jerusalem and the temple, princes have departed from among the Jewish people. The coming of the promised one must have already occurred, then, and that could only refer to Jesus. Origen adds a web of additional texts, but this is the base of his argument. Both the reality of events, as against the philosophers, and the witness of Scripture, as against the Jews, show the divine power at work in the spread of Christianity.

It is this evidence of divine activity that shows the inspiration of the Scriptures. Prior to the coming of Jesus, the predictions of Scripture could not be either fully established nor completely denied; there was simply not enough evidence. Once it becomes possible to compare Jesus' career and the further spread of his teaching with the biblical witness, Scripture assumes a different aspect, and its divine character "is put in the clearest light" (1.6). There is of course one immediate problem with this line of argument, inasmuch as the Christian reading of a given biblical passage may be far from obvious to an inquirer. It would be "too laborious" for Origen to explain every single instance, though, and he thinks such a procedure unnecessary. The texts are open to all, and anyone can assemble the array of proofs. If they are sometimes difficult to perceive at first, this speaks more to the spiritual status of the reader than to any failing in the text, "because divine matters are brought down to men somewhat secretly and are all the more secret in proportion to anyone's disbelief or unworthiness" (1.7). This argument may beg the question, but Origen follows it immediately with an analogy that sheds some light upon his meaning.

If we look to the operations of divine providence, there is another mixture of clarity and obscurity. Some things are clearly the result of God's activity, such as the arrangement of the heavenly bodies, and others less so, as with the variety of human events.[5] Depending upon native ability and training, one person will be able to perceive these things more clearly than another. This distinction seems to be in accord with common experience, as it is a rare human who never meets someone superior in learning or intellect. It is important to note, however, that Origen makes it clear that no rational creature (including angels) can fully plumb the depths of God's ordering of the world. There is an irreducible core of mystery that will always remain obscure.

The unspoken presupposition that both the created universe and the books of Scripture serve as media of divine revelation grounds the comparison, and at the same time accounts for human failure to perceive the revelation in particular cases. Just as the existence of a divine care and watchfulness pervading the world is not (or ought not to be) denied through an inability to explain an individual exercise of it, so also the divine message given in Scripture ought not to be rejected "because the weakness of our understanding is not strong enough to discover in each verse the obscure and hidden meanings" (1.7).

Principles of understanding

Origen identifies failures of interpretation, rather than simple disbelief, as the main source of error for those who fail to grasp the meaning of Scripture. All the various people whom he takes as examples here profess the divine origin of the texts: Jews and heretics (more properly Gnostics in modern parlance) as well as the less per-

5. The examples are taken from the Greek text.

ceptive within the Great Church.[6] Yet this alone does not lead them to a correct understanding. The Jewish reading insists on understanding the figural statements of the prophets literally, and fails to acknowledge the reality of Jesus as the Christ as long as certain material signs are lacking ("the lion shall eat straw like the ox," Is 11.7, etc.). The heretics adopt much the same procedure, although to a different end, by reading references to God's anger or jealousy literally. Rather than reject Jesus when faced by apparent incongruities, they instead reject the God of the Old Testament and distinguish the merciful Father of Jesus from the more stern and just Creator. Certain simpler believers, while affirming that the Father and the Creator are one, yet seem to read Scripture in the same way and so "hold opinions about God that should not be held concerning the most unjust and cruelest man" (2.1).

There is a common thread uniting these three groups, which Origen identifies as interpreting Scripture "according to the sound of the letter" (2.2).[7] The qualification is important, for Origen is not about to reject the letter of the text in an absolute or excessive way. His intent is to provide a way of understanding that encompasses both the literal and the "spiritual" meanings, a way that holds to "the rule of Jesus Christ according to the succession of the heavenly church of the apostles" (2.2 Greek).[8] In agreement with this design, he deliberately confines his intended audience to those who already believe that Scripture is inspired by the Holy Spirit and given us through Christ according to the will of the Father. Even though he has cited them as examples of an excessively literal reading, he makes no further attempt to respond to Jewish concerns. Whatever subsequent misunderstandings there may be, a basic adherence to Christ appears to be indispensable; it serves as a first principle for any later progress.

6. See Henri Crouzel, *Origen,* trans. A. S. Worrall (San Francisco: Harper and Row, 1989), 153–56, for a brief overview of Origen's opposition to Gnostic ideas.

7. Greek: according to the naked letter.

8. The canon, which is sometimes of faith, of Christ, or of the Church, is extremely important to Origen throughout his work. Fidelity to the rule of faith (as he understands it) is central to his self-understanding; cf. pref.2 and elsewhere. The matter is treated at length in Henri de Lubac, *Histoire et Esprit* (Paris: Aubier, 1950), 55–69, esp. 61–63.

Another principle that Origen sets out as basic in the search for understanding is the element of mystery in the scriptural texts. After adducing several already classic difficulties such as the incest of Lot and his daughters, he confesses his own ignorance when it comes to determining the precise significance of these matters. This ignorance relates to the specific instances, however, and not the general idea. The simple existence of spiritual meanings is too clear to miss:

> Indeed, the entire narrative, which seems to be written about weddings or the births of sons or different battles or whatever other stories one wishes, what else must it be believed to be than the forms and types of hidden and sacred matters? (2.2)

The same principle extends even to the Gospels and apostolic letters. Even though they may appear more clear than the older writings, there is still a realm of inner meaning that is accessible only through participation in the Spirit.[9] Anyone seeking to enter that realm must do so, according to Origen, by taking into account the intended purpose of the Bible together with its audience.

> Just as a human being is said to be made up of body, soul, and spirit, so also is sacred Scripture, which has been granted by God's gracious dispensation for man's salvation. (2.4)

The salvific intent behind Scripture requires that the text be adapted to the humans whom it is meant to help. Everyone, whatever their spiritual state, ought to be able to find something of help in it. Consequently, Origen measures the levels of meaning according to his anthropology.

To say that the tripartite anthropology of body, soul, and spirit is used to explain Scripture may be slightly misleading. There is an intermediate layer, where Origen distinguishes different levels of Christian progress according to the different levels of human being. Just as an individual human is composed of these three elements, so also is the Church made up of different types of Christians who can

9. At this point Origen refers again to 1 Cor 2, which serves as a key text throughout these chapters. Paul's explanation of the spiritual wisdom to be found by those who advance in the Christian life helps provide a program for Origen as well as an assurance that there are mysteries to be understood.

rightly be called bodily, psychic or "soul-like," and spiritual. It is this taxonomy of spiritual growth that is directly applied to the meanings of Scripture. Some Christians who are simpler or less mature cannot see beyond "the ordinary and narrative meaning," which corresponds to the body of Scripture (*communem istum et historialem intellectum,* 2.4).[10] Those who are beginning to advance may profit from the "soul" of Scripture (usually the most obscure of the three categories in Origen's explanations). The highest of the three levels is reserved for those "perfect" or advanced believers who can receive the "secret and hidden wisdom of God," which corresponds to the "spirit" of the Scriptures (again with a citation of 1 Cor 2, here vv. 6–7).[11]

After simply affirming the existence of three levels of understanding within Scripture, Origen moves on to more clearly establish the levels' existence and some of their characteristics with the aid of a few biblical examples. The bodily level would appear unproblematic, but Origen here offers one of his most criticized teachings. It is a crucial (if not notorious) part of Origen's way of understanding that there are passages without a "bodily" meaning. The literal sense of the text, in these cases, either is logically incoherent or somehow contradicts other portions of the same Scripture (2.5). He seems to be aware of the dubious character of the assertion, as he follows it with a promise to explain more fully later on, and turns directly to the "great profit" that lies in this prima facie meaning.

There is only one example given of the psychic or "soul-like" meaning, which we have already called the least defined of the three. However, the nature of that example together with the little that Origen says about it may show why this sense is less relevant to his aims

10. Greer consistently translates *historia* and cognate terms by "narrative meaning" or some such phrase. This is not objectionable, since it accords better with the usage of Latin, and modern English gives somewhat positivist connotations to "history."

11. See Karen Jo Torjesen, "'Body,' 'Soul,' and 'Spirit' in Origen's Theory of Exegesis," *Anglican Theological Review* 67 (1985): 17–30. One should note that, for Origen, these levels represent stages on the one path of spiritual progress (an idea rooted in Philo). The Gnostics known to him understood these levels to refer to essentially different types of human beings, with little or no transfer from one level to another (cf. *De prin.* I.8.2, III.1.23).

in *De principiis.* The passage is Paul's defense of his right to support from his congregations, where the apostle cites the injunction of Deuteronomy 25.4 against muzzling an ox treading grain.

"Is it for oxen that God is concerned? Does He not speak entirely for our sake? It was written for our sake, because the plowman should plow in hope and the thresher thresh in hope of a share in the crop" (1 Cor 9.9–10). Moreover, a great many other sayings like this one, which are interpreted from the Law in this way, bestow the greatest instruction upon those who hear them. (2.6)

The thrust of the text is greater in Greek, where Origen's comment reads: "And most of the interpretations adapted to the multitude which are in circulation and which edify those who cannot understand the higher meanings have something of the same character." This character is not spelled out further, but it seems as though the psychic meaning is understood mainly as an indication of what we must do rather than what we must know; its primary goal is to teach and inculcate correct behavior. If that is its purpose, then it becomes more clear why Origen has little to say of it. *De principiis* is concerned with what today we would call issues of systematic theology or foundations rather than ethics. With the exception of Origen's uncompromising insistence on "free will," there are no topics in the book that can rightly be called ethical.[12] Origen simply assumes that the reader is already familiar with such subjects, as one of "those who train themselves to become worthy and capable of receiving wisdom" (pref. 3).[13] There is little need to say more than he does on the psychic sense, if the work is intended for those who have already grasped its lessons.

Though Origen does not give an explicit definition of the spiritual meaning, one can be pieced together from his discourse with little effort. Spiritual understanding refers to the "secret and hidden wisdom

12. This is a decidedly poor way to translate *autexousion* or *liberum arbitrium,* which do not have the connotations of virtually monadic isolation that "free will" tends to have in modern parlance. Unfortunately, the habit is probably too ingrained in English discourse to be eradicated.

13. Quotations from *De principiis* other than IV.1–3 are drawn from Origen, *On First Principles,* trans. G. W. Butterworth (Gloucester, Mass.: Peter Smith, 1973).

of God," which consists primarily in learning the "heavenly things" through their copies and shadows present in Scripture and also through the experiences or types of the OT "written down for us" (2.6). This wisdom, grasped in the relation between type and typified or shadow and reality, seems to be accessible only through Christ. More precisely, perhaps, our minds may be directed to these things by looking at them in the light of Christ (who serves as the personal embodiment and realization of the mystery of salvation).[14] Here one should note that the account given thus far serves mainly to show the existence of these multiple senses together with some examples of them. In themselves they are not a way of understanding but only the raw material for it.

"How we should understand divine Scripture in particular points"

The heart of book IV lies in the next two sections, 2.7–9, where Origen sets out his considered views on the correct approach to the Bible. Scripture takes its beginning from the Spirit enlightening "prophets and apostles" so that they can understand the "mysteries of those events or purposes that happen among human beings or from human beings." Those mysteries are then narrated as stories or portrayed in types so that only someone who is already prepared for such knowledge by study and virtuous practices will be able to find these spiritual mysteries within the guise of "an ordinary narrative looking in another direction." Inasmuch as this hidden meaning is spiritual in the full sense of the word, being revealed and guaranteed by the Spirit, anyone who comes to grasp it will become "an ally of the Spirit's knowledge and a participant in the divine counsel" (2.7). Since this description might also be applied to the writers of Scripture themselves, it appears that coming to understand the Bible and its higher teachings assimilates one in some degree to its writers. Origen does say that only those inspired "by the truth of divine wisdom" reach the

14. *Commentary on John* I.8, where Christ's advent causes all Scripture to be seen as Gospel in some sense. See Crouzel, *Origen*, 186–98, for some consideration of Origen's Christology.

summit of knowledge, which implies that one who understands Scripture is experiencing anew, albeit in a lesser way, the same event or charism that gave birth to the text in the first place.

The "lesser way" should not be overlooked here, lest Origen seem to place the spiritual interpreter on too high a pedestal. The biblical authors are said to be filled with the Spirit, and Origen will go on to speak of the Holy Spirit as composing and determining the aims of the text (2.9). His usage shifts from the terms of human authorship to those of divine authorship without a clear explanation of the relation between the two. It is possible that the concern with human authors is a way of showing that they fully grasped what they were writing, spiritual meanings included, regardless of any failures of perception on the part of their contemporaries.[15] Origen's constant concern for freedom of the will may prevent him from ascribing any lack of self-knowledge to the biblical writers, lest they be taken for simple mediums or sibyls.[16]

The content and sequence of the wisdom that the inspiring Spirit places within the scriptural texts bears a close resemblance to the order of treatment Origen himself follows in *De principiis.* It begins with the knowledge of God as Father, Son, and Spirit; the Incarnation of the Son; the nature of the rational creatures to be saved through that incarnation; and the sort of world in which this drama is played out. This may lend credence to the notion of *De principiis* as Origen's explanation of his own work of interpretation: he is gathering and setting out in a more systematic, cohesive, and open way the wisdom that the Spirit has woven into the texture of Scripture.

This is not the Spirit's sole aim in the composition of Scripture, however, for all will not "give themselves to the effort and diligence" needed to reach this wisdom (2.8). This may be due either to lack of will or simply to lack of ability, but Origen seems to regard the situa-

15. See Enrique Nardoni, "Origen's Concept of Biblical Inspiration," *Second Century* 4 (1984): 9–23, for an examination of Origen's sometimes complicated understanding of inspiration.

16. The whole of III.1 is an extended defense of free will, and the topic often surfaces elsewhere.

tion itself as a simple fact. The accounts of the visible creation, the history of subsequent events, and the deeds of people both good and bad are intended as a garment and a veil for the spiritual wisdom of the deeper meanings. Yet as the work of the Spirit, even these narratives are filled with wisdom of a sort. Though not complete, it is still capable of giving instruction to the many people (perhaps most) "who otherwise would be unable" to learn and advance (2.8).

The existence of valuable and needed elements in the surface reading of the texts does create a potential danger, however. If there are fruitful meanings to be gleaned here, it may be that the reader will think that there is nothing further to be learned from Scripture. Consequently, the narrative meaning of Scripture is not a complete work. Occasional problems of various types lead the attentive reader to seek another way of understanding the Spirit's intent in a given passage. Origen cites this pedagogical concern on God's part as the reason for incongruities or impossibilities in the sacred texts. These difficulties are needed to induce the human interpreter to undertake the hard road that leads to the higher wisdom that is the ultimate goal of the biblical witness:

> All these things the Holy Spirit arranged so that from them, since what first appears cannot be true or useful, we might be called back to examine the truth to be sought more diligently, and might seek a meaning worthy of God in the Scriptures, which we believe were inspired by God. (2.9)

Origen sees the revelation of the spiritual meaning as the primary purpose of Scripture, to which the Spirit subordinates the literal or narrative sense of the texts. That understanding may sometimes be entirely true, a mixture of the correct and incorrect, or impossible. Whatever the situation, the narrative is always "fitted to the spiritual meaning" (2.9). This strong statement will be qualified in what follows, but it does express the basic attitude that Origen expects of the interpreter.

The examples of false literal meanings are drawn first from narratives of events and then from various commandments. It may be that they fall into two types, the impossible and the merely irrational. Origen regards as impossible according to the literal meaning such things as God walking in Paradise during the evening (Gn 3.8), Cain's departure "from the face of God" (Gn 4.16), and Jesus looking upon all the kingdoms of the earth from a mountaintop (Mt 4.8). Although couched in the same form as events that he does not question (e.g., the building of the Temple by Solomon), these reveal at once that they could not have occurred. They either speak of God with anthropomorphisms that cannot simply be applied to the divine nature, such as "face," or involve some bodily difficulty, such as the impossibility of seeing all the kingdoms of the earth from any mountain no matter how high. The case is similar with actual commandments, where he takes as examples impossible to fulfill both the rules regarding the Sabbath ("no one shall move from his place on the seventh day," Ex 16.29) and Jesus' order not to have two tunics or sandals (Mt 10.10). No one can go for a whole day without moving in any way, and Origen criticizes Jewish attempts to determine someone's "place" as a given area with a defined extent. Similarly, while having only one tunic and pair of shoes may do well for Palestine, how can it be managed in colder climates? Such passages, and others like them, only confirm his judgment that

> the aim of the Holy Spirit is that we should understand that there have been woven into the visible narrative truths that, if pondered and understood inwardly, bring forth a law useful to men and worthy of God. (3.4)

Here the objection arises that if some texts are not to be taken in their plain sense, then none of them should be. Origen responds that passages where both the truth of the narratives and the literal meaning of precepts ought to be maintained "are far more numerous than those that contain only the spiritual meaning" (3.4). The criterion for judgments of plausibility and implausibility is usually found outside the biblical text, in what one can know from other, more general sources. It is basically a common-sense approach. No one is in doubt that Jerusalem was the capital of Judah, or that it contained the temple of God, just as there is no doubt that the Ten Commandments or many instructions in the New Testament ought to be observed as they stand. The problems arise in ambiguous cases, and for them Origen can give no infallible rule. Only zealous effort and prudent understanding can distinguish whether the literal meaning is to be retained at a given juncture. Throughout Origen's discussion there is an awareness of the fragility of human speculation. Ultimately, he reaffirms the essential limitations faced by any created intellect in understanding divine truth:

> in all these speculations let our understanding have sufficient coherence with the rule of piety, and let us think of the Holy Spirit's words not as something that shines as a speech fashioned by frail human eloquence, but [as a place where] the treasure of divine meanings is confined, shut within the frail vessel of the common letter. (3.14)

One should always keep in mind this singular character of "divine letters," and measure one's understanding of them by the whole body of Christian teaching. The final words that Origen gives here may be taken as symbolic of his whole approach, as he recalls "the divinity of the Holy Spirit, who inspired their writing" (i.e., the Scriptures).

Origen's principles of exegesis

The framework laid out in *De principiis* may be summed up in a few words: inspiration, applicability, and the rule of faith. This particular list is not found in his text, but it is clearly implied in his discussion. Inspiration, the traditional term by which the work of the Spirit in the witness of Scripture is understood, serves for him as a guarantor of the divine character of these writings. There is a real sense, not excluding the role of human authors, in which God through the Spirit is the author of Scripture. It is God's Word in a way that nothing else is, and this requires that it be read in a way "worthy of God." There must be a reason and a meaning, however obscure, behind each detail of the text (even down to individual words and phrases). One can find here a parallel to the way in which God is the "arranger" of the events of human history, both personal and collective. In addition, Scripture must be read as a whole with each part in relation to every other. From Genesis to Revelation, there is one and the same God proclaimed by the text as well as one and the same Spirit active in it.

If inspiration is understood to refer to some trait or aspect inherent in Scripture, applicability (as it is called here) looks more to the relation between Scripture and the humans reading or hearing it. The Bible is written for them and for their instruction, and that end should be kept in view throughout. Just as God wishes all to be saved, whatever their placement in time and space, so also Scripture is meaningful for all and not solely for the Israelites under Ezra or the inhabitants of Corinth in the days of Nero. No matter how time-bound it may seem at points, the witness of the text is intended to transcend its circumstances in some way, as a word addressed to everyone. In addition to such differences of locale and era, there are also different levels of intellect, learning, and spiritual development from person to person. Origen expresses this in terms of the Pauline anthropology of flesh, soul, and spirit; just as each individual has these three elements, so also do they describe different levels of progress in the journey of faith. Scripture speaks on each level, so that everyone may find in it something of help to them. The interpreter's duty is to adjust each discourse to the needs and natures of the audience at hand, with confidence that such efforts are in accord with the Spirit's intention throughout the biblical text.

The final and overarching principle, which after a fashion embraces and supports the first two, is the rule of faith. By this Origen means the entire body of basic Christian belief as handed down through the tradition of the Great Church. Coherence with this foundation, which can be understood as a patristic outline of Christian doctrine (also exemplified in traditional baptismal creeds), is a basic presupposition for any correct reading of the sacred texts. It also fills out in greater detail the content of the teaching (i.e., Creation, Providence, the unity of Old and New Testaments, and so forth), as both inspiration and applicability are somewhat abstract and lacking in concrete implications. This provides an element of control against wild or excessive speculations (although it is precisely this question of exegetical limits that will spur further developments).

AQUINAS

Thomas Aquinas embarked on his career as a Christian teacher a full thousand years after Origen's death. The development of exegetical thought in that intervening millennium is complex, but remained largely within Origen's framework. The basic principles outlined above, and the distinction between the literal and spiritual senses in which they found expression, provided the axis around which interpretation turned. There remained significant variations in the precise configuration of spiritual senses, as well as the explanations that writers provided for them. One also finds an enhanced focus on the literal sense, due to Origen's reputation as a promoter of untrammeled speculation and the consequent turn toward Antiochene exegetes such as Chrysostom, but the spiritual sense continued to occupy the primary interest of most commentators.[17] The literal sense, and serious study of that aspect of Scripture, would come much more to the fore in the generations immediately preceding Aquinas's work, with the "sprouting of interest in the Gospel and the intense curiosity about Scripture that then take hold of the Christian conscience, affecting the plain faithful as well as the professional master."[18] We mention it here to ward off any impression that Aquinas's explanations on these matters are sui generis; without some prepared materials, even the finest of architects remains helpless. Thomas's contribution is a clear and lucid explanation of scriptural meaning and its multiplex senses. It is precisely this that makes it valuable.[19]

17. See Beryl Smalley, *The Study of the Bible in the Middle Ages* (Notre Dame: Notre Dame University Press, 1964), 1–36, for a concise summary of the Western exegetical tradition as it reached the forerunners of the scholastic masters. For Chrysostom's views on the literal sense, see J. N. D. Kelly, *Golden Mouth: the story of John Chrysostom* (Ithaca: Cornell University Press, 1995), 95ff.

18. M.-D. Chenu, *Toward Understanding St. Thomas,* trans. A. M. Landry and D. Hughes (Chicago: Regnery, 1964), 234. One can also find a discussion of the developments in Andre Vauchez, *The Spirituality of the Medieval West* (Kalamazoo: Cistercian Publications, 1993), 75–145.

19. Marc Aillet, *Lire la Bible avec S. Thomas* (Fribourg Suisse: Editions Universitaires, 1993), 161–62, points out the disarray among Aquinas's contemporaries on the question.

A thing to bear in mind as the discussion progresses is that while today we may tend to think of Thomas as "professor of theology," the designation he himself would have applied is ***magister in sacra pagina***. The greater amount of his efforts as an active teacher were devoted to lectures on the biblical text itself, rather than systematic treatises such as the *Sentences* or his own *Summa*.[20] The reflections that he offers on the proper way of reading are those of someone in daily contact with the text, at the highest level of his time, and not separated from it by academic specialization as often happens today.

Thomas's *ex professo* discussions of the multiple senses of Scripture and its proper reading may be found in the *Summa theologiae* I.1.10, and in *Quodlibet* VII.14–16. The three questions of the latter text are misplaced, as they are more properly disputed questions dealt with by Thomas during his inception as ***magister*** and later inserted into the collection of quodlibeta.[21] Notwithstanding the eleven years separating this disputation from I.1.10, the substance remains the same. The disputed question is more extensive, as befits an exercise conducted on such an occasion, and adds some valuable details. Some ancillary passages will also be used, where circumstances lead Aquinas to insert some theoretical observations into his discussion. While far from exhaustive, these texts suffice for a basic grasp of his principles.[22]

Literal sense reconsidered

While Thomas is often portrayed as a champion of the literal sense, it is interesting to note that by Origen's standard he would be considered rather unliteral. The point can be illustrated with one of the Dominican's own examples: the literal sense of biblical phrases such as "the arm of God" is not that God is corporeal but that he possesses active power, which is signified among humans by the arm

20. See Torrell, *Saint Thomas,* 55–59, and also Terence McGuckin, "Saint Thomas Aquinas and Theological Exegesis of Sacred Scripture," *Louvain Studies* 16 (1991): 99–120.

21. Torrell, *Saint Thomas,* 51–52, relying on Weisheipl, *Friar Thomas,* 104–7.

22. A full treatment would have to roam through the length and breadth of Thomas's work, which would take us too far afield. The reader is referred to Aillet's work.

(I.1.10 ad3). This is precisely the opposite of Origen's understanding. Part of the reason may lie in differing audiences. Theological reflection was not yet philosophically advanced in Origen's day; his literal sense often appears to be defined by what the average Christian of Alexandria or Caesarea would grasp in a given passage.[23] As noted above, there is often a pedagogical and practical inspiration at work when he comes to roots and methods. Thomas, on the other hand, functions in a much more specialized environment oriented first toward understanding the *veritas rerum* and expressing it as clearly as possible.[24] These questions of milieu and training are not the only factors involved. Thanks to Augustine and Aristotle, Aquinas has at his disposal a more sophisticated understanding of the ways words function as signs of thought.[25] The understanding of the letter gains in depth when the focus shifts from letter as a sort of lowest common denominator to letter as the vehicle of intended meaning.

Among humans, external signs and symbols are required for meaning to be communicated from one to another. Those signs are most commonly "some words or imagined similitudes" (VII.16).[26] Their only importance is that their value as signs is known to all parties involved (ideally). As signs, the words are subordinate to what they signify; e.g., it matters little to a bilingual person if one says "the king has died" or "el rey ha muerto." The signs themselves are subject to subtle and flexible adjustment to persons, places, and circumstances that go far beyond such flat relations as that between "king"

23. Or so the often crude anthropomorphisms in his understanding of the literal sense would indicate. See Henri Crouzel, "Origéne et le sens literal dans ses homelies sur l'Hexateuque," *Bulletin de littérature ecclesiastique* 70 (1969): 243–49.

24. Pastoral concerns and interests were still important, but functioned in a different arena.

25. *De doctrina christiana* II.1–4 lays out Augustine's understanding of things and signs, with a modern review in John Rist, *Augustine: Ancient Thought Baptized* (New York: Cambridge University Press, 1994), 23–40. See Smalley, *Study,* 292–307, and T. F. Torrance, "Scientific Hermeneutics according to St. Thomas Aquinas," *Journal of Theological Studies* 13 (1962): 259–89, on the Aristotelian influence.

26. *Aliquas voces vel aliquas similitudines fictas.* Translations from works other than the *Summa* are my own, and so the Latin will be given in the notes; the English Dominican translation is used for the *Summa.*

or "rey" and the particular individual. There are also metaphorical or figurative significations whose meaning can be expressed over or even against the definitions of the words involved, for example, "living water." The importance of this development lies in the way that it removes the *litterae* themselves from the literal sense, which finds its locus instead in "the reality intended by the author and signified by those words."[27] Thomas expressed the underlying principle thus: "the literal sense is not the figure itself, but that which is figured" (I.1.10 ad3). The transition from text to authorial meaning also prevents Thomas from following Origen in denying a literal sense to any text. Where for Origen this would be to say that the words do not make sense, for Thomas this is to say that the author is irrational. (It is noteworthy that one of the longest questions in the *Summa* is I–II.102, where Thomas defends the literal reasons behind the ceremonial precepts of the Mosaic law in some detail.)

This focus upon grasping the author's intended meaning raises further questions when applied to the Bible, where authorship is not a simple category. Though I.1.10 states that "the author of Holy Writ is God," the *quaestio disputata* reveals a more complex situation. In that presentation, Thomas refers to the Holy Spirit as the *auctor principalis* with the human author serving as an *auctor instrumentalis* (VII.14 ad5).[28] Taken over from his teaching on prophecy,[29] the distinction posits a real divine/human collaboration in the production of Scripture that allows authorship to be ascribed to both God and humans. With this comes the possibility of different (but not discordant) intentions at work in the *litterae* of the text, implying the existence of multiple literal senses in one and the same passage.[30]

27. John F. Boyle, "St. Thomas Aquinas and Sacred Scripture," *Pro ecclesia* 4 (1995): 95.

28. The same distinction also appears in *De potentia* IV.1, which dates from the same period as the *Prima pars*. Its omission in I.1.10 is most likely due to reasons of pacing and pedagogy. The notion of dual authorship is reminiscent of Origen but worked out more fully with the notion of instrumental causality.

29. Expressed in II–II.171–78, and discussed at some length in Pierre Benoit and Paul Synave, *Prophecy and Inspiration*, trans. Avery R. Dulles and Thomas L. Sheridan (New York: Desclée, 1961).

30. That implication has called forth a vigorous controversial literature, which

Thomas spells out this implication in two of the passages under consideration here. The explanation in I.1.10 is straightforward, in keeping with the lack of regard for the human author in that article:

> Since the literal sense is that which the author intends, and since the author of Holy Writ is God, Who by one act comprehends all things by His intellect, it is not unfitting, as Augustine says (*Conf.* xii), if, *even according to the literal sense* [emphasis mine], one word in Holy Writ should have several senses.

The discussion is somewhat deeper and more explicit in *De potentia* IV.1, where the topic is the proper interpretation of the creation account in Genesis. Aquinas is concerned with potential presumption on the interpreter's part, who may force the text to a favored meaning and so exclude other equally true possibilities. There are good reasons for Scripture to admit more than one sense: everyone should be amazed at being able to always draw new truth from it, and this multiplicity also allows one to more easily defend the biblical witness. If one understanding should fall (a warning particularly apt to Genesis 1), recourse can be had to another sense. Yet if multiple senses are so explicitly endorsed, authorial intention here becomes a question. Being reluctant to ascribe ignorance to the human authors, Thomas first says that God may have so enlightened them that they grasped all the multiple senses of their words. Thus, every true understanding would be "the sense of the author." But even if they did not understand the full meaning of their words,

> there is no doubt that the Holy Spirit understood, who is the principal author of divine Scripture. Wherefore every truth which can be adapted to divine Scripture, keeping the circumstances of the letter, is its sense. (*De Pot.* IV.1)[31]

---

will not be explored here. It has been summarized in Mark F. Johnson, "Another Look at the Plurality of the Literal Sense," *Medieval Philosophy and Theology* 2 (1992): 117–41. The primary texts discussed in the main body, particularly *De potentia* IV.1, clearly show that Thomas envisioned a multiple literal sense.

31. *Non est dubium quin Spiritus sanctus intellexerit, qui est principalis actor divinae Scripturae. Unde omnis veritas quae, salva litterae circumstantia, potest divinae Scripturae aptari, est eius sensus.*

Though Aquinas increases the role and function of the literal sense, while providing a far more satisfactory explanation of it, this acceptance of multiple literal senses should serve as a cautionary note. One shares Thomas's understanding of the literal sense only if one shares his understanding of the biblical text as a joint production of divine and human authors.

Spiritual sense refocused

The basic explanation of literal sense given above is one that might be applied to any text, presuming only an author with an intent to communicate. Scripture, however, possesses a spiritual sense or senses in addition to the literal signification of the words. This statement was a matter of wide acceptance in the tradition as it came to Thomas, but the precise explanation of it was still a matter of discussion. For him, the answer is found in the same ideas that serve to explain the literal sense: signs as intentional bearers of meaning, and God as the ultimate or primary author of Scripture. They provide the foundation, while the finer structure is derived from what we would call the history of salvation.[32]

The discussion here has already touched upon the unique status that the Bible possesses, thanks to God's work as its author, as the basis for speaking of multiple *literal* senses. Striking as that may be, it is much the same as authorship in general. God may deliberately intend all the meanings that may be drawn from the words, but the words themselves are functioning as they might in any other work. They are signs, which signify the things about which their author intends to communicate. Yet where humans are confined to the use of written or unwritten signs as expressions of their meaning, God has additional options.

Being a provident Creator, God can as easily form the course of events and the creatures of the world in order to convey a given meaning as a human author can the course of a sentence.

32. There is a fine treatment in M. D. Mailhiot, "La pensée de S. Thomas sur le sens spirituel," *Revue Thomiste* 59 (1959): 613–63.

For as a human can employ some words or imagined similitudes for signifying something, so God employs for signification the course of things subject to his providence. (VII.16)[33]

Everything mentioned in Scripture is potentially a bearer of meaning in itself, and not only according to the use made of it in the literal sense of the words. The use of things in order to signify other things constitutes the spiritual sense, named thus because "the visible things are commonly the figures of invisible things" (VII.15).[34] This requires some expansion, however, for while words have the grammar and syntax of a particular language to govern their use as signs of meaning, the grammar and syntax of things is not readily apparent.

Two overarching rules limit the boundaries of the spiritual sense. The first states that nothing is taught under the spiritual sense in a given passage that is not taught openly elsewhere in Scripture; it follows that "a spiritual exposition should always have support from some literal exposition" (VII.14 ad3).[35] There is no explanation of this apart from the authority of Augustine, but it may be that one finds reasons in the next point. There the discussion turns to the related principle that spiritual senses are not a proper source for theological argumentation. While this is put forth as an objection, implying some lack or defect in spiritual interpretation, for Thomas it is intrinsic to the basic character of spiritual senses as likenesses or similitudes. "For one thing can be similar to many other things; hence there can be no fixed advance from something mentioned in Scripture to some one of those others" (VII.14 ad4).[36] That is to say,

33. *Sicut enim homo potest adhibere ad aliquid significandum aliquas voces vel aliques similitudines fictas, sit Deus adhibet ad significationem aliquorum ipsum cursum rerum suae providentiae subiectarum.*

34. *Visibilia solent esse figurae invisibiliae.* The explanation given in the disputed question is easily the most complete in Thomas's work, and therefore the one followed here. It is surprising that one author can say that "the text that serves Thomas as a base for his theory of the senses of Scripture is *In Epistola ad Galatas,* 4.24" when this much shorter and later text only summarizes the lengthier account offered earlier; Waclaw Swiezawski, "L'exégèse biblique et la théologie speculative de S. Thomas d'Aquin," *Divinitas* 18 (1974): 149 n. 11.

35. *Spiritualis expositio semper debet habere fulcimentum ab aliqua litterali expositione.*

36. *Una enim res pluribus similis esse potest; unde non potest ab illa, quando in Scriptura sacra proponitur, procedi ad aliquam illarum determinatio.*

borrowing his example, that the lion as it appears in Scripture may signify either Christ (e.g., the Lion of Judah) or the devil (e.g., "who goes about as a roaring lion"). The mere appearance of a lion in any given passage offers no help in determining whether either of these significations exists there. Another factor must intervene for exegesis to proceed, whether it be the literal interpretation of other texts or additional knowledge of lions and their nature.[37] The *res* of Scripture are at the mercy of an interpreter's fancy without that sort of framework, much as the words of a language are subject to distortion at the hands of someone unskilled in grammar or deficient in vocabulary. Both of the explicit strictures that Thomas mentions can be reduced to this one consideration.

The contrast with Origen here is instructive. As observed above, Origen makes use of spiritual interpretation with great freedom. The measure appears to be his perception of the church's rule of faith, rather than factors intrinsic to the specific text he considers. The Scripture that originated from the Spirit remains an instrument of the same Spirit working through the exegete for the benefit of others and so remains somewhat open (though the text does serve to guide reflection). While Thomas would be far from denying the importance of the Bible as a means of spiritual growth, for him that is less its primary function than something consequent upon it. His description is precise, even clinical: "Sacred Scripture has been divinely ordained so that the truth necessary for salvation may be manifested to us through it" (VII.14).[38] The focus shifts toward Scripture per se and what is taught through or learned from a passage. While for Origen the spiritual sense is grounded in the interaction between the text and its audience, bearing wisdom at a level appropriate to everyone who comes to it, Thomas would see it as a framework of relationships and significations inherent in the matters discussed. He embeds the spiritual sense more deeply into the biblical text, and so

37. The text fails to specify; but see the remark of an earlier *magister* in Smalley, *Study,* 258–59, with reference to Nm 11.7 *(the manna was like coriander seed):* "We could discourse lengthily on this, if only the nature and quality of *coriander seed* were known to us."

38. *Sacra Scriptura ad hoc divinitus ordinata est ut per eam nobis veritas manifestetur necessaria ad salutem.*

makes spiritual interpretation less a matter of charismatic reading on the part of the exegete and more a matter of investigation and analysis. This change of emphasis becomes even more apparent when one examines his way of explaining the different types of spiritual senses.

The spiritual sense was divided traditionally into three subtypes; moral, allegorical, and anagogical. Aquinas accepts this structure and accounts for it within his own understanding of spiritual senses. The truth that Scripture manifests under the figures of the spiritual sense may concern either matters of right conduct or matters of right belief. Right conduct as the concern of spiritual interpretation constitutes the moral sense, where we may draw instruction from the examples of the *res* narrated in the Bible and preeminently from that of Christ or those things that signify him (I.1.10). Here it is important to note that the moral sense, like the other spiritual senses, can be drawn only from the significations inscribed in the *res* themselves. Passages put directly, such as the Sermon on the Mount, or couched openly in parable, such as the story of the Good Samaritan, bear their moral teaching in their literal sense; strictly speaking, they have no moral sense. Spiritual interpretation as focused on matters of belief has a more complicated structure that mirrors what is believed, which Thomas explains in a unified and ecclesiocentric way in *Quodlibet VII* (as opposed to the somewhat scattered account in the *Summa*).[39] The grounding insight is that:

> the state of the Church is a medium between the state of the Synagogue and the state of the Church triumphant. Therefore the Old Testament was the symbol of the new, and the Old and New Testaments simultaneously are the symbol of the celestial. (VII.15)[40]

39. Ecclesiocentric should not be understood here in opposition to Christocentric; as the balance of the question will go on to show, Thomas is operating here under the most comprehensive category. The idea of Christ as head of the Church, which is his mystical body, and ourselves as members of that body plays an important structural role.

40. *Status Ecclesiae medius est inter statum Synagogae, et statum Ecclesiae triumphantis. Vetus ergo testamentum figure fuit novi; vetus simul et novum figura sunt caelestium.*

Spiritual interpretation as focused on the relationship between Old and New Testament then leads to the allegorical sense, where the happenings of the Old Testament serve as figures of Christ and the Church, while the anagogical sense is founded upon the ways in which each testament foreshadows the heavenly reality of the world to come.

One gains an additional understanding of the spiritual senses in operation from the response to an objection, where Aquinas explains that all senses are not to be sought in every individual passage of the Bible. While earlier things and events may signify later ones, as the Old Testament does the New, such significations are not fully reciprocal; one cannot say that the New Testament is the figure of the Old. The *res* at hand in the literal sense of a passage control the sort of spiritual interpretation that may be drawn from them. All three spiritual senses may be found in "the deeds of the Old Testament" *(facta veteris testamenti),* which may symbolize any of the later things. Passages whose literal sense deals with Christ can also be expounded in all three senses: moral insofar as we have an example of how to live in his life, allegorical insofar as things said or done concerning him may be understood of the Church that is one body with him, and anagogical "insofar as the road to glory has been shown to us in Christ" (VII.15 ad4).[41] Passages that deal directly with the Church are not open to allegory, but can be interpreted either anagogically with reference to the future state of the Church in heaven or morally with reference to ourselves as members. As noted earlier, texts whose literal sense is concerned with moral instruction do not themselves have a moral sense, though they may have an allegorical or anagogical significance. Those passages that speak literally of heaven and the world to come have no spiritual sense at all because, in a beautiful phrase, "they are not symbols of other things, but symbolized by all others" (VII.15 ad4).[42] For Thomas as for Origen, that heavenly fulfillment is the ultimate goal toward which the Bible directs us in all its senses.

41. *Inquantum in Christo est nobis iter gloriae demonstratum.*
42. *Ipsa non sunt figura aliorum, sed ab omnibus aliis figurata.*

Basic agreement

The fundamental principles of Origen's exegesis were earlier identified as inspiration, applicability, and the rule of faith. Thomas shares those core principles, with the exception of applicability. For Thomas, the fact that Scripture has something to say everywhere and to all is rather a consequence of its function in conveying "the truth necessary for salvation"; his attention is much more focused on the different ways the Bible communicates that truth. The role applicability plays for Origen in the structure of his spiritual reading is filled for Thomas by God's ability to make use of things as well as words to signify meaning. As we have seen, this change reduces the opportunity for subjective caprice by linking spiritual meaning more closely to realities discussed in the text.

The crucial agreement between Origen and Thomas, one that is emblematic of the tradition that they represent, lies in the emphasis on inspiration.[43] They share a conviction that Scripture is from God in a unique way, so much so that God stands behind its words and can be called its author (without denying the human role in the composition of the various biblical texts). This is the greatest influence upon the ways in which they approach the Bible, whether it finds expression in Origen's quest to read "in a way worthy of God" or Thomas's analysis of divine authorship and the ways God is able to convey meaning. One might even say that Thomas's explanation of the spiritual senses, which flows more clearly and directly from the idea of divine authorship, concentrates the basic insight of inspiration while avoiding the lack of control to which Origen is often subject. When that view of the spiritual senses is combined with his more sophisticated treatment of the literal sense, Aquinas lays out a fully developed way of reading that constitutes a high point within the tradition established by Origen.

43. One can understand the rule of faith, or less concisely, the coherence of a given interpretation with the whole body of Christian teaching developed over time, as secondary to inspiration; the same God who is the ultimate source and authority behind Scripture is also the one guiding the Church as its understanding of faith grows. See II–II.1.7–9 and, more broadly, Per Erik Persson, *Sacra Doctrina: Reason and Revelation in Aquinas* (Oxford: Oxford University Press, 1970), 58–60.

SPINOZA

Spinoza's biblical thought is contained in his *Theologico-Political Treatise,* published anonymously in 1670. The work quickly gained distinction as one of the most denounced books of the seventeenth century. Spinoza himself soon shared that reputation, as the fact of his authorship was open knowledge in the learned community. He had undertaken the composition when already engaged in writing his *Ethics,* in order to clear the ground and prepare an audience more receptive to his substantive philosophy.[44] In line with this purpose, the *Treatise* is not composed in the *more geometrico* fashion of the *Ethics.* It is rather a sustained exercise in persuasive rhetoric, using many elements of classic rhetorical structure.[45] There is also some rhetorical play involving such basic and commonplace religious topics as God or providence. Part of Spinoza's project is to subtly redefine these terms and others in a way that "exploits the connotations of familiar words to serve radically new purposes."[46] This requires a more cautious and synthetic approach in presenting his ideas; Spinoza is much less straightforward than either Origen or Aquinas. To recognize Spinoza's place as the founder of a new way of reading, one must read the discussions of interpretation and Scripture in light of the restructured ideas of prophecy and providence. It is in the changes wrought upon those ideas that his differences from the older tradition become most clear.

44. See letter 30 (Oct. 1665) to Henry Oldenburg. In the short to medium term, at least, his effort must be judged a failure: for a summary of the violently hostile reaction, see Brad S. Gregory, introduction to *Tractatus Theologico-Politicus,* by Baruch Spinoza, trans. Samuel Shirley (Leiden: E. J. Brill, 1989), 27–32.

45. Fokke Akkerman, "Le caractère rhétorique du Traité théologico-politique," in *Spinoza entre lumière et romantisme* (Fontenay-aux-Roses: E.N.S., 1985), 382–83.

46. Yirmiyahu Yovel, *The Marrano of Reason,* vol. 1 of *Spinoza and Other Heretics* (Princeton: Princeton University Press, 1989), 136. The entire fifth chapter, "Spinoza, the Multitude, and Dual Language," is an excellent discussion of Spinoza's art of writing. See also J. Samuel Preus, *Spinoza and the Irrelevance of Biblical Authority* (Cambridge: Cambridge University Press, 2001).

"On the Interpretation of Scripture"

The only way to avoid theological prejudice and superstition when approaching the Bible is to study it in precisely the same way that one studies natural phenomena. Close and detailed examination, unimpeded by any outside considerations, provides "assured data" from which definitions and axioms may be constructed. The inquirer then possesses a set of fixed principles for explaining a given subject, be it natural science or biblical meaning. In adopting this method, Spinoza carefully segregates the scriptural text from other sources of speculative or practical knowledge. Revelation and miracle, which one can know only from Scripture, play so significant a role in its witness as to constitute "almost all the contents of Scripture" (142).[47] Natural sources of knowledge are irrelevant to either of these supernatural events, which go beyond nature in their action and in their content. Biblical teaching regarding ethics, though not supernatural in the same way, is also marked off as sui generis; since it is only from the truth and correctness of its moral doctrine that we recognize Scripture as divine, that doctrine must be established in an integral way without influence from natural reasoning (prior to the judgment that acknowledges the superiority of biblical morality). Biblical interpretation is to be practiced in what one might call a "clean room," shielded from potentially contaminating knowledge. An effect of this is to place the question of truth outside the realm of interpretation. As Spinoza will note, the important question is not truth but meaning:

> in seeking the meaning of Scripture we should take every precaution against the undue influence, not only of our own prejudices, but of our faculty of reason in so far as that is based on the principles of natural cognition. In order to avoid confusion between true meaning and truth of fact, the former must be sought simply from linguistic usage, or from a process of reasoning that looks to no other basis than Scripture. (143)

47. All page citations of Spinoza's *Treatise* in the text are drawn from Baruch Spinoza, *Tractatus Theologico-Politicus,* trans. Samuel Shirley (Leiden: E. J. Brill, 1989).

This search for meaning is guided by three main prerequisites. First and most important is an exact and precise knowledge of the biblical languages of composition. Spinoza here tends to speak always of Hebrew (and the difficulties involved in mastering it), with little attention to Greek. This may be due to his personal background or to the greater currency of Greek among his audience. The second prerequisite is the correlation of texts so that all an author's statements on any given topic can be compared and ambiguities or contradictions investigated. That investigation is to be conducted on a purely internal level, however. What a given author means "must in no wise be decided by the rationality or irrationality of the belief, but solely from other pronouncements" of the same author (143). The final requirement is as much knowledge as possible not only of the biblical authors and the circumstances of their lives and writings but also the subsequent history of the text and its reception into the biblical canon. Study of these things is necessary to weed out textual corruption or the personal idiosyncrasies of author or audience in order to clearly discern "teachings of eternal significance" (145).[48] Once these historical and linguistic preliminaries are firmly in hand, substantive interpretation of the biblical text becomes possible. The idea that the procedures of biblical study should follow and parallel those used in studying nature here exerts an important influence; only things that are taught universally and without exception through Scripture are to be taken as its core teaching, just as the rules that "Nature always observes and through which she constantly acts" are the basic principles of science (145). The universal teaching, together with due attention to the historical context, can then be used in resolving ambiguous or contradictory passages stemming from different authors.

Spinoza goes on to examine much of Scripture in light of his new historical framework. This leads to the attack on Mosaic authorship

48. This concern for avoiding personal traits and focusing only on the universal prevents the use of one author to clarify another. Without a prior understanding of what each author teaches or merely accepts from their environment, Spinoza finds such mutual clarification unreliable (151–52).

of the Pentateuch that is so famous a part of the *Treatise*. Though outrageous to many of Spinoza's contemporaries, doubts or even outright rejection were not new.[49] However, Spinoza's denial of Mosaic authorship as well as his other historical analyses take place in a context that makes such statements more than mere issues of proper bibliography. That is part of the reason that the treatment of biblical interpretation is held back until the seventh chapter; the historical/philological framework does not stand on its own.

Prophecy and providence

As we turn to the underpinnings of Spinoza's interpretive structure, it is important to keep in mind that these topics are brought up only in order to clarify his view of what Scripture is and how it functions. The *Treatise* is a complex work, and the amount of time and space required for a full treatment of Spinoza's ideas regarding God and God's interaction with the world goes far beyond the limits of our present concern.

Spinoza defines prophecy as "sure knowledge of some matter revealed by God to man" (60). Inasmuch as he holds that all knowledge depends in some way on the presence of "the idea and nature of God" within the human mind, knowledge acquired by the use of natural reason should have an equal claim to prophetic and divine status. Yet since "the multitude" are less impressed by the familiar, his discussion of prophecy passes over natural knowledge and reason to focus on other ways used by God to reveal things that exceed the grasp of human understanding. This investigation is confined to scriptural data, that being our sole source for information on prophets and prophecy. The term "scriptural data," however, is subjected to an important qualification. According to Spinoza, it is a Jewish habit to attribute everything that happens to God while neglecting inter-

49. In reviewing prior discussions of Mosaic authorship, Richard Popkin notes that a traditional doctrine of inspiration could rather easily cope with such difficulties: "the petty difficulty that Moses could not have written line x did not matter, if the author was also in contact with God." See Richard H. Popkin, "Spinoza and Bible Scholarship," in *The Cambridge Companion to Spinoza*, ed. Don Garrett (Cambridge: Cambridge University Press, 1996), 396.

mediate causes. A good harvest, commercial success, or some fortunate stroke of genius are all ascribed immediately to God. This turn of speech requires that only express statements or the clearest possible context can serve to establish biblical references to divine communication as true prophecy.

With this proviso in mind, the remaining treatment of prophecy is concerned with two major points. The first concerns the cognitive status of prophecy. After a review of various and sundry prophetic incidents, Spinoza concludes that "God's revelations were received only with the aid of the imaginative faculty, to wit, with the aid of words or images" (65).[50] The effect of this is to remove prophecy from the realm of reason and make of it a matter of imaginative flair or sense perception; the intellect of the prophet is not directly engaged. The only other topic considered is the meaning of the phrase "Spirit of God" and its role in prophetic revelation. Spinoza goes through a number of etymological points regarding each half of the phrase before grouping various biblical uses under differing parts of the definition. While these points are interesting in terms of the overall project of the *Treatise,* the constraints of time and space limit us here to his conclusion regarding the role played by the Spirit in prophecy. Since Spirit of God can simply be another way of referring to the divine mind, "the imaginative faculty of the prophets, insofar as it was the instrument for the revelation of God's decrees, could equally well be called the mind of God, and the prophets could be said to have possessed the mind of God" (70). As with the initial definition of prophecy, Spinoza notes that this understanding could also be referred to our natural knowledge (which "has the mind of God and his eternal thoughts inscribed" within it) were it not for the fact that people regard what is common and universal as of little importance. Another reason that prophecy was ascribed to the Spirit of God is that

50. Revelation is confined to dream or vision apart from Moses, who "spoke with God face to face," or Christ, who "communed with God mind to mind" (65). It is open to doubt how seriously Spinoza took either of the exceptions he stated here.

men did not know the causes of prophetic knowledge, which evoked their wonder. They therefore referred it like all other portents to God, and were wont to call it divine knowledge. (70)

Spinoza shares this ignorance of the causes underlying the prophetic phenomenon, but dismisses it. Once it is established that biblical prophecy takes place solely in the imaginative faculty, "the causes of these Scriptural teachings are not our concern" (71).

The discussion of prophets takes up and expands upon the idea of prophecy as purely a matter of imagination. Since prophecy has little or nothing to do with reason, it follows that the ideas held by the prophets are unchanged by their prophetic experiences. The prophets continue to share the common conceptions of their day and age, and their beliefs on those matters differ just as their historical circumstances and personalities do. The only element of importance for Spinoza is their common focus on how "to live the true life [which he identifies with the basic requirements of justice and charity], for that alone is the object and the substance of the revelation, which does not teach free will or philosophic doctrine" (86). The trappings with which these exhortations to morality are clad are irrelevant; they are all arguments of convenience aimed at producing conviction in the immediate audience or at the refutation of opponents based on their own premises.

The point of Spinoza's treatment is to entirely remove prophecy from the realm of knowledge. There is no rational content conveyed under the prophetic imagery that is not equally accessible to pure human reason, as is shown by his insistence that human knowledge acquired by normal means has a claim to the status of divine truth as good or better than anything conveyed by prophecy.[51] To use a modern idiom, prophets under this scheme become advertising agents. Except insofar as we learn from them how to deal with and convince "the multitude," there is no prophetic teaching in the strict sense of the word.

51. Better, for the human knowledge that is based on "clear and distinct ideas" carries its certitude and proof with it. Prophetic knowledge, as a matter of imagination, can achieve a practical, moral certainty only on the basis of extrinsic indicators such as signs or the individual prophet's upright manner of life (74–75).

Scripture's *ad hominem* focus and lack of concern for speculative truth also figure prominently in Spinoza's discussion of providence. Although he sets the discussion within a much broader indictment of the common notion of miracle, what concerns us here is the way in which he identifies divine providence with the order of nature.[52] "When Scripture tells us that this or that was accomplished by God or by God's will, nothing more is intended than that it came about in accordance with Nature's law and order" (132). The whole body of references to God's doing or acting that one encounters in the biblical text is dismissed as another instance of the peculiarly Jewish tendency to neglect other causes and ascribe things directly to God. Therefore, "we need have no hesitation in believing that what truly happened, happened naturally," that is, following universal and immutable laws of nature (133).

Spinoza's analysis of prophecy and divine interaction with the world has the cumulative effect of "naturalizing" the Bible.[53] As we have seen, his explicit treatment of biblical interpretation is careful to separate the text from other areas of human knowledge (except for the linguistic and historical study necessary to grasp the context and meaning of individual books). The six chapters prior to that point serve to separate Scripture from God's knowledge. As an entirely imaginative experience, the prophetic impulse that lies behind the words of Scripture is void of revealed truth. It cannot and does not convey any information that is not accessible to natural reason, and whatever cognitive content it does have lacks the intrinsic proof offered by the "clear and distinct ideas" of reason. Nor can one adopt a Thomist perspective that finds a divinely intended meaning in the biblical persons and events, if not in the records of prophecy. If "providence" is nothing more than a synonym for a fixed and univer-

52. The eternity and immutability of natural laws are, for Spinoza, so directly derived from the divine immutability and eternity that to question or weaken the one is to make an assault on the other. For the broader question of his precise meaning in such well-known phrases as *Deus sive natura*, see Yovel, *Marrano*, 146–50.

53. The principle that providence and the fixed natural order are identical lies behind portions of his discussion omitted here, such as his rejection of a special election of the Jewish people, or the idea that humans are the object of special care on God's part (88–100, 131).

sal natural order, to which there are no exceptions, the idea that specific things or events have anything to teach regarding God or humans in a way that others do not is no longer tenable.[54] This naturalizes the Bible, because there is no longer any possibility of learning anything supernatural from it; "the 'truth' of scripture is that which is recognizable to unaided human reason."[55] This fundamental rejection of revelation is much more crucial to the argument of the *Treatise* than the particulars of authorial attributions.

Function of Scripture

With Scripture no longer a medium of divine revelation in the strict sense, one may ask what role Spinoza allots for it. This is best disclosed through his reformulated ideas of the Word of God and Divine Law. The traditional understanding of them would seem to have little place in a framework that has so carefully ruled out that tradition's understanding of revelation. The version presented in the *Treatise* continues the "naturalization" process, as Spinoza identifies God's word with the universal morality of philosophy.

There are three meanings given the phrase "Word of God" in this analysis, with two of these being metaphorical. The prophets understood the order of things as directly dependent upon divine will rather than natural causes, and so offered predictions of future events as decrees of God. This is merely a Hebrew figure of speech that they absorbed from their environment. More broadly, they also tended to represent whatever came from their prophetic gifts as the words of God. Neither of these usages is a proper one since they derive from the particular imagination and circumstances of the prophets. The primary meaning of "Word of God" in the *Treatise* is "the Divine Law . . . that is, religion universal to the entire human race" (208). That is the core of the Bible, wound about with prophetic and historical narrative, and so lends its name to the whole text.

"Wound about" is an image that may fit here, inasmuch as that

54. One should note that any specific meaning found in the *res* of Scripture under a Thomist reading depends on some literal reading; once the literal sense is deprived of revelatory content, the extended or spiritual sense loses its foundation.

55. Harrisville and Sundberg, *Bible in Modern Culture*, 42.

prophetic and historical narrative is separable from the philosophic and universal morality. The *summum bonum* of human life consists in the intellectual cognition of God, a cognition that necessarily evokes our love inasmuch as it perfects the intellect that is our highest faculty. We attain that love and cognition through the study not of Scripture, but of Nature: "the greater our knowledge of natural phenomena, the more perfect is our knowledge of God's essence, which is the cause of all things" (103). The means required to achieve this end are, for Spinoza, the true divine law inasmuch as they are derived from the inner dynamism of the mind toward God. One can even consider them to be ordained by God, "in so far as he exists in our minds" (103). That qualification is important, because God cannot be a lawgiver in the strict sense of the term. The sort of hypothetical necessity involved in legislation is incompatible with the divine eternity and immutability, since "God's affirmations and negations always involve eternal necessity or truth" (106). A truly divine law would impose necessity and not merely obligation on those subject to it. The numerous biblical references to God as a lawgiver are due to misconceptions on the part of prophets or their audiences. The rules of morality are simply the practices and actions that fit us for the study and contemplation in which our ultimate happiness consists. They are "law" only in the same extended sense as the training regimen of an athlete.

Spinoza draws some interesting consequences from this philosophic understanding of divine law. The consideration of humans as intellectual beings extends as far as human nature itself. There is no need of special revelation. Similarly, as the basic human nature is the same in whatever circumstances it is found, there is a radical lack of serious interest in history. Historical narrative cannot lead to the sure knowledge of God, since knowledge in the strict sense is based on "general axioms that are certain and self-evident" (105). There is a use for history, but it has no direct value.[56]

56. The disdain for history also extends to ceremonies of any kind (which are often grounded in historical narratives). Those observances are ascribed to simple tradition or to symbolic representations of some good; in either case, "they are mere shadows" and as such irrelevant to anyone possessed of "intellect and sound mind" (105).

Spinoza will go on to assert that "Scripture unreservedly commends the natural light and the natural Divine Law" (111). This agreement between the biblical teaching (in this presentation) and the philosophic morality of reason is significant, inasmuch as it serves to popularize morality for those unable to grasp it in a purer form. That category embraces most people, who lack the ability to follow "a logical chain of reasoning" based upon certain axioms (120). That philosophic approach demands a rare level of concentration and dispassion, in addition to sheer intellectual acuity. The (much) greater share of the human race draw their knowledge, such as it is, almost entirely from experience.[57] This is where the historical and prophetic narratives of Scripture come into play; they offer grounds attainable by the average run of people for the core beliefs on which this moral vision depends. More precisely, they offer grounds for believing the conclusions which ground that vision: the existence of a God who sustains and directs all things, ensuring that those who do good also do well and those who do evil do badly. Operating without reasoned discourse, as well as being adapted to the common understanding, these narratives fail to adequately explain those concepts, but they do engender a simple affirmation that suffices for "obedience and devotion" (121). As a result, both the multitude and the small minority capable of emulating Spinoza can agree on the fundamentals of correct behavior and conduct themselves accordingly. Once that agreement is produced (a task Spinoza hopes to achieve through his own work), one can then lay out the principles of a rational political order that will not be open to the disruption and turmoil caused by religious dissension.

A striking feature of the analysis given in the *Treatise* is the fundamental dispensability of Scripture. As we have seen, the biblical text does not serve to reveal truth but rather to provide salutary beliefs for those who lack the intellectual stature to grasp reasoned proofs. Those beliefs are conveyed in a variety of fashions adapted to the

57. Yovel's discussion on the role of the multitude, and the ways of dealing with it, in Spinoza is precise and interesting in the links it finds with Spinoza's Marrano background (*Marrano,* 128–52).

original circumstances of biblical authors and the common understanding of their day. Historical study serves to pin down those adaptations and pierce through them in order to forestall the rise of the "superstition" that Spinoza takes as his primary enemy from the very beginning of the *Treatise* (49–51). This sense of an apparent or surface reading of the text, which must be transcended in order to make progress, bears some similarity to Origen's idea of "the letter." However, with an idea of God carefully set up to exclude the possibility of revelation, it is not the Spirit that leads beyond that surface reading. Philosophy, understood as logical reasoning with "clear and distinct ideas" based upon certain axioms and concerned with the study of nature and humanity as part of nature, is the ultimate guide. With its aid one can perceive the universal morality whose basic conclusions (if not the reasons supporting them) are endorsed under the historically conditioned veils given it by Scripture. This account makes the Bible both dispensable, since different types of imaginative narrative may be needed to convey the same message in different historical situations, and disposable, at least for those capable of learning philosophy directly.

TROELTSCH

Ernst Troeltsch was first a professor of systematic theology and then of philosophy, not a biblical scholar by trade. The essay "Historical and Dogmatic Method in Theology" belongs to an early period of his career, as one stage in a running polemic that followed his attempts to set up an independent and objective path for the study of religion.[58] Here as elsewhere the marks of academic specialization are deceptive, for the essay continues to be cited as "an unexcelled explanation of the structure of historical criticism."[59] The clarity and concision that have made the essay a near classic fit it well to our present

58. See Hans-Georg Drescher, *Ernst Troeltsch: His Life and Work*, trans. John Bowden (Minneapolis: Fortress Press, 1994), 70–97, regarding Troeltsch's thought and career at this point.

59. Peter Stuhlmacher, *Historical Criticism and Theological Interpretation of Scripture*, trans. Roy A. Harrisville (Philadelphia: Fortress Press, 1977), 45.

purposes, as does its date. Published in 1898, it has no engagement with the doubts and questions that began to be raised about the significance or value of "history" as such.[60] Those concerns more properly belong with the contemporary figures treated in subsequent chapters; what Troeltsch enables us to see is the outlook to which they respond. Historical method, of course, was not his creation; but he did provide a clear analysis of the principles involved while highlighting their theological consequences.

Basic principles

For Troeltsch, the historical approach is constituted by three essential ideas. First among them is the principle of criticism, understood as the recognition that "in the realm of history there are only judgments of probability . . . and that consequently an estimate must be made of the degree of probability attached to any tradition" (13).[61] The importance of this lies more in the general attitude spawned by it than the particular judgments to which it might lead. The fundamental relationship between present and past texts or traditions changes from trust (or at least acceptance) to a rather skeptical detachment. There is also a certain amalgamation of different traditions into one mass of data to be subjected to the critical gaze; the tradition of the Christian religion is not exempt from the scrutiny accorded tradition per se.

The main tool used in reaching these critical judgments is provided by the second of Troeltsch's three ideas. The principle of analogy states that "agreement with normal, customary, or at least frequently attested happenings and conditions as we have experienced them is the criterion of probability for all events that historical criticism can recognize as having actually or possibly happened" (13–14). Analogy in this usage is another way of affirming a continuity among human affairs across time, so that we can formulate an explanation of past

60. There is a reference to Nietzsche's *On the Advantage and Disadvantage of History for Life,* but there is no sign that Nietzsche's arguments made any impression upon the essay.

61. All page citations of Troeltsch's essay in the text are drawn from Ernst Troeltsch, *Religion in History,* trans. James Luther Adams and Walter F. Bense (Minneapolis: Fortress Press, 1991).

events through comparison with the present. As with criticism, an immediate effect of the analogical principle is to bring "Jewish and Christian history" into conjunction with history as a whole; the same analogies function in the same way for whatever branch of history one may study.

The final concept that Troeltsch sets up is that of interaction or correlation. Once religious history has been brought into the orbit of universal history by application of the other two principles, it follows that "there can be no change at one point without some preceding and consequent change elsewhere, . . . inevitably forming a current in which everything is interconnected and each single event is related to all others" (14). Put more directly, the events of history form a comprehensive causal structure in which the present is conditioned by the past and the future by the present. No particular occurrence stands out as a source of significance or meaning, apart from its place within the context of the whole. Eliot would later write (with specific reference to the Incarnation) "a moment in time but time was made through that moment; for without the meaning there is no time, and that moment of time gave the meaning," but Troeltsch instead would say that it is the history of the world as a whole that explains and gives significance to the moments.[62]

These three principles lend a certain expansionism, if you will, to historical method that does not permit anything to stand outside its reach. Spinoza displays a similar tendency in his attempt to bind the varied biblical witnesses to their original historical contexts. However, with that binding achieved, he began to interpret Scripture in terms of his own strongly ahistorical philosophy. History itself remained a tool used to neutralize his opponents so that the real work of philosophy could begin. Troeltsch, on the other hand, disclaims any ulterior philosophic motive; the elements of historical method lead "with irresistible necessity" to the vision of history as a "seamless web of correlated effects and changes," while the method itself is confirmed by the massive and undeniable advance in our knowledge of the past that it has produced (15).

62. T. S. Eliot, *Choruses from "The Rock,"* VII.

Once the founding principles of that vision are laid out, they possess some noteworthy consequences. If historical study leads us to a reasoned skepticism about particular facts, "it becomes impossible to base religious faith on any single fact" (17). To draw a Kantian analogy, it is almost as if facts are the noumena of history. Since they are more or less inaccessible in themselves, thanks to the critical principle, we can be sure of their influence upon the present only through the phenomena of historical process. With that process serving as the essential mediator in our knowledge of the past, and history as a unified structure of interacting causes, one can attempt to understand the historical role of any given event or personage only in light of the broadest possible context. Nor is it only understanding that depends on that context; it is even more important from Troeltsch's point of view that our *evaluation* of the past be derived from the perspective of universal history rather than any particular tradition. "Standards of values cannot be derived from isolated events but only from an overview of the historical totality," as he puts it (18). This is an important component of his particular historical relativism, which weighs and explains any given aspect of the past only in relation to the whole movement of history.[63] It is also the core of the historical method to which his three principles lead: when consistently applied, he is confident that it will more and more clearly reveal "the glory of God in history" (19).

Standards of judgment

The essay's positive account of the historical approach ends with this vigorous affirmation of history as the revelation of the divine. The balance of the text is occupied with an attack upon the older tradition, which Troeltsch labels dogmatic, and in replies to various objections. Those replies further illuminate Troeltsch's views by showing some of the concrete standards used in the development of the

63. Troeltsch's epistemological framework and the precise character of his relativism are complex, going well beyond the bounds of the essay under consideration here. There is a careful and detailed analysis of the matter in Sarah Coakley, *Christ without Absolutes: A Study of the Christology of Ernst Troeltsch* (New York: Oxford University Press, 1988), 5–44.

universal viewpoint. Here if anywhere he begins to make use of philosophic ideas that are not easily or immediately drawn from the principles of his method.

The objections single out two pitfalls that any attempt to draw "standards of values" from the total context of history must face, one concerning human ability to grasp those standards and the other concerning history as a proper source for them. With respect to the first, its essence is suggested by an old Latin proverb: *tot capites, quot rationes* (so many heads, as many explanations). Experience shows how widely human judgments regarding meaning and significance of past events can vary. What is to ensure that any significant degree of consensus can be achieved on the precise character of the values provided by history? Here Troeltsch stands upon a non-historical idea: "the essential uniformity of human nature" (25). Despite the possibility of error, people of good will can come to agree on common values through the basis of their shared humanity. Though it is perhaps based in part on the principle of analogy, it still seems fair to consider this a non-historical idea because it implies some fundamental core within humans that is not subject to the conditioning effects of historical progress.

The substance of these agreed-upon values is drawn from within the sequence of history, or more precisely, said to be drawn from it. No reasons are brought forth to justify the axiomatic statement that "history is not a chaos but issues from unitary forces and aspires towards a unitary goal" in which the "essential truth and profundity of the human spirit" grow ever deeper. There is no attempt to develop a more detailed scale of values from this source, but it may be unfair to demand more from what remains a relatively brief essay. The progressive principle at work in history is something that one is simply expected to understand and accept, even though on a prima facie level there is only an "apparent chaos" (27).[64] Christianity remains an

64. Troeltsch praises the Hegelian doctrine of history while dismissing such pillars of Hegel's system as "its metaphysics of the absolute, its dialectic of opposites, and its specifically logical conception of religion" (27). This displays a notable lack of concern for the very foundations on which Hegel built his idea of history in the first place.

important agent in this process, inasmuch as Jesus himself represents the highest expression thus far of the human spirit, but there is nothing in principle that would forestall the advent of another religion with a greater contribution.[65] It is telling that the one objection here that Troeltsch does acknowledge is that of being too free in referring to the absoluteness of Christianity in his earlier work; he should have highlighted the role of history more clearly. As a recent biographer notes,

> He does not begin from the truth of the Christian principle of faith, and go on from there to examine the possibility of the truth or correctness of modern conceptuality or ideas, but takes the opposite course, moving from the assumption of the correctness of the concept of development to the Christian faith and its possible implications for the truth.[66]

It seems correct (albeit odd) for us to say that by taking the idea of development as a basis for argument rather than a conclusion, Troeltsch's reliance on progressive history is itself ahistorical. The elements of historical method fail to provide a justification, because there is a significant gap between affirming the unity of history and showing an intrinsic progress at work within it.

Biblical implications of historical approach

Although Troeltsch says little explicitly about Scripture, that does not mean it falls outside his concern. The Bible continues to be one of the prime objects with which the historical approach has to concern itself (18–19). The need to focus on issues of method and the more formal aspects of history as an approach to human affairs obscures this. When one juxtaposes his essay with Spinoza's *Treatise*, though, two common factors begin to emerge as characteristic of the modern approach. The most noticeable is the embrace of history as

65. If the Eastern religions have not already taken that role: while pointing out the vast ignorance of Asian religious thought in the West, Troeltsch observes that "we can persevere in our traditional faith and leave further developments to the future" so long as our culture continues to find the "decisive and elevating forces of religion" within the bounds of Christianity (28). If those forces manifest themselves more strongly elsewhere, there seems to be no reason why Christianity could not be abandoned as merely another stage within the march of history.

66. Drescher, *Ernst Troeltsch*, 74.

the master key for understanding the biblical text; each individual book must be studied within its original context. Spinoza's turn to history as the antidote to superstition and Troeltsch's application of criticism and analogy cause the texts to be seen as human compositions coming from a specific situation and directed to a specific audience, both of which are now gone (and possibly forgotten beyond retrieval). Spinoza does this in a less pure and integral way than Troeltsch, since history is for him a rhetorical weapon more than an intrinsic object of study, but the result in either case is to transform the Bible from revelatory text to historical artifact. The other crucial element follows naturally since a Scripture whose main focus and intended message are in the past requires interpretation and guidance in its relationship with the present. Spinoza makes use of a rationalist philosophy that dismisses history in order to focus upon the eternal principles of Nature, while Troeltsch looks to the ideal of progress and development within history; other options could be devised. This is where the classic formulations of modern biblical study leave their greatest mark; guidance can no longer be derived from the Bible itself or religious traditions based upon it due to the distancing effects of history, and so it must be supplied by more comprehensive frameworks drawn from other sources.

CONCLUSION

The exposition of these two differing streams of thought is not intended merely as a historical exercise. To do that well would require a book in itself, if not a life's work. The aim here has been to fill in vital background, and a recognizable sketch serves that purpose well enough. Now that it is complete, it is time to step back slightly and consider each side's strengths and weaknesses in its approach to the Bible. The contemporary figures to whom our attention next turns have been singled out due to their conscious efforts to combine Christian faith with modern historical practice; in whole or in part, they stand as heirs to both traditions. One element that must come into play as we evaluate them is their degree of fidelity to both forebears.

The central guiding idea that occupies the classic Christian tradition in its approach to Scripture is inspiration, here understood broadly to indicate that the Bible is derived from God in a unique way. Scripture not only speaks about God as its object, but has God for a source. The prophets or prophetically inspired individuals who produced the text wrote and recorded under the immediate direction of God, "sure and genuine scribes of the Holy Spirit"; what they taught, God taught.[67] That divine influence safeguards and guarantees the biblical witness against falsehood and internal confusion, as well as uniting it with the ongoing development of Christian thought. The same Spirit who stood behind Scripture was also at work leading the community "into all truth" (Jn 16.13). As a consequence, the entire body of authoritative Christian teaching served as the proper context within which the text was read and difficulties resolved.

Neither the virtues nor the vices of this orientation are insignificant. It stands in clear continuity with the way in which apostolic Christianity treated the Jewish Scriptures, which were its only Bible, and extends over more than fifteen hundred years of Christian life and teaching.[68] It also promotes a most serious concern for ascertaining what the text says to the present, exploring all its implications as a guide for thought and practice. Yet the emphasis on understanding Scripture as a unity, intended for our instruction, can lead to a disregard for historical situations that obscures what a text has to say.[69] Even apart from such considerations of history, a Bible read in close union with the whole of Christian teaching can easily be homogenized as the theology of the day blends and subordinates the differing scriptural voices and concerns in the service of its own goals.

If the classic approach is characterized by the emphasis on God as

67. These precise words are Calvin's (*Institutes* IV.viii.9), but the sentiment is common; translation from *Institutes of the Christian Religion,* ed. John T. McNeill, trans. Ford Lewis Battles (Philadelphia: Westminster, 1960).

68. A point to which we will return in discussing de Lubac.

69. This tendency as it appeared in Thomas is shown by Otto Hermann Pesch, "Paul as Professor of Theology: The Image of the Apostle in St. Thomas's Theology," *Thomist* 38 (1974): 584–605.

the ultimate authority and source behind Scripture, it would be fair to say that the modern way of reading lays almost all its stress upon Scripture as the product of history. The Bible is seen as an assemblage of diverse texts from diverse historical circumstances that convey the concerns and thoughts of their authors from within their own particular situations. Our understanding of a given biblical passage must depend upon our ability to recover that historical context and read the text in its light, just as it does with any other historical text; we are no more the intended audience of the Bible than we are of Herodotus. The historical study needed for that recovery is to be conducted along the same lines and with the same critical tools that one brings to historical research in general.

It is important not to minimize the real gains achieved by modern historical studies; the use of critical methods and techniques affords us a greater and more detailed grasp of the biblical text, history, and languages than ever before. Even apart from the value of knowledge for its own sake, research conducted *sine ira et studio* has enormous potential for clarifying obscurity or correcting errors that have crept into traditional readings. An example of this with particular relevance in our century is the recent emphasis on the Jewish background of early Christianity, which has gone far toward eliminating hackneyed stereotypes of a legalistic first-century Judaism and highlighted much apparent anti-Semitism in the New Testament as intra-Jewish polemic.[70] However, the growth and increase of knowledge produced by this attention to history can lead to an overemphasis that binds biblical texts to their historical circumstances.[71] The importance given to original context tends to overshadow the possibility that Scripture might have its own teaching for our present situation. With that possibility obscured, the Bible becomes merely one historical source among others. Any meaning it has for us apart from that is accidental; it may provide illustrations of more general theories, or serve as a

70. The various works of E. P. Sanders provide a signal instance of this, most notably *Paul and Palestinian Judaism* (Philadelphia: Fortress Press, 1977).

71. A binding deliberately intended by Spinoza, and taken as an inevitable effect of historical method by Troeltsch.

sort of cultural influence, but other works of history or literature could do so as well.

These particular advantages and disadvantages are not isolated accidents, but flow from the fundamental principles involved. They are difficult to avoid once one takes either God or history as the ultimate source of the biblical texts. Though fidelity to both these traditions will play a crucial role as we consider contemporary authors, the obstacles involved should not be underestimated.

CHAPTER TWO

RAYMOND BROWN

Raymond Brown was a leading Roman Catholic New Testament scholar for over thirty years, whose significant exegetical labors on the Gospel (1966–70) and Epistles of John (1982), the Infancy Gospels (1977, rev. 1993), and the Passion narrative (1994) established his reputation across the scholarly community.[1] Among the modern writers to whom we now turn, he is the clearest exponent and most active defender of the approach and assumptions of mainstream twentieth-century exegesis. A Sulpician priest, Brown began his academic career at a time when Catholic biblical scholarship was only starting to take advantage of the increased freedom offered by *Divino Afflante Spiritu (DAS)* (1943).[2] His work played a major role in establishing the parity of Catholic and Protestant biblical scholarship.[3] In addition to the specialized scholarly studies mentioned above, he produced a number of books aimed at bringing the practice and results of modern biblical studies to a broader audience.[4]

1. *The Gospel according to John* (Garden City: Doubleday, 1966–70); *The Epistles of John* (Garden City: Doubleday, 1982); *The Birth of the Messiah,* rev. ed. (New York: Doubleday, 1993); *The Death of the Messiah* (New York: Doubleday, 1994). His last major book was *An Introduction to the New Testament* (New York: Doubleday, 1997).

2. Gerald P. Fogarty, *American Catholic Biblical Scholarship: A History from the Early Republic to Vatican II* (San Francisco: Harper and Row, 1989), is particularly helpful on this development. He shows there that the opportunity offered by *DAS* remained in considerable jeopardy throughout the years from 1943 through 1965, when it was confirmed and extended by the Vatican II document *Dei Verbum.*

3. A parity symbolized by his own service as president of major ecumenical biblical societies (Society of Biblical Literature, Society for the Study of the New Testament), as well as his tenure on the Pontifical Biblical Commission.

4. Such as *An Introduction to New Testament Christology* (New York: Paulist Press, 1994); *Biblical Exegesis and Church Doctrine* (New York: Paulist Press, 1985); *The Churches the Apostles Left Behind* (New York: Paulist Press, 1984); with John

These popular writings are more directly concerned with issues of hermeneutics and theological use of the Bible than are the exegetical commentaries, although the revised edition of his *Birth of the Messiah* includes important replies to criticisms from the Catholic right.[5]

We begin with his assessment of the contemporary situation of biblical studies. As we will soon see, Brown regarded the era following *DAS* as a rare chance for the Church to integrate historical approaches to Scripture into the structure of its theology and preaching. One could say that the raison d'être for his activity was the need to ensure that the chance would not be squandered as it had been in the past. He sought to avoid this outcome by providing an example of modern exegesis at the service of the community of faith and by correcting misapprehensions on both right and left. The two principal deviations that drew his attention were rejection of historical criticism on the one hand and rejection of the New Testament canon on the other. In both cases, the remedy is less an abandonment of modern biblical study than a proper application of it.

PRESENT CIRCUMSTANCES

Background

Brown's assessment of the situation is formed by the way he understood the history of critical exegesis within the Catholic Church and his fear that a familiar pattern might again repeat itself. The engagement with the Bible as a historical text, whose modern inception may be dated by the founding of the École Biblique (1890), is an opportunity that the Church has in the past neglected or suppressed. Three lost chances in particular stood out for him: the later years of St. Jerome, in which he turned away from Origen and toward the *hebraica veritas;* the revival of Hebrew study around the abbey of St. Victor in the twelfth century, with a renewed focus upon the literal sense; and Richard Simon's research into the origins of the Penta-

---

Meier, *Antioch and Rome* (New York: Paulist Press, 1983); *The Critical Meaning of the Bible* (New York: Paulist Press, 1981).

5. See especially *Birth,* 573–83, but responses to criticism appear intermittently throughout the Supplement containing the revised material.

teuch.[6] "In each of these instances biblical criticism was suffocated by pietism and exaggerated traditionalism, ultimately on the grounds that it could not be right because it differed from what Catholics had been saying before."[7]

The more recent course of Catholic biblical studies provided further cause for concern, particularly for an exegete of Brown's generation with personal experience of its fluctuations. The vigorous repression associated with the Modernist crisis (1907), and its perceived roots in biblical scholarship, virtually snuffed out the incipient use of critical methods among Catholic scholars. The most active phase of the reaction, which even led to the creation of a network of concealed spies and informers, lasted less than ten years, but an atmosphere of fear and apprehension, reinforced by continued vigilance among both official and unofficial authorities, extended for decades.[8] Pius XII's 1943 encyclical *Divino afflante Spiritu,* which opened new avenues for study of the Bible as a historical document, was a welcome but largely unanticipated reversal. While this new openness encouraged a less hesitant scholarship, and Catholic students began pursuing advanced degrees in biblical studies at non-Catholic institutions, a vigorous opposition led by those whose attitudes had been formed in the earlier period inhibited the growth of the biblical movement in many ways. Following the death of Pius XII, a period of retrenchment, symbolized by the dismissal of prominent faculty at several institutions, gave the appearance of a return to a more repressive climate. The eventual outcome was unclear for several years, and the anxiety among biblical scholars intense, until the Pontifical Biblical Commission's 1964 "Instruction on the Historical

6. The reader is referred to J. N. D. Kelly, *Jerome* (New York: Harper and Row, 1975); Smalley, *Study;* and John D. Woodbridge, "Richard Simon le 'père de la critique biblique,'" in *Le Grand Siècle et la Bible,* ed. J.-R. Armogathe (Paris: Beauchesne, 1989), 193–206, for specific studies.

7. *Critical Meaning,* 81.

8. See Gabriel Daly, *Transcendence and Immanence: A Study in Catholic Modernism and Integrism* (Oxford: Clarendon Press, 1980), particularly chapters 8 and 9, for official reaction to Modernism. A review of the anti-Modernist campaign in the United States may be found in Fogarty, *American Catholic Biblical Scholarship,* 171–98.

Truth of the Gospels," followed a year later by Vatican II's document on divine revelation, *Dei Verbum,* made it clear that "the Church officially espoused historical criticism."[9] While sufficient to remove fears of outright rejection or condemnation, the conciliar development did not eliminate all uncertainty. The degree to which this espousal has matured in the time since the Council, particularly with regard to the influence of exegesis upon systematic theology, remains an open question.[10]

Problems

History and memory combined to produce in Brown a keen sense of how fragile the standing of historical criticism is, leaving him with a particular concern to ensure and extend its full acceptance in the ongoing life of the Church (as opposed to a merely notional acknowledgement that does nothing to correct a naive pre-critical approach). His popular works pursue this goal by "showing how contemporary scriptural research can enrich our doctrinal heritage rather than threaten it," and also by opposing various distortions "in order to assist Catholics who are seeking to understand modern biblical research."[11]

One constant problem is disengagement from historical-critical method and failure to engage the insights it offers, whether expressed in a blunt or a subtle way. Though Brown considered simple denial of modern biblical studies "the enduring and recurring question" in pastoral terms, it flows from a naive approach to Scripture as a source of proof-texts for later theology, an approach that draws encouragement from the fundamentalist strains abroad in the American environment rather than from reasoned opposition.[12] An investiga-

9. Fogarty, *American Catholic Biblical Scholarship,* 343. The abbreviated summary given above may be filled out in detail by 250–350.

10. For an example of the difficulty with specific reference to Christological issues, see John P. Meier, "Jesus among the Theologians," in *The Mission of Christ and His Church* (Wilmington: Michael Glazier, 1990), 33–69.

11. *Biblical Exegesis,* 8.

12. Richard John Neuhaus, ed., *Biblical Interpretation in Crisis* (Grand Rapids: Eerdmans, 1989), 132.

tion devoted to figures who, whatever their other differences, stand together in accepting the basic legitimacy of historical-critical exegesis need not linger over this problem.

Attention is better spent upon more adroit forms of rejection, where the validity of historical method is admitted in principle but denied in practice. This tends to happen through omission or forced harmonization of certain texts, as when Mark's negative portrayal of Jesus' family (including Mary) is ignored or explained away in favor of Lukan and Johannine portrayals more favorable to later Mariology. One also finds positive results derived through arguments from silence, or later doctrinal formulations being used to resolve historical problems, as when the NT's apparent lack of interest in designating the celebrant of the Eucharist is taken for evidence that "*only* those ordained by the apostles" presided.[13] Brown sees this less as fundamentalism than as a failure to understand the relationship between Scripture and subsequent Church teaching, which leads to the dangerous pretense "that our status as Catholics enables us to find more historical information or evidence in the literal sense of the text than can our Protestant brothers and sisters."[14] As we will see below, the link between an acknowledgment of the insights of historical criticism and a proper appreciation of doctrinal development is a crucial element of his outlook.

At a more academic and less popular level, "modern tendencies to disintegrate the canon" of Scripture have become an area of distortion.[15] These tendencies, in Brown's analysis, flow not from a rejection of historical-critical method, but from a use of it that stresses the critical element at the expense of the historical. The clearest explanation is given in his Presidential Address to the SNTS, which identified the fundamental problem as rejection of the canonical texts of

13. *Critical Meaning,* 77; though Brown does not dream of denying legitimacy to later teaching about the celebrant of the Eucharist, that teaching must be seen as the fruit of development and not retrojected into the past.

14. *Biblical Exegesis,* 73. There is a particular focus upon this flaw in the responses offered here to John McHugh and René Laurentin; the point is made anew in *Birth,* 573–77.

15. Neuhaus, *Biblical Interpretation,* 42.

the New Testament in favor of alternative visions of early Christianity.[16] Those alternative visions are derived from reconstructed situations prior to the composition of the NT texts, as well as apocryphal texts taken to reflect earlier views suppressed by the forebears of those who would become "the catholic church" of Irenaeus's day.

A wide variety characterizes the individuals whom Brown places within this movement; while his specific critique of Crossan's work on the *Gospel of Peter* is intended as a test case, he recognizes that such a restricted analysis cannot do full justice to the spectrum of approaches.[17] He does, however, identify several widely applicable points of criticism. One is that extensive and far-reaching reconstructions based upon slender evidence are taken as self-evident to anyone not biased by an attachment to Christian orthodoxy. This in turn leads to casual dismissal of detailed criticism of the reconstructions as the fruit of prejudice, without pausing to consider that prejudice can run in many directions.[18] An additional concern is what one may call the reductionism that often serves as a guiding principle; Walter Bauer's thesis (1934) that "orthodoxy" emerged only near the end of the second century as the result of purely political struggles, leaving the losers to be retrospectively portrayed as heretical enemies of the Gospel, itself becomes an orthodoxy. The diversity of early Christianity, as further revealed by sixty years of subsequent research, does not exclude the presence of widely accepted core beliefs by which one may measure later developments.[19] The last of Brown's general ob-

16. Later published as "The *Gospel of Peter* and Canonical Gospel Priority," *New Testament Studies* 33 (1987): 321–43. Though his specific objections to J. D. Crossan's position have been set out in more detail elsewhere (*Death,* 1317–49), this essay remains his best statement of the larger difficulty.

17. "*Gospel of Peter,*" 323.

18. A trend that continues; see Robert W. Funk, *Honest to Jesus* (San Francisco: Harper Collins, 1996), 65, which sweepingly dismisses the work of both Brown and John Meier as "an apologetic ploy." Apart from a reference to *Death* on a minor issue of chronology, Funk's book makes no further reference to the extensive works of either man.

19. "*Gospel of Peter,*" 324; Brown points to Paul's admitted differences with James and Peter (Gal 2.11–14), which coexist with affirmations of a more basic unity (1 Cor 15.11), as evidence that "let a thousand flowers bloom" cannot be regarded as a motto of first-century Christianity.

servations reflects his aversion, noted earlier, to arguments from silence; the existence of "sayings collections," such as Q or the *Gospel of Thomas,* that lack a biographical framework does not justify the notion that earliest Christianity was "concerned only with understanding Jesus the Lord" and devoid of interest in the career of the earthly Jesus as it led up to passion, death, and resurrection. This view is an overstatement, inasmuch as it fails to consider why such sayings would be considered worthy of collection in the first place.[20]

One should note that Brown's response to this more recent problem is far less grounded in theology than is his defense of historical criticism. All of these responses, as well as later expansion upon them, are essentially exhortations in favor of objectivity and attention to historical evidence. Their failure to make any noticeable impression upon their main targets may indicate some difficulty with the notions of history and objective judgment, on either a practical or a theoretical level, which leads to an overconfidence in the possibilities of historical criticism.

LITERAL AND HISTORICAL

Literal sense

The justification for historical-critical method as applied to Scripture is "the recognition that, as a set of written documents, the Bible is open to the same methods of study as any other collection of literature."[21] As ancient writings produced in specific contexts of place, time, and historical situation, they are open to study by all the various historical and literary means devised for the interpretation of such texts. Those methods themselves are rarely a topic of explicit reflection in Brown's work, apart from cautionary remarks against taking any particular technique as all-sufficient or absolute.[22] His interest turns more around historical criticism's goal than its tools. That

20. *"Gospel of Peter,"* 324.

21. *Birth,* 26.

22. See Brown and Schneiders, "Hermeneutics," 1158, for warnings against exclusive reliance on one particular method. Different types of criticism (form, redaction, etc.) are discussed in 1149–52 and 1158–62, with an eye toward establishing the role of specialized knowledge in approaching the biblical text.

goal is the literal sense of the biblical text, understood as "the sense which the human author directly intended and which the written words conveyed."[23] Though the definition is simple on its face, both its elements require some explanation.

The idea of a human author with a definite intention is difficult to apply directly to Scripture, and not only as a result of modern literary hermeneutics.[24] The ordinary modern sense of the term *author* is highly specific, enforced with copyright or threat of lawsuit; it is "the original writer of a literary work." The Bible is less clear, as is ancient literature in general, embracing five different ways in which someone may be known as the author of a text: by writing with one's own hand, by dictating, by providing a summary of ideas to a subordinate who then produces a complete text, by being a revered figure whose disciples write under the guidance of his thought, and finally by being the biblical archetype for a particular form (e.g., Davidic authorship of Psalms, or Solomonic authorship of the wisdom literature). This has more in common with Latin *auctor* (in the sense of "author of a piece of information, warrant for its truth, authority") than the English word.[25] Biblical texts whose composition extended through multiple stages across significant lengths of time give rise to a further problem, as the relation between substantial writer(s) and the final redactor/editor becomes an issue.[26] Brown notes these difficulties almost without taking pause, as he confines the significance of authorship to an affirmation that "those who produced the biblical books had in their times a message to convey to their readers and that it is important for us to have this message in mind when we read the

23. Brown and Schneiders, "Hermeneutics," 1148.

24. Hermeneutical reservations about the possibility, let alone the reality, of author as a significant idea for interpretation will be discussed in the concluding chapter.

25. Brown and Raymond F. Collins, "Canonicity," in *New Jerome,* 1051–52; *Oxford Latin Dictionary. The American Heritage Dictionary* has an emerging verbal use of the word, with overtones of taking responsibility for some text or statement, that is more akin to Latin; e.g., "the Senator authored a bill limiting uses of desert lands," even though the written text itself would crafted by legislative staff.

26. The issue will reappear with our consideration of canonical criticism in the next chapter.

texts."[27] If that production involved multiple stages and/or multiple writers, the literal sense sought by exegesis should take some account of the individual parts or stages; understanding the modifications worked upon earlier texts through revision or addition can do much to illuminate the final version.

The second element of the definition, regarding the sense "which the written words conveyed," guarantees a focus upon the text as it stands. Helpful though diachronic study of a work's development may be, such reconstructions are more or less hypothetical. The element of control provided by an extant text that serves as both a starting point and a terminus is necessary to restrain speculation and ground at least the hope of a common understanding. A focus upon the written text also takes into account the audience that the author(s) had in view, since their ability to grasp the text to some extent influences its composition. Difficult as discerning this may be, "it must be attempted to supply a control on the tendency of scholarly commentators to assume that what they have learned . . . was surely known by the ancient audience."[28]

One feature in Brown's account of the literal sense is its lack of engagement with such *topoi* of literary criticism as the fallacy of searching for authorial intent or Northrop Frye's description of literary works as picnics "to which the author brings the words and the reader the meaning." While part of this may be simply a disinclination to involve himself with what he clearly regards as obscure jargon, there is something else at work. We noted above that the role of "the human author" in the literal sense can be reduced to the affirmation that the various biblical books had a message to communicate in their historical setting and that later readers should keep that message in mind even as they find additional avenues of meaning that arise from their own situation. This serves the original setting rather than the author's intent; the author is little more than an anchor that fixes the text in a specific historical location. There is a similar historical anchor in the "written words" portion of the definition, though

27. "Hermeneutics," 1148.
28. *Death,* 11.

to a lesser extent, as it is used to bring in the reception of the text by its first audience. The priority given the original circumstances is due less to interpretive theory than to a theological judgment that "what the biblical text said to its first readers should be related to what the text says to me, because I am a Christian heir to the people of Israel and the people of the early church, and not independent of them."[29] The importance of continuity with the past, and especially the past out of which the Bible came, is an enduring part of Christian awareness that appears in the credal reference to an apostolic church and expresses the ancient distrust of "a different gospel" expressed in various parts of the NT.[30] The literal sense of Scripture, focused upon the historical setting and original meaning given the biblical texts, is for Brown an instrument of that continuity. As a result, in a move reminiscent of Irenaeus's stress on plain sense readings against the gnostic predilection for complex allegories, literary modes of reading that devalue historical meaning are more dismissed than disproved.

Continuity must be distinguished from identity, however; one primary function of literal exegesis is to serve as "an obstacle toward substituting a self-composed word for the word given so long ago."[31] Any given book of the Bible comes out of a specific set of historical circumstances that partially condition the message it conveys and the questions it answers. Failure to attend to them can lead to the easy harmonization of the biblical texts in the interests of later doctrine (or the causes of the day), often under the guise of exegesis. Brown identifies this as a significant problem. Historical-critical study highlights the "clear difference between the thoughts of the various biblical authors . . . and the subsequent use and development of those thoughts in divergent theologies" in a way that forces one to recog-

29. Neuhaus, *Biblical Interpretation,* 46, with much the same thought in *Death,* 7; it is worth noting that this theological commitment also works in favor of authorial meaning and against literary ways of portraying all meaning as the work of the reader.

30. Gal 1.6, though the Galatians themselves would have disagreed; less polemically, 1 Cor 15.11; Mk 13.5–6, 21–22; Acts 21.29–30; Heb 13.7–8 et al.

31. *Biblical Exegesis,* 20; see also *Birth,* 664.

nize the *brutum factum* of doctrinal development along with diversity among biblical writers themselves.[32]

Role of history

Concern for the literal sense of the Bible understood against its historical background is an interesting way to integrate modernity's characteristic stress on history and texts as historical artifacts into a theological framework applied to Scripture. It guards against anachronistic readings and does an admirable job of highlighting both the cultural and the theological differences between the biblical situation and our own. However, the incorporation of historical study may become difficult when the focus shifts away from understanding the biblical texts and toward the history and character of the underlying events. The question unavoidably changes from "what does this mean?" to "what happened?" due either to conflict between different biblical texts or to the drive of critical history (as seen in the previous chapter with Troeltsch) toward the events behind its sources.

Brown is far from rejecting this shift, since "to ignore questions like historicity that come spontaneously out of our times would be irresponsible," but his main interest lies elsewhere.[33] There is little or no consideration of the wider epistemological issues involved in historical knowledge; he presents history in a straightforward fashion as a true or accurate account of events in the past. The basis for such accounts lies in scientifically controllable evidence, understood as "the type of evidence constituted by tradition from identifiable witnesses of the events involved, when that tradition is traceably preserved and not in conflict with other traditions."[34] These three elements of witnesses, chain of transmission, and degree of conflict with other tradition are all open to testing and criticism. Once evaluated for reliability, such evidence grounds

32. *Gospel of John,* vi.

33. *Birth,* 517; his prime goal is always understanding the text at hand, with historicity an ancillary concern. He even refers to "obsessive history-hunting" (*Death,* 24).

34. *Birth,* 527.

a range of judgments: certain, very probable, possible, not impossible. "Certain" has nothing to do with the certitude of mathematics or the physical sciences; it refers to the certitude we have in ordinary experience about the things we encounter or are reported to us in writing or orally.[35]

The temporal separation between ourselves and the events recounted in Scripture, not to mention any distance between the underlying events and the composition of the texts, places significant limits on the extent of the evidence available to us. Dealing with ancient history requires a nearly Socratic willingness to admit ignorance in cases where the evidence is insufficient or confused.[36] One can still reach some conclusions (e.g., "Jesus was crucified") of near-certain probability, along with others that enjoy greater or lesser degrees of probability, and Brown does not try to avoid doing so.

This focus upon witnesses and testimony enables Brown to put aside the classic concern over miracles. Difficulties with the notion of miracle per se are based upon prior philosophical or theological ideas regarding God's interaction with the world rather than historical evidence.[37] Such a focus also marks the extremely limited role allotted to the investigator's personal subjectivity. Despite the rejection of a positivism derived from the natural sciences, the recognition that objective study without presuppositions is impossible serves only as a reminder to watchfulness; such presuppositions may "become total prejudices, distorting evidence rather than accepting it."[38] Objectivity here remains, if not a real possibility, at least an ideal one with a regulative function.

This understanding of history, a concept treated with such brevity in Brown's published work as to be taken for granted, reveals a striking lack of engagement with contemporary reflection on the nature of historical knowledge and the inescapable role played by the histo-

35. *Death*, 22.

36. *Biblical Interpretation*, 125; these limitations are not at all unique to biblical study, but apply to ancient history in general. Cf. John P. Meier, *A Marginal Jew*, vol. 1, *The Roots of the Problem and the Person* (New York: Doubleday, 1991), 23–24.

37. Spinoza illustrates the point above. As for Brown, see Neuhaus, *Biblical Interpretation*, 46.

38. Neuhaus, *Biblical Interpretation*, 45.

rian's personal horizon in setting the limits of research pursued or results judged credible.[39] When he does take notice of differing horizons, it is typically done as a way of dismissing such concerns. One response to accusations of pro-traditional bias in *Birth of the Messiah* is to highlight the biases of the critics; with bias conceded as a universal possibility, attention turns elsewhere.[40] The topic itself has no place, leaving Brown in the position N. T. Wright describes as "chastened positivism": evidence requires evaluation, and some will be rejected or found insufficient, but what survives analytical inspection provides a basis for dispassionate statements of descriptive historical fact.[41] It may be that this nearly nineteenth-century ideal of objectivity is an inheritance of the struggle to secure official Catholic acceptance of modern biblical studies in the twentieth century, where presenting historical research as the fruit of an unblemished intellectual neutrality served as a defense against theological attacks.[42]

Whatever the source, such an understanding gives rise to several difficulties. One is the illusion that different opinions arising from differences of horizon can be settled by appeals to objectivity rather than a critique aimed at the opposed horizon. An increase in the level of rhetoric between the first and second detailed analyses of Crossan's *Gospel of Peter* / Cross Gospel hypothesis seems to reflect at least some frustration with the first's apparent lack of impact.[43] The

39. See Ben F. Meyer, "The Relevance of 'Horizon,'" *Downside Review* 112 (1994): 1–14, for an excellent review of the topic.

40. *Birth,* 701–4; though followed by a defense of ecclesial context as an aid to exegesis, that defense turns around the role of the Holy Spirit in the development of tradition and so is theological rather than historical.

41. N. T. Wright, *The New Testament and the People of God* (Minneapolis: Fortress Press, 1992), 81; following Bernard Lonergan and R. G. Collingwood, Wright would find it preferable to speak in terms of data (manuscripts, archaeology, etc.) and interpretation; fact appears only as the end of a process where data and interpretation mutually influence one another and the subjective horizon of the investigator is very much taken into account.

42. Robert Bruce Robinson, *Roman Catholic Exegesis since* Divino Afflante Spiritu: *Hermeneutical Implications* (Atlanta: Scholars Press, 1988), 53.

43. The first being *"Gospel of Peter"* and the second being *Death,* 1317–49. As for rhetoric, see *Death,* 1342 n. 45: "To my mind this shows the utter implausibility of Crossan's thesis . . ."; 1347: "a simplistic tendency to regard extracanonical works as the key to true Christianity." Luke Timothy Johnson, *The Real Jesus* (San Francisco:

critique also demonstrates Brown's tendency to convert aspects of his own horizon into points of method. Examples of this include the insistence on the community of faith as the most appropriate background for exegesis, as well as a greater willingness to suspend judgment regarding the historical implications of crucial theological points (i.e., virginal conception or "brothers" of Jesus understood as compatible with Mary's perpetual virginity) than a strictly historical perspective would allow.[44]

This lack of interest in deeper and more subtle accounts of historical knowledge may be explained through the following passage:

> Historical questions are not the only questions one can put to Scripture; but once historical questions are posed, historical investigation must enter into the solution. *That investigation is concerned with the meaning the author's words had when they were written and first read* [emphasis mine].[45]

Others would say instead that historical investigation is concerned with history, understood as the course of human events and reconstructed as best one can; the same theological focus upon authorial meaning that leads Brown to reject aspects of literary criticism also diminishes concern for the historicity of underlying events. While he does engage in detailed historical work, with concern for discerning the actual political situation in Galilee and Judea during 6 B.C.–A.D. 41 (*Death* 21 and *passim*) as a prime example, history itself functions rather as the handmaid of exegesis than an independent object of inquiry.[46]

HarperCollins, 1996), 44–50, shows how crucial a role the underlying horizon plays in Crossan's historical work.

44. The question of Jesus' siblings is particularly strong as an example, following Brown's stated explanation of historical investigation; a historical inquiry concerned with NT witnesses and traditions is hard put to deny the prima facie meaning of "brothers" and "sisters." See *Birth*, 606, and Meier, *Marginal Jew*, vol. 1, 318–32.

45. Neuhaus, *Biblical Interpretation*, 27; while it is possible to make too much of something written as a lecture, the observations provoked by this passage fit well into the broader context of his thought.

46. This is not to say that Brown does not engage in detailed historical work while pursuing exegetical ends; a prime example is the concern for discerning the actual political situation in Galilee and Judea during 6 B.C.–A.D. 41 displayed in

BEYOND THE LITERAL SENSE

One distinguishing feature of Brown's career is a more receptive attitude than some of his colleagues toward the role of extra-literal senses within Scripture.[47] His first major publication was focused on the *sensus plenior* approach, which saw "additional meaning . . . in the words of a biblical text (or group of texts, or even a whole book) when they are studied in the light of further revelation or development."[48] The existence of this additional meaning was grounded in the Thomist notion of dual authorship; *sensus plenior* was intended by God, even if it went beyond the scope of the human author. The theory was first aired in 1925, with clearly apologetic intentions, as a way of clearing space for both modern and traditional views. While the focus on God's intended meaning reached back to classical exegesis, there was an attempt to meet some standards of modern scholarship by introducing specific controls such as substantial homogeneity between the literal and *plenior* meaning of a text and a requirement that an extended reading be grounded in some literal sense or in light of authoritative teaching.[49] Here, as elsewhere, the evangelical counsel on the folly of serving two masters proved true. *Sensus plenior* did not last once the apologetic necessity for it lapsed. "The scholastic and peculiarly Catholic origins and formulation of this theory" left it unable to take a broader perspective or answer serious objections brought against it.[50] Brown's interest in extra-literal senses survived the demise of his initial approach, even though the principal focus of

---

Death (21 and passim). However, the underlying motivation always has better exegesis in view.

47. For example, Joseph A. Fitzmyer, *Scripture, The Soul of Theology* (New York: Paulist Press, 1994), 90–92, displays a strong and vivid hostility to the idea (even though his longer discussion in 62–72 shows more balance).

48. *The* Sensus Plenior *of Sacred Scripture* (Baltimore: St. Mary's University, 1955), 92.

49. See Robinson, *Roman Catholic Exegesis*, ch. 2; the criterion of "substantial homogeneity" in particular goes beyond Aquinas.

50. See Brown, "The Problems of the *Sensus Plenior*," in *Exégèse et théologie: Les Saintes Écritures et leur interprétation théologique*, ed. Raymond E. Brown and Gustav Thils (Gembloux: J. Duculot, 1968), 81.

his scholarly work continued to be literal commentary. The topic receives enough treatment to provide matter for discussion here, despite a certain lack of detail.

Levels of meaning

The traditional teaching of inspiration led to all the books of the Bible being seen as God's word, even if some texts make no claim to such status. Various theories attempted to explain just how this inspiration worked, but Brown finds them "scarcely adequate" to account for many aspects of Scripture highlighted by modern scholarship, such as the complex and often lengthy history of composition for many books or the wide diversity in content and style.[51] His response is to narrow the notion of inspiration as much as possible, making it an a priori axiom of Christian theology; it signifies the unique status of Scripture as the Word of God, produced and understood with the guidance of the Holy Spirit, for the use and instruction of the Church. That unique and authoritative status establishes a structure of multiple meanings:

> For this Bible to be normative for Christian life, it has had to be accepted by the church and proclaimed as part of a living tradition in the community of believers. "Biblical meaning" is not simply what a passage meant to the author who wrote it (literal meaning), or what it meant to those who first accepted it into a normative collection (canonical meaning); biblical meaning is also what the passage means today in the context of the Christian Church.[52]

For Brown all three types of meaning are inspired, insofar as one affirms the role played by the Holy Spirit in the genesis, collection,

51. *Critical Meaning*, 7, 14; with the latter reference Brown quickly runs through options focused upon inspiration of the author, of the words, or of the community within which the writing was produced. Most of the theories concerned are reviewed in James Tunstead Burtchaell, *Catholic Theories of Biblical Inspiration since 1810* (Cambridge: Cambridge University Press, 1969), while a more recent discussion of the topic may be found in Paul J. Achtemeier, *The Inspiration of Scripture* (Philadelphia: Fortress Press, 1980).

52. *Critical Meaning*, 20; Brown largely, though not entirely, avoids speaking in terms of "senses" of Scripture, perhaps to avoid confusion with views he rejects, and instead uses "meaning" or "levels of meaning."

and ongoing reception of the biblical texts, but the main locus of inspiration lies in the whole complex taken together. Neither literal, canonical, nor present meaning is sufficient in itself; an exclusive focus on any one of them inevitably leads to distortions.[53] Reading only on the literal level runs the risk of confining the text's message to a past now long gone or becoming absorbed in the minutia of historical investigation. Concentration upon individual books can also overlook the fact that they come down to us only as elements within a larger collection and overemphasize discontinuities. Correspondingly, readings that take the canonical level as absolute can homogenize the biblical writings so that the voices of individual authors are lost and their particular historical situations neglected. This neglect of the particular may also fail to consider the ways in which the biblical books developed a tradition of interpretation once the canon had stabilized.[54] The main problem with an exclusive concern for what the Bible means "today" has already been noted: it is a tendency to read and understand in a way that confirms current preoccupations and interests rather than challenging them.

The exposition as a whole suffers from a lack of concrete illustrations; no one biblical text is interpreted on all three levels of meaning. This lacuna, together with the explicit confinement of Brown's major exegetical works to the literal sense, makes it difficult to understand how "the interaction of these various senses provides the excitement and wealth of exegesis."[55] It is also interesting to note that

53. Despite this caution, Brown reserves a primacy for the literal sense: "One may never ignore the literal sense . . . and Christians must be aware of and justify instances in which they seriously differ from it." Here as elsewhere he fears "an innate tendency to skip over lightly the quest for the literal sense" (*Critical Meaning*, 35).

54. Brown does not explicitly consider the canonization process or the understanding of the Bible operative at that time in conjunction with canonical meaning; his later *Introduction to the NT* (10–15) provides a brief statement of the standard account where the process takes place over the course of the second, third, and fourth centuries. He is unsure whether for canonical critics such as Brevard Childs "such an ongoing process is only a matter of 'receiving and transmitting the authoritative Word' or is actually formative of biblical meaning" (*Critical Meaning*, 34, and also *Biblical Exegesis*, 21–22). This probably reflects underlying differences between Catholic and Reformed traditions, as well as a certain confusion in Childs himself.

55. *Critical Meaning*, 35.

the framework set up in *Critical Meaning* is not mentioned in Brown's later works, particularly since *Biblical Exegesis and Church Doctrine* deals with similar themes.[56] Canonical meaning as a separate level tends to disappear. While the fact of the canon together with the role of the Spirit in its establishment is not denied, it is absorbed into the ongoing movement of Christian teaching. This may reflect some hesitation about using "canonical" as a term, due to the increasing prominence of Childs's thought, but it is more likely due to a narrowing focus on Brown's part. As with the topic of inspiration, there is a drive toward a simpler and sparer account.

Doctrinal development as an issue

Canonical meaning falls by the wayside because its concern with the operative understanding of the Bible when the canon developed does little to address the central problem spurring Brown's interest in what lies beyond the literal sense: the distinction between what Scripture meant and what Scripture means. "What Scripture meant" is the province of the literal sense, focused upon the meanings understood by author and audience in the historical context of each book. "What Scripture means" refers to the present context, in which the Bible serves as both kindling and fuel for Catholic theological reflection in light of centuries of tradition. Over the course of those centuries a systematic structure has developed whose relationship to the literal sense "is not simple"; the biblical basis for a given doctrine may range anywhere from strong to nonexistent.[57] The complexity increases further when one recognizes the substantial diversity among the NT authors themselves. This only adds another difficulty, inasmuch as one has to decide "which NT voices, among different NT voices, should be taken as an authentic guide" before

56. For instance, apart from a discussion of Childs (20–22), the canonical meaning makes no clear appearance in *Biblical Exegesis*. Neither is there any mention of it in his contribution to Neuhaus, *Biblical Interpretation*. Brown's differing context as a Catholic exegete, with a correspondingly greater openness to development within tradition, contributes to this.

57. *Biblical Exegesis*, 49. Other Christian bodies, of course, have their own theologies, but Brown's primary frame of reference is always Roman Catholic.

considering the precise relation of the NT text and contemporary teaching.[58]

Brown addresses the issue of development by affirming the importance of continuity within difference; the proper response denies neither the reality of development nor the importance of maintaining substantive links with the witness of the first Christian generations given in the Bible. Instead, he insists "that a doctrinal trajectory should be traceable from the NT outlook to the later dogma, even if the connection between the two goes beyond pure logic."[59] Examples of such trajectories include the movement from the biblical presentation of Father, Son, and Spirit to the Nicene account of three Persons in one Nature as well as from the Lukan portrayal of Mary the first disciple down to the definition of the Assumption. The controversies attendant upon these teachings also illustrate that one can draw different accounts, and plot different trajectories, from the same biblical texts. The mere fact that one can give an intelligible account linking a given biblical teaching and the current doctrine of the Church does not, in itself, justify that doctrine as a legitimate development; any two points suffice to define a line. There is a further need of standards to discriminate among trajectories.

A limited guidance in making these judgments may be found in the literal sense of the NT. (One should say NT here, rather than Scripture simply, because Brown acknowledges contradictions between the two Testaments as well as the normative role of the NT in any disagreement; one should also note that others do not acknowl-

58. *Biblical Exegesis,* 40. This may be an additional problem with the canonical sense; the existence of a canonical list has a formal character that fails to address the material problem of different views within the books making up the list.

59. *Biblical Exegesis,* 28, and also Neuhaus, *Biblical Interpretation,* 29. The qualification is intended to reject an older view that tried to portray later doctrines as implicitly contained within the biblical understanding, awaiting only the discovery of proper terminology. One finds something of that view in Newman's idea of logical sequence as the fourth note of development, although the other notes qualify it in some ways: "the holy Apostles would without words know all the truths concerning the high doctrines of theology, which controversialists after them have piously and charitably reduced to formulae, and developed through argument," *An Essay on the Development of Christian Doctrine* (Notre Dame: University of Notre Dame Press, 1989), 191–92.

edge such contradictions and assume a linear continuity, as the discussion of Segundo in chapter 4 will illustrate.) The NT offers a negative criterion, hedged with qualifications: later developments that lead to the affirmation of "a position contradictory to a major, formal teaching of a NT author" should be rejected.[60] Here the key aspect is the reference to major, formal teaching, which is sufficiently stringent to turn back most challenges. For example, Hebrews places great emphasis on the unique priesthood and sacrifice of Christ. The later development of a Christian cultic priesthood, in a tripartite form of bishop, priest, and deacon that has visible links with the high priest, priest, and levite found in the Old Testament, is sometimes seen as a direct contradiction of the epistle's teaching.[61] While Brown considers it extremely difficult to envision the author of Hebrews receiving this favorably, it is enough to say that he "probably never thought of such developments; and so in the technical sense they are not contradictions of his thought."[62] There is no instance in which Brown finds a later doctrine formally accepted by the Church to be in direct contradiction with such a "major, formal teaching" of the NT. While this should not be wondered at in a reputable Catholic scholar, the utility of a negative standard that has never been violated is questionable. It seems to be more of a postulate or axiom than a working criterion.

The basis for this confidence lies in what is for Brown the ultimate guarantee of continuity and consonance between current Catholic teaching and the witness of the NT: "the Spirit working in the Church and speaking through its leaders."[63] Though he rejects an ex-

60. *Critical Meaning,* 79 n. 14, and also *Biblical Exegesis,* 42, where the same idea is identified as "an exceedingly important component of the development of doctrine."

61. For example, by James D. G. Dunn, *The Parting of the Ways* (London: SCM Press, 1991), 88–93, 96–97, who concludes that a primary message of the epistle is that "*a distinct priesthood is no longer necessary*" (90, emphasis his). He goes on to say that any other interpretation is "tradition riding roughshod over scripture" (97).

62. *Biblical Exegesis,* 129; Hebrews does continue to serve as a reminder of "the primacy of Christ's priesthood." See also his *Priest and Bishop: Biblical Reflections* (Paramus: Paulist Press, 1970).

63. *Biblical Exegesis,* 50; see also Neuhaus, *Biblical Interpretation,* 138: "the teaching church is the only thing that is going to work in the long run."

trinsic view of Church authority that would put aside the need for biblical foundations altogether, authority does play a crucial role in guiding the developments built upon those foundations. This may happen through preferring some biblical voices to others, as when texts much used by Arians that indicate limited knowledge and subordination to the Father on Jesus' part are integrated within a Nicene structure that affirms the consubstantial nature of the Persons and that is based upon other texts.[64] It also occurs when questions arise that Scripture fails to address; recognizing the importance of the literal sense must also be accompanied by recognition of its limitations. The meaning intended as part of the original dialogue between author and audience addresses the questions and concerns of their time. Other eras may have similar questions, but some of their questions will be different in new and unforeseen ways. Rather than reading later doctrines back into the biblical text, or rejecting any attempt to settle questions left open by Scripture as illegitimate, one must recognize the Church's "right to teach definitively and infallibly on matters not settled in the NT" with some confidence that the abiding presence of the Spirit will ensure that those teachings are "consonant with the values of Jesus."[65]

While this is a brief and sketchy treatment of a complex issue, doctrinal development is not our topic. The main point to be noted is the general movement of Brown's thought away from the idea of multiple senses and levels within the Bible itself and toward an emphasis on Spirit-guided continuity that looks outward from the literal sense to present authoritative teaching. Although there continues to be a benevolent if rather vague acceptance of different modes of reading, which may be drawn from a variety of sources, there is little guidance in how to combine those modes with historical-critical exegesis and less of a sense that Scripture differs from other books in any way that should affect our reading of it.[66]

64. *Biblical Exegesis,* 33 nn. 18, 19.

65. *Biblical Exegesis,* 51–52; Brown presents Reformation disputes on the notion of sacrament (45–48), or present debates regarding the ordination of women, as situations where such missteps have occurred (50–51).

66. See "Hermeneutics," 1158–62, for acceptance of other modes; nota bene that

EVALUATION AND COMMENT

In many respects, both the strengths and the weaknesses of Brown's account are ones to be expected in someone whose life was given to historical-critical study of the NT and to establishing a firm place for that study within Roman Catholicism. His explicitly hermeneutical and methodological statements are somewhat fragmentary and occasional because he takes up these topics not as a systematic theologian or philosopher, but by way of his exegetical work. Our observations here are intended as part of an effort to find more adequate ways of integrating modern biblical studies into a broader theological framework, and not as a dismissal of his attempts. That we are able to speak of integration at all is due in significant part to the work, and perhaps even more to the example, that he and others offer of modern exegesis and orthodox faith working in harmony.

The strongest element of Brown's presentation concerns the nature of the literal sense, and its continuing importance. Once the literal sense is defined as "the sense which the human author directly intended and which the written words conveyed," the way is clear to focus upon each biblical text within a specific historical context where the interpreter can bring in all the resources of philology and historical scholarship.[67] Emphasis falls first on what the text itself is intended to convey, and not upon questions of a different order (e.g., miracles, historicity), which more properly follow an understanding of the text than precede or condition it. This is the basis for his well-known statement that there is "no reason why a Catholic's understanding of what Matthew and Luke meant in their infancy narratives should be different from a Protestant's."[68] Judgments may differ as to whether what Matthew, Luke, or other biblical authors meant is true, but that meaning is in principle accessible to everyone.

---

this is not to say that Scripture does not enjoy a unique status or authority for Brown, merely that whatever unique character it possesses has no apparent effect on how it should be read.

67. "Hermeneutics," 1148.

68. *Birth*, 8.

Its particular value for Christians lies in the enduring desire to maintain continuity with the people of Israel and with the apostolic church from which the Bible came; what they had to say cannot be a matter of indifference or merely antiquarian interest. Literal exegesis helps prevent us from twisting their witness to suit ourselves.[69] Awareness of the literal sense also highlights the reality of doctrinal development against a naive fundamentalism that would fail to see any difference between the questions and concerns of the NT and our own.

Once one moves beyond the literal sense, seeking either underlying history or alternate forms of meaning, Brown's account falters. This is not surprising; efforts to extend and defend modern exegesis depend upon the role allotted to the literal sense, and his central agenda continues to turn around those efforts. Although he is capable of exacting and precise historical investigation, the nature of historical knowledge is never a concern. There is a confidence in the objectivity and reliability of what disciplined historical work may discover that shows little trace of more nuanced modern reflections. This confidence hampers his efforts to deal with scholars whose approach derives from a radically different horizon, and also conceals ways in which he makes aspects of his own horizon into rules of method. As for senses other than the literal, one can trace a gradual abandonment of specific interest in them over the course of his work. In his most recent treatments of hermeneutical issues he does not set up a specific structure of extra-literal meanings as he once did, but instead he focuses on establishing developmental links from the literal sense of NT books to current Church teaching, with the integrity of those movements formally guaranteed by the ongoing presence of the Holy Spirit. While doctrinal development is an important topic, it does not in itself constitute part of exegesis, nor does it provide any guidance in seeking a disciplined and theologically justified way of going beyond the literal sense.

69. Inspiration, in Brown's discussion, seems a theological label for the uniquely authoritative status of the Bible as a whole and less a reason to ascribe particular importance to the literal sense of individual books.

The value of Brown's work does not lie with these topics, but with his account of the literal sense. The clear explanation he offers regarding the role of the literal sense as a vehicle of intended meaning within a particular historical context makes it possible to use all the resources developed by modern historical scholarship in search of that meaning, while excluding a great deal of philosophical baggage (e.g., doctrinaire rejection of the miraculous). Though the literal sense itself is defined in a neutral way, its importance is based on the traditional Christian desire for continuity with "those who were from the beginning eyewitnesses and servants of the word" (Lk 1.2) rather than on a progressive idea of history or a specific philosophy. The first point opens the biblical text to a historical reading, and the second provides a Christian warrant to do so. While these two points are by no means a complete answer to the question with which we began, what they do provide will be a crucial element in that answer.

CHAPTER THREE

BREVARD CHILDS

Brevard Childs has long argued that modern biblical studies must be reconfigured in significant ways if we are to understand the role and function of the Bible as Scripture. Where Brown intended to secure the practice and integrate the results of historical-critical exegesis, Childs aims to shift the prime focus of exegetical concern away from the sources or historical circumstances of individual texts toward their function and meaning within the context of the Bible as a whole. Though he ascribes an explicit and essential role to historical study, it is only when historical criticism functions in the service of this integral reading of the Bible that one is engaged in biblical interpretation proper rather than one form or another of ancient Near Eastern history. This interest in the canonical texts is shared to some extent with forms of narrative criticism inspired by literary theory, such as one sees in his Yale colleague Hans Frei, but Childs takes care to distinguish himself from these by the explicitly theological justification provided for his own approach. He stands upon an acceptance of the canon, which for him means the recognition that the Bible is the end result of a long process that has intentionally shaped the text and underlying traditions in ways that enable it to function as *Scripture;* that is, as an enduring and normative witness for subsequent generations of the believing community in a variety of historical circumstances differing from those in which the individual books were composed.[1] Formal canonization of a given list of books is merely the last and in some ways the least important stage of a much longer development.

1. This stress upon the canon as theological touchstone has caused Childs's method to be known popularly as "canonical criticism," a label that he rejects inasmuch as it gives the impression that he is proposing merely one type of criticism

The primary context of exegesis for Childs is the full canon of the Christian Bible understood as a coherent and unified (but not uniform) whole in which both Old and New Testament "witness to the one Lord Jesus Christ, the selfsame divine reality. The Old Testament bears testimony to the Christ who has not yet come; the New to the Christ who has appeared in the fullness of time."[2] The diverse voices found within the canonical witnesses each present a partial perspective on the divine reality, which the exegete should try to discern through attention to the text and whatever guiding elements it may offer the reader. Attention should also be paid to the ways in which the canonical text adjusts and integrates prior historical or literary sources inasmuch as this contributes to a deeper understanding of the text's aims and concerns. At the end of the exegetical process stands biblical theology, which he presents as a discipline aimed at relating those different voices to one another and building up an understanding of the whole of Scripture.[3]

Childs has laid out this approach in numerous articles and four major books, which have drawn an extensive scholarly response. There has been some development within his thought, as is natural, sparked by both critical observations and internal pressures.[4] With that in mind, it seems fair as well as practical to focus upon *Biblical Theology of the Old and New Testaments,* the work that "implements Childs's methodological proposals in their fullest extent."[5]

---

among others; cf. Brevard S. Childs, *Introduction to the Old Testament as Scripture* (Philadelphia: Fortress Press, 1979), 82.

2. Brevard S. Childs, *Biblical Theology of the Old and New Testaments* (Minneapolis: Fortress Press, 1993), 85.

3. This formulation of course stands in direct continuity with traditional Protestant theology, and in particular the biblical theology movement of the mid-twentieth century in which Childs finds his roots. It is his perception of that movement as a failure that spurs his later work; cf. *Biblical Theology in Crisis* (Philadelphia: Westminster, 1970).

4. In addition to *Biblical Theology* (1993) and *OT as Scripture* (1979), there is also *The New Testament as Canon: An Introduction* (Philadelphia: Fortress Press, 1985. Both his major commentaries, *The Book of Exodus: A Critical, Theological Commentary* (Philadelphia: Westminster, 1974) and *Isaiah : A commentary* (Louisville: Westminster John Knox, 2001), are applications of ideas presented more clearly and succinctly elsewhere.

5. Paul R. Noble, *The Canonical Approach: A Critical Reconstruction of the*

We begin with Childs's assessment of the current situation of biblical studies, particularly the division between various forms of historical criticism and narrative/literary reading. An analysis follows that presents some of the foundational terms in Childs's understanding, such as "witness," "canon" with its cognates, and the Christian Bible as constituted by the juxtaposition of Old and New Testaments. We then turn to aspects of canonical exegesis, in particular the function of history, the canonical context, and the relationship of OT and NT in light of the whole Christian message. Though hostile to traditional allegory, Childs does allow for a specifically Christian reading of the OT that he distinguishes from the "discrete witness of the Old Testament" itself.

CRITIQUE OF THE PRESENT SITUATION

Serious dissatisfaction with the predominant directions of modern biblical study has remained a consistent feature of Childs's work even as those directions themselves have varied. Despite this consistency, the criticisms made in his two *Introductions* and *Biblical Theology* remain somewhat obscure because they are expressed within reviews of current approaches to the areas of biblical introduction or biblical theology rather than consideration of the discipline as a whole. Examination shows that those different approaches fall into two main types; one derived from historical studies, and the other from literary theory.

Historical criticism

As we saw with Spinoza and Troeltsch, historical-critical scholarship has from its inception rejected theological categories in order to recover the original voice of each biblical book or author as understood in their own historical context. This change of focus has pro-

Hermeneutics of Brevard S. Childs (Leiden: E. J. Brill, 1995), 2. The first two chapters are the most thoughtful and complete review of Childs; the author then goes on to offer independent solutions to perceived flaws within Childs's program. (The discussion of Childs in Harrisville and Sundberg, *Bible in Modern Culture,* 304–28, should also be mentioned; however, it was an addition to the second edition [2002] and came into my hands too late to be of use here.)

duced significant gains in our knowledge of the biblical texts and the circumstances and stages of their composition, as well as the history of Israel and early Christianity. Childs never fails to acknowledge this as a real advance that makes essential contributions. "From it the interpreter learns a multitude of things about the text, its meaning, history, and audience. Exegesis performed without its aid seems naive, often crude, and flat in its dimensions."[6] Historical investigation per se does not pose a problem for him in the way it does for evangelical or fundamentalist scholars.[7]

The difficulty with historical method lies much more with the priority it is commonly given, so that it sets the terms of discussion.[8] Its concern for historical circumstances of individual texts results in a division of the Bible that the complex history of composition behind many biblical books only worsens. There are several negative consequences in this as far as Childs is concerned. In the first place (*pace* certain forms of redaction criticism), historical-critical methodology neglects analysis of the texts as they stand to focus upon reconstructed stages within the history and development of biblical literature. Such reconstructions are unavoidably hypothetical and, most importantly for Childs, do not represent the texts actually received and used as Scripture by the community. In the second place, interpretation conducted exclusively within historical contexts often fails to see or admit the "dimension of resonance within the Bible which issues from a collection with fixed parameters."[9] Finally, the operating principle that historical context is the touchstone of interpretation leads to a reductionism that envisions social or political factors as the primary determining forces behind the text.

6. *NT as Canon,* 45; *Biblical Theology,* 4, which sets Gabler's essentially Spinozist approach at the genesis of biblical theology.

7. As Carl Henry is quick to point out in his review of Childs ("Canonical Theology: An Evangelical Appraisal," *Scottish Bulletin of Evangelical Theology* 8 [1990]: 76–108).

8. As a result, Childs dismisses Brown for "giving over the basic task of exegesis to the usual methods of historical criticism" (*NT as Canon,* 47).

9. *OT as Scripture,* 40. One should note that these criticisms of historical-critical method are rather lacking in concrete examples, perhaps because Childs regards his criticisms as sufficiently fundamental that examples would be redundant.

The initial rejection of ecclesial and theological structures by critical methods, when combined with these fragmenting effects of a historical orientation, leaves the Bible without a unifying principle. Such a situation is inherently unstable, and Childs identifies several approaches used to impose some order on the biblical material without turning away from historical-critical insights. One seeks to isolate universal ideas and themes in a fashion more or less reminiscent of Spinoza. Though few modern scholars are "completely comfortable with . . . this idealistic philosophical tradition," the danger of distortion remains in that the selection of supposedly universal ideas is often guided by the reigning philosophy of the day or a preference for one portion of the Bible over others.[10]

Another approach, more familiar to Childs from his early training in German Protestant biblical theology, looks to biblical history as the progressive history of salvation in which God is revealed. The unifying principle lies neither in timeless ideas nor in the Bible, but in the underlying events. This option has the merit of taking history seriously, but different meanings are given to "history" as a term. In some instances (e.g., Troeltsch), biblical history simply forms part of the ongoing movement of universal history as it reveals the development of humanity. The message drawn from the biblical history is subordinated to whatever philosophy of history is animating the interpreter. In other cases, biblical history is set apart as *Heilsgeschichte:* a salvation-history extending through Old and New Testament that is "intertwined but distinct from ordinary history." Childs finds this special type of history difficult to justify on historical grounds, and also lacking sufficient biblical foundation. Some texts reflect an interest in such a redemptive history, but many do not (at least not as a primary category) (*Biblical Theology,* 16).

Childs groups several other modes of interpretation, such as liberation or feminist theology, as sociological interpretations. They are dismissed with the same central objection, for he is consistent in rejecting any approach that embraces "a process of critical reconstruc-

10. *Biblical Theology,* 15, with Bultmann as a prime example.

tion to extract the real theological data from the biblical text."[11] Such approaches confirm and extend the tendency of historical study to break down the Bible into ever-smaller constituent portions. The extant text is treated as a source, raw material that must be processed and sifted to provide building blocks for theological structures whose blueprints are drawn from other sources.

Literary criticism

Literary modes of interpretation share aspects of Childs's concern for an integral reading of the Bible. The main interest falls upon the texts as works of literature, with theological and historical concerns held in abeyance if not dismissed. "The language itself, rather than some form of history, provides the realm in which the events occur through the medium of human experience" (*Biblical Theology*, 19). Poetic metaphor, narrative, and imagery present a symbolic vision that the reader is invited to enter and appropriate (just as one might immerse oneself in *Hamlet* or *Crime and Punishment*). A wide variety of tools adapted from literary studies can then be applied, not to elucidate the prehistory of the texts, but to highlight the avenues used to convey meaning.

Childs recognizes that "the study of biblical texts in their own right has greatly benefited" as a result of this literary focus (*Biblical Theology*, 20). A greater emphasis on the literary features of the Bible has done much to clarify the structure of extant texts and provided a counterweight to the disputes over background and sources that he finds so unproductive. Despite this appreciation of literary readings, though, he ultimately finds them nearly as wanting as purely historical modes of interpretation. Treating the Bible as a work of literature brings in its wake the conscious or unconscious conception that it is solely a literary work, self-contained and with little reference to realities outside itself. That notion finds expression in proposals to read Scripture as a "classic," which places it on the same level as other classics, or in "viewing the Bible [as] akin to a realistic novel."[12] Literary

11. *Biblical Theology*, 17; and see *Biblical Theology in Crisis* for a more lengthy critique.

12. *Biblical Theology*, 20; Childs is here referring to Hans Frei, thus making the criticism more noteworthy. He is otherwise quite appreciative of Frei's work.

readings do attend to the integral text at one level, and so perceive the intended message in a more complete way than historical readings whose focus lies behind the text, but they fail at another level by implicitly characterizing the Bible as a form of fiction rather than an authoritative Scripture deeply involved with the world beyond the text.[13]

This assessment of the present situation of biblical studies functions at a high level of abstraction, because Childs is rejecting foundational elements of modern scholarship in both historical and literary modes. His tendency to brusque dismissal of competing views further clouds the matter. As one largely favorable critic has said, "Childs proceeds as though 'canonical' were a self-evident reading that anyone can see."[14] The best statement of the point he is trying to make may be this: "the theological issue turns on doing full justice to both text and reality which remain dialectically related, neither to be separated nor fused" (*Biblical Theology*, 22). Standard forms of historical criticism separate the biblical text from the objects of its witness by treating it as a source to be processed and reduced to its component elements, while more literary treatments turn the text in upon itself and so lose sight of the difference between the witness and the realities that evoked that witness in the first place.

FUNDAMENTAL DISTINCTIONS

Several terms or relations require explanation before we examine individual stages within Childs's account of the interpretive process. Some of the contention raised by his proposals has been due to neglect of the specific meanings that he employs.[15] A clear statement of

13. The lack of connection between the Bible and extra-biblical reality also leads Childs to reject the "cultural-linguistic" approach proposed by George Lindbeck (also of the Yale faculty). The notion that "it is the text, so to speak, which absorbs the world, rather than the world the text," so that one can speak of the text itself as creative, is unsustainable to the extent that it disregards the question of theological realities (and particularly the reality of God) to which the biblical text bears witness (*Biblical Theology*, 21–22).

14. Walter Brueggeman, "Against the Stream: Brevard Childs's Biblical Theology," *Theology Today* 50 (1993): 281.

15. Most notably the polemic attack upon Childs in James Barr, *Holy Scripture: Canon, Authority, Criticism* (Philadelphia: Westminster, 1983), which does not

the basic trio of witness, canon, and Christian Bible as constituted by the juxtaposition of Old and New Testaments contains his whole approach *in nuce* and sets the governing conditions for concrete exegetical work.

Neither historical source nor imaginative narrative is adequate as a primary category in approaching the Bible; as seen above, both fail to catch important aspects of the biblical text. Childs prefers to speak in terms of witness, a term that on its face implies the statement of one's own knowledge or experience. Hearing the biblical text in that way respects the "theological intention of bearing its testimony to a divine reality which has entered into time and space" that governs the development and collection of both Testaments (*Biblical Theology,* 98). Each presents accounts of God's decisive actions to bring together, redeem, and sustain the covenant people (together with various forms of commentary and reaction). The OT finds those acts within the history of Israel as that history was received and transmitted by later generations, while the NT looks to the proclamation of Jesus in the practice and memory of the apostolic church. They express the community's self-understanding of its encounter with God; emphasis upon the biblical texts as witness helps ensure that the primary object of study remains the community's testimony to itself and to its God.[16]

That testimony is constituted by a lengthy and complicated process involving "the reception and acknowledgment of certain religious traditions as authoritative writings within a faith community" (*Biblical Theology,* 70). Childs employs the term "canonical" to characterize the process of reception as a way of emphasizing that theological concern for the text's ability to serve as a rule or canon is deeply embedded within the biblical tradition. ("Canon" itself refers

appreciate the structure of his thought and so "his expositions of Childs often descend into caricature and misrepresentation" (Noble, *Canonical Approach,* 3). Cf. Stephen E. Fowl, "The Canonical Approach of Brevard Childs," *Expository Times* 96 (1985): 176 n. 13; "one gets the impression that both scholars are talking round each other."

16. At least, the primary object of biblical study *qua* biblical. One can approach the Bible from other perspectives (e.g., comparative religion or ancient Near Eastern history), as Childs freely acknowledges (*OT as Scripture,* 76).

to the final, stable form of the text produced by the canonical process, understood as the "received, collected, and interpreted material of the church" [*Biblical Theology*, 71].) Earlier texts and traditions used in the formation of the canonical material were adjusted and reformed in a variety of ways to better serve a normative function for future generations:

> Often old material has been given a new redactional framework (e.g., Judges), or an interpretive commentary added (Ecclesiastes), or originally separate entities combined into a single composition (Philippians). There are also a few examples within both Testaments in which there is no sign of explicit redactional layering, but a new way of reading the literature has emerged from the larger canonical context (Daniel, Romans). (*Biblical Theology*, 73)

Childs insists on this "canon-consciousness," rather than scribal conventions or political struggle, as the main factor governing the redaction and compilation of the biblical texts. Guidelines for interpretation are to be sought more from the structure of the collection itself and less from the historical circumstances of particular texts. The study of Paul, for example, should begin with Acts and take into account the complete range of epistles canonically ascribed to him. That is the Paul remembered by the Church, even though in doing so it extended "the profile of Paul far beyond that of his historical ministry."[17] The acknowledged differences between the canonical presentation of figures or events and the results of historical study highlight the shaping given the authoritative traditions.

It is crucial for Childs that this shaping culminates not in Scripture simply, but in an Old Testament and a New. He sees OT and NT as the fruit of distinct processes of canonization (in his sense of the word), since the OT had already reached its final form within the Jewish environment prior to the rise of Christianity. There is not a specifically Christian text of the OT, nor have its books been subjected to Christian editing.[18] Instead, the Church's own writings that came to form the NT were joined to the OT collection inherited

17. *NT as Canon*, 426; also 240 (the Pauline corpus exists "within the framework of Acts, which provides hermeneutical guidelines for their interpretation").

18. *Biblical Theology*, 74–77. The Christian ordering of the OT books is seen as a

from Judaism and already acknowledged as Scripture. The Christian Bible is constituted by this juxtaposition of OT and NT in order to assert that both should be understood as witnesses to Jesus Christ. The precise way in which these witnesses are related to their common subject remains open, however, so long as both the continuity in the object of witness and the genuine differences between the witnesses themselves are maintained.[19] Childs himself clearly prefers a structure of promise and fulfillment but admits other options such as law and gospel, shadow and reality, or certain types of salvation history (*Biblical Theology*, 77, 84–85).

Within his methodological framework, however, the main emphasis falls upon the distinction between OT and NT rather than their eventual unity (without ignoring or underestimating the latter). This is intended to correct the tendency of both ancient and modern Christian interpreters to read the OT almost exclusively through the lens of the NT. While it is true that the NT does cast its own witness largely in OT terms, Childs finds that influence operating in the composition of individual books rather than in "the formation of the Christian Bible *qua* collection" (*Biblical Theology*, 76). The existence of two Testaments within the collected Scripture establishes a new canonical context for later Christians that the early church did not possess and in doing so "asserts the continuing integrity of the Old Testament witness" (*Biblical Theology*, 78). Submerging the OT within the NT destroys that integrity, as is the tendency of traditional allegory, and also obscures the latter's character as a true *novum*.

STAGES OF INTERPRETATION

With these basic distinctions set up, we may review steps within the exegetical process where the particular emphases of the canonical approach stand out. These are the role of historical knowledge, the

---

selection among already extant options, and the role of the LXX minimized. As we will see later, there is some difficulty with such a reading of the situation.

19. For example, the Church turned away from Marcion due to his rejection of the OT as unchristian while also separating itself from Torah-observant Jewish Christians who failed to perceive the real novelty of the NT.

use of the whole canon as the context of interpretation, and the role of typology in Christian appropriation of the OT. The explanation given here is drawn from Childs's general discussion together with the two examples he provides of "exegesis in the context of biblical theology": the Akedah (Gn 22.1–19) and the parable of the wicked tenants (Mt 21.33–46).[20] The examples themselves appear in a separate chapter, without introduction or methodological commentary; this is a serious flaw given his somewhat diffuse and extended style. A concise and concrete account of exegetical procedure would have been valuable.

Historical investigation

One must acknowledge that historical study of the canonical text does play an important role for Childs. Exegesis involves the use of historical tools from the outset, but this is integrated with his focus upon the text's character as witness. The recovery of a "depth dimension," as he calls it, advances the understanding of that witness in several ways.[21] Most important among them is the light shed on the development of the tradition. The canonical approach is founded upon the idea that the final form of the text is the result of a process where the community and its authoritative traditions mutually influenced one another; "it seems obvious that this final form can be much better understood . . . if one studies carefully those hundreds of decisions which shaped the whole."[22] This is not only a question of the history of composition behind given texts, whether complex as with the Pentateuch or relatively straightforward as with Romans. Important though it is to grasp particular witnesses, with the historical fea-

20. The examples appear in *Biblical Theology,* 322–47.

21. Though Richard Bauckham, Review of *Biblical Theology of the Old and New Testaments* by Brevard S. Childs, *Biblical Interpretation* 2 (1994): 248, makes the critical observation that one need not employ history to find a "depth dimension" within *Hamlet,* Childs would most likely see this as a confusion of literary and canonical concerns. Understanding the place of a given witness within the developing biblical tradition is different from perceiving the multiplex grasp of the human condition in a literary work.

22. *Biblical Theology,* 104; see also 217.

tures behind them, each witness represents one element within a wider development and not an isolated block. Childs emphasizes that the canonical tradition terminates in the OT as a whole and the NT as a whole rather than in individual books. The proper role of history lies not in disassembling the end products of the tradition, but in understanding how and with what purpose they came together. "The crucial test is the extent to which the recognition of the parts aids rather than impairs the hearing of the whole."[23]

Beyond the development of the texts, historical inquiry serves to place different witnesses in the concrete historical situations that elicited their testimony. The interpreter can then correlate stages in the growth of the tradition with external circumstances, as well as with different canonical responses to the same problems. Recovery of the eighth-century understanding of covenant, for example, enables us to hear more clearly the changes rung upon that understanding by a prophet such as Hosea. Similarly, once the composition of Matthew and Luke is seen to be post–A.D. 70, the ways in which they adapted Mark and other sources to fit their perceptions of the problems then facing the Church stand out. This concern for circumstances also helps forestall what Childs calls biblicism, that is, the error of "assuming that every time-conditioned feature" of the Bible remains normative apart from reflection upon the text's primary function as "kerygmatic witness" (*Biblical Theology,* 84–85). Though that witness remains authoritative and unique, it is nevertheless influenced by the historical situation in which it arose; hearing that witness in different situations is a matter for theological reflection rather than simple repetition.

In light of these rather positive statements, it is unfortunate that the readings that Childs gives of the Akedah and the wicked tenants are nearly devoid of these historical considerations. With regard to the parable in particular, while a disregard for potential *Sitz im Leben Jesu* is not surprising, there is also a lack of interest in the specific circumstances of the evangelist. Nearly all of his interest turns around

23. *Biblical Theology,* 105; note that the main use for history seems to be in the service of source and redaction criticism.

the parable's relationship to the song of the vineyard in Isaiah 5, together with Matthew's redactional changes vis-à-vis Mark.[24] This lack may be due to the nature of the text being examined, but it may indicate a gap between theory and practice with regard to the function of historical knowledge.

Canonical context

The exegetical weight that Childs places upon the shape and features of the canonical text is clear. Understanding the witness of the text is founded upon a reading of passages as they stand. Redactional adjustments or additions provide the interpreter with valuable hints, as does the placement of a book within the broader structure of Old or New Testament. This latter element is more uniquely characteristic of Childs, and deserves mention here, inasmuch as his concern for the extant biblical text as the main object of interpretation is shared with others (including both literary critics and at least some historical-critical exegetes).[25]

We have already noted one way in which he employs the larger canonical collection as an interpretive aid, with Acts serving as introduction and framework for the Pauline epistles. His discussion of the Akedah provides an additional example. After tracing canonical guideposts within the text of Genesis 22 (e.g., the superscription in v.1 introducing the story as God's test of Abraham), he notes that "ram," "burnt offering," and "appear" make up a cluster of significant terms within the story. The same cluster reappears only in Leviticus 8–9 and 16, which discuss respectively the institution of the Aaronic

24. Bauckham (Review, 249) is left with the impression that "Childs seems to treat as insignificant for biblical theology any relationship of the theological witness of the texts to the concrete historical circumstances in which that witness originated." The treatment of Matthew in *NT as Canon* (57–73) is similarly lacking in consideration of those circumstances. Although one could ascribe this to Childs's formation as an OT scholar, he himself would not attempt to take advantage of that excuse. His introduction to the NT volume stresses that the NT was his primary research focus for a period of years, together with his "effort to do justice to the integrity of this discipline" of NT studies (*NT as Canon,* xvi).

25. One need only think of Brown's statements on the importance of the extant text; cf. *Biblical Interpretation* 46, with related thoughts in *Death* 7 and 11.

priesthood and the day of atonement. The canonical echo links Abraham's testing with the later worship of Israel "and conversely Israel's sacrifice is drawn into the theological orbit of Abraham's offering: 'God will provide his own sacrifice'" (*Biblical Theology*, 328). A similar use of key words guides Childs's theological reflections upon the divine attributes, as he brings witnesses from both OT and NT to bear (*Biblical Theology*, 371).

Use of typology

Childs's strong concern to maintain the integrity of the OT as a discrete witness within the biblical canon, which leads him to reject the predominant ways in which the NT itself uses the OT, appears to set the canonical approach firmly against allegorical or typological readings. Once the diverse voices within Scripture have been heard and understood as types of witness borne to the one divine reality, unified in their common object, the movement of interpretation should come to an end. As natural as this conclusion is, though, Childs does reserve a place for reflections that return to the text of Scripture "in the light of the full reality of God in Jesus Christ" (*Biblical Theology*, 87). He distinguishes this return from traditional allegory and NT practice by reiterating his insistence that such a move take place only after full examination of each passage within its own proper context. No one witness within the canon offers more than a partial and limited view; naively reading the broader perspective offered by the whole canon back into individual texts destroys their unique voice. This is a particular danger with respect to Christian use of the OT, because it separates the OT from the historical community of Israel by insinuating that "the Old Testament's hidden agenda was always Jesus Christ" (*Biblical Theology*, 87).

Childs offers a different role for typology that does not oppose readings focused on the historical and canonical sense of the text or work in isolation from them. He considers the typological figures and metaphors as ways of linking the partial perspectives of a given text with the full biblical truth, which seems to depend upon a literary or aesthetic sensitivity to patterns of imagery of the sort that has often found expression in the Church's liturgy. Typology then finds its foundation in the power of biblical words to echo and resound in new ways as the reader brings in a more complete apprehension of divine truth. That apprehension is not solely a matter of discursive knowledge, for

> the reality of God testified to in the Bible, and experienced through the confirmation of God's Spirit, functions on a deeper level to instruct the reader toward an understanding of God that leads from faith to faith.[26]

Emphasis on the charismatic foundations of typology renders the statement of definitive guidelines for its practice difficult if not impossible. The suffering servant of Isaiah 53 appears as the sole example in his main discussion. There is no question of portraying the text as a direct witness to the sufferings of Christ, given its canonical function as a word directed to Israel within the context of the OT. However, the Christian interpreter recognizes "an immediate morphological fit" with the Passion.[27] Such typological resonances serve not as opposition to readings based on the historical and canonical setting of the biblical text, but as an additional avenue for spiritual growth by making clear "the inexpressible *texture,* and composition of [God's] *Word.*"[28]

EVALUATION AND COMMENT

This brief review of the canonical approach's distinguishing features has suffered from a certain vagueness characteristic of Childs's thought, despite his lengthy works.[29] Nonetheless, it does provide sufficient basis for some observations regarding the actual role played

26. *Biblical Theology,* 382; Noble, *Canonical Approach,* 290, notes that while "the illumination of the Spirit is indispensable for a proper understanding of the Scriptures . . . [Childs's] comments are extremely cryptic."

27. *Biblical Theology,* 382. The word "immediate" should not be lightly overlooked. On the same page, Childs explicitly rejects the idea of an "objective criterion" for such judgments apart from the Spirit-informed perception of interpreter and audience. The importance of "the continuing work of the Spirit" is mentioned earlier at 215.

28. *Biblical Theology,* 382, with words borrowed from John Donne.

29. Hans M. Barstad, "Le canon comme principe exégétique. Autour de la contribution de Brevard S. Childs à une 'herméneutique' de l'Ancien Testament," *Studia theologica* 38 (1984): 85–87.

by historical study and also the foundation provided for the idea and function of canon. Both are crucial for the success of canonical interpretation. Acceptance of modern historical tools sets it apart from the classical readings, on the one hand, and the reformulated notion of canon separates it from standard historical-critical exegesis, on the other. Unfortunately, Childs's entire system is vitiated by significant flaws in the application or explanation of just these ideas, which neither his seriousness of purpose nor depth of learning can overcome.

Historical and canonical dissonance

A vigorous polemic against the use of Scripture as a source for historical reconstructions, and the shift of interest away from the canonical texts to those reconstructed situations, dominates Childs's treatment of history. This vigor obscures an important distinction between indirect and direct historical references within the Bible. For example, the sociological structure of ancient Israel or the roles of women in that admittedly patriarchal society are not a primary concern of the biblical authors. Their texts may often reveal significant amounts of information on such topics, but they do so by the way and in the course of pursuing different ends. In other cases, a variety of historical points are the object of direct affirmations. It is quite central to the canonical witness of the Pastorals, for instance, that they are letters of Paul, and Childs criticizes attempts to interpret them as pseudepigraphical compositions within a later historical context (while acknowledging that Pauline authorship is most unlikely).[30] Elsewhere he refers to "a series of revelatory events which entered Israel's time and space" (*Biblical Theology,* 91). That series includes creation, the call of Abraham, the exodus, Sinai, occupation of the land, and the destruction of Jerusalem, among others. While some of these events, particularly the destruction of Jerusalem, are undoubtedly historical, one can raise legitimate questions about others if regarding them as events in Israel's time and space requires an acceptance of the numerous details that modern research has rendered questionable.

30. *NT as Canon,* 378–95, especially 380–86.

Without taking explicit note of the difference between direct and indirect references, Childs attempts to resolve the problem of historical and canonical conflict over the actual historicity of events by tracing "both an inner and an outer dimension" within biblical history.[31] The outer dimension operates from the modern historical-critical perspective, with its concern for neutral and objective evaluation of all possible data, whether derived from biblical or from extra-biblical sources. The inner dimension is the perspective taken by the community of faith working from an explicit and committed position in which canonical traditions and texts serve as authoritative witness to the past. Here past events have been interpreted and evaluated according to the theological significance found in them; some are highlighted, some reshaped to match a larger pattern, others left unmentioned or even suppressed.[32] The relationship between these two dimensions is variable; some events (e.g., the fall of Jerusalem) may be clearly affirmed from each side, while for others (e.g., the Red Sea) one is totally dependent upon the biblical view. Most cases will fall somewhere within these two extremes, leaving the interpreter with a "genuine dialectical tension" between an intra-biblical and an extra-biblical viewpoint (*Biblical Theology,* 101). Childs's intention in using terms such as "dialectical" is to indicate the lack of a complete and systematic framework for resolving these tensions. The best one can do is to explain problems or potential problems clearly, "and then seek to work in a theologically responsible exegetical fashion" (*Biblical Theology,* 99).

This discussion of the historicity problem suffers from a flaw noted above in dealing with the issue of typology. A general explanation of the methodological issue is left with little substantive illustration

31. *Biblical Theology,* 100–101, which is the primary discussion within that book. Though expressed solely in relation to the OT, the passage is taken here as applicable to biblical history per se. A subsequent excursus on Old Testament history as a theological problem (*Biblical Theology*, 196–206) is almost entirely a review of the literature. Attempt at reflection on the problem itself is confined to the last paragraph, which only "suggests that the church's path of theological reflection lies in its understanding of its scripture, its canon, and its Christological confession which encompass the mystery of God's ways in the world with his people."

32. No examples are provided.

of the points of method applied to concrete particulars. In the abstract, Childs clearly affirms that the biblical testimony "continually points outside itself to extrinsic reality" and that the tools and results of modern critical history are vital.[33] Yet in practice, there never appears to be any question of historical truth or falsehood influencing his interpretations. "It often seems as though . . . the theology of a text is expounded *just as if* [italics his] everything had happened as the text portrays it, with no significance being allowed to the question of whether it really did or not."[34] There is a clear example of this in his treatment of Acts and the Pauline corpus, where Acts and the pseudepigraphical epistles are joined with Paul's own letters as the basis for a "canonical Paul" who is taken as normative. The existence of tensions and differences between the canonical and the historical Paul is recognized, in the abstract, but has no evident consequences.[35] When it comes to the actual work of interpretation, the distinction Childs lays out between the inner and outer dimensions of biblical history fails to function. There is an appearance of engaging the problem, without the reality.

Problems of canonical process

Despite all the weight attached to the idea of canon, and the crucial function that it plays, examination reveals gaps or inconsistencies in the foundations supporting it. Childs's idea of canon, and the way in which he applies it, has certain historical and theological questions

33. "Response to Reviewers of *Introduction to the Old Testament as Scripture,*" *Journal for the Study of the Old Testament* 16 (1980): 57. Here one notes again that the acceptance of modern historical tools is most clearly integrated into Childs's thought when it comes to the use of source and redaction criticism, i.e., when those tools are directed at the biblical text rather than biblical history or events.

34. Noble, *Canonical Approach,* 60. The same tendency is visible in Childs's Exodus commentary: "There is no special interest here in *bruta facta;* the problem seems simply not to arise," James A. Sanders, Review of *The Book of Exodus* by Brevard S. Childs, *Journal of Biblical Literature,* 95 (1976): 289. Cf. also Katharine D. Sakenfeld, Review of *The Book of Exodus* by Brevard S. Childs, *Theology Today* 31 (1975): 276; "the consistent refusal to deal with any context of known ancient history leaves the reader with the impression that it makes little or no difference whether any of the events took place at all."

35. *NT as Canon,* 422–27. Noble raises similar questions regarding the issue of Mosaic promulgation of Torah at Sinai (*Canonical Approach,* 84–88).

that must be addressed before one can acquiesce in his dismissals of alternative views. The historical issues turn around the process of canonization together with the understanding of Scripture in operation at that time. Theological difficulties arise with his rejection of NT modes of interpretation and the role of canonical process as a substitute for inspiration. He does not overlook these problems, for the most part, but he has a tendency to resolve them through magisterial statements rather than argument. The judgment of one critic, though harsh, is not altogether unfair: "the term 'canon' functions as a type of magic formula."[36]

Reviewers have often remarked upon Childs's lack of interest in the actual formation of the canon of Scripture (i.e., the process by which certain books came to be regarded as Scripture in preference to others). "Canon for Childs is a hermeneutical device, not a distinctive historical phenomenon."[37] There is one historical question, however, that does concern him. He devotes some effort to establishing the existence of a sharply defined canon of Scripture within Judaism prior to the rise of Christianity. Though direct evidence is lacking, he finds that early signs of the stabilization of the Masoretic text combined with Josephus's mention of a twenty-two-book canon and a few other factors show that Pharisaic Judaism (at least) possessed a clear canon even in the first century B.C.[38] An early closure of the OT canon is of some importance; a prime reason to exclude the NT use of the OT as a practice to be followed by later Christians is that such usage "cannot be directly related to the formation of the Christian Bible *qua* collection."[39] If the formation of that collection involved anything more than simple juxtaposition of the recent NT writings

36. Barstad, "Le canon," 87. Bruce M. Metzger notes that Childs attaches the adjective "canonical" to over thirty different words in a "seemingly indiscriminate way . . . creating a kind of mystique" (*The Canon of the New Testament: Its Origin, Development, and Significance* (Oxford: Oxford University Press, 1987), 30).

37. M. O'Connor, "How the Text Is Heard: The Biblical Theology of Brevard Childs," *Religious Studies Review* 21 (1995): 94; see also Harry Gamble, Review of *The New Testament as Canon* by Brevard S. Childs, *Journal of Biblical Literature* 106 (1987): 332.

38. *Biblical Theology*, 56–68, and to a slightly lesser degree in *OT as Scripture*, 62–67.

39. *Biblical Theology*, 76, and also 62, where all the characteristic interpretive

with the OT inherited en bloc from Judaism, it seems that Childs feels that the Christian understanding of the OT would assume a more significant role in the canonical shaping.

There are difficulties that can be raised at this point. Few would follow Childs in assigning so early a date to the closure of the OT canon, especially with regard to the Writings portion. Early signs of the Masoretic text there may be, but there are also "markedly different text types" and traditions (as Qumran shows).[40] The majority view, embodied in standard reference works, does not place so much weight on indirect signs of closure: "Our evidence for a date earlier than the end of the first century C.E. is at best weak and unconvincing."[41] Childs's sweeping references to "pharisaic" or "rabbinic" Judaism in the first century are also worrisome. Recovering an accurate perception of the range and diversity of Jewish thought, at least prior to the fall of Jerusalem, is one of the signal achievements of recent scholarship. One would have thought that the work of E. P. Sanders and others had rendered it impossible to speak casually of "rabbinic Judaism" in a first-century context.[42] The notion of a consistent and unified rabbinic entity, much less one with a clear canon, is a significant anachronism. This carelessness, when combined with the ques-

moves of the NT in relation to the OT are ascribed to a period in which "Christians abandoned the strictures of rabbinic Judaism such as limiting canonical authority to Hebrew writings."

40. Richard J. Clifford, Review of *Biblical Theology of the Old and New Testaments* by Brevard S. Childs, *Theological Studies* 54 (1993): 729. Despite a measure of agreement with Childs, Clifford admits some uncertainty regarding the edges of the canon in addition to text-critical concerns.

41. James A. Sanders, "Canon, OT," in *Anchor Bible Dictionary,* s.v. Childs himself acknowledges that his evidence is "indirect" (*Biblical Theology,* 59). It is noteworthy that Sanders's own form of canonical criticism pays significantly more attention to the actual history of canonization; cf. *From Sacred Story to Sacred Text* (Philadelphia: Fortress Press, 1987), 166–70.

42. E. P. Sanders, *Judaism: Practice and Belief, 63 BCE–55CE* (London: SCM, 1992), 3, who begins by noting that "Judaism . . . was dynamic and diverse." Earlier, in *Paul and Palestinian Judaism,* 33–76, he had devastated a tendency to portray first-century Judaism en bloc as a sterile and static religion of works-righteousness particularly common in German biblical scholarship. Though Childs is far from that substantive error, his early training in Germany may well be the reason why he seems to consider first-century Judaism as a monolithic block. Similar sweeping references appear throughout his discussion in *Biblical Theology,* 56–68.

tionable arguments for the early dating, illustrates the special pleading that Childs is forced to employ in order to sustain his preferred schema of the canon's development.

Childs altogether avoids a related issue concerning the canonical collection. An additional reason for rejecting NT modes of interpretation as a model for Christians to follow in reading the OT is that Scripture as it stands now embraces both Testaments, and so makes later situations fundamentally different from that of the apostolic church.[43] The theological issue that this raises will be taken up in a moment, but there is a historical point worth comment. When Childs reviews the formation of the whole Christian canon, he does so with a focus upon the differing opinions regarding the use of the LXX or Hebrew canon of the OT (*Biblical Theology*, 59–63). There is another aspect where there was much less diversity. Extant witnesses from the second and third centuries, when the canon was taking shape, demonstrably understood the OT along lines laid out in the NT. Irenaeus and Origen, for example, both employed arguments from typology and prophecy and portrayed the OT as bearing direct witness to Christ: "the new covenant having been known and preached by the prophets, He who was to carry it out . . . was also preached."[44] In putting aside their mode of reading the OT, Childs indicates that "the very same generation of Christians who fixed the main outlines of the canon is also a hopelessly unreliable guide to the correct way of reading that canon."[45] While there may be arguments in favor of this (and a blind endorsement of patristic exegesis surely has its own difficulties), none are given. One is left with the impres-

43. *Biblical Theology*, 244. The point is significant, but not in the way that Childs thinks; cf. the concluding chapter.

44. Irenaeus, *Adversus Haereses* IV.9.3; translation from *The Ante-Nicene Fathers*, vol. 1, ed. Alexander Roberts and James Donaldson, rev. A. Cleveland Coxe (Peabody: Hendrickson, 1994, repr.). He is particularly significant, given his position in the period when the unity of the Christian Bible was most under attack from Marcion and others; cf. Hans von Campenhausen, *Formation of the Christian Bible*, trans. J. A. Baker (Philadelphia: Fortress Press, 1972). Origen has been treated above.

45. John Barton, *Reading the Old Testament* (Philadelphia: Westminster, 1984), 96–97.

sion that the concrete circumstances of canonical development are being cut to fit a Procrustean bed of canonical theory.

Beyond these historical questions, dismissing the NT's modes of biblical interpretation raises a more significant theological problem, which appears clearly in Childs's various discussions of Paul. He begins by stating that Pauline exegesis must be evaluated in its historical context; unsatisfying though that exegesis may be when judged by modern standards, the apostle works with accepted methods of Hellenistic interpretation in confidence that the entire revelation of the Gospel has happened in fulfillment of the Scriptures. "That Paul is not following modern exegetical rules is clear, but this acknowledgment is far from saying that he is willful, inconsistent, or irrational" (*Biblical Theology,* 241). True, but this is not the point. Granted that Paul did his best to understand Scripture and followed methods accepted in his day, a more fundamental question "is whether Paul ***really did*** hear the Old Testament."[46] Childs's criticism of modern figures "who simply adopt Paul's method" reveals a negative answer. That method is wanting historically and theologically: historically inasmuch as "it changes the voice of the original witness," and theologically because it illegitimately conflates the Old Testament with the New (*Biblical Theology,* 84). He also warns against taking Paul as the supreme hermeneutical guide in isolation from other biblical witnesses; important though the apostle is, he "must be heard in concert with the entire Christian canon."[47]

The rest of the NT, however, reveals a remarkable degree of agreement with the basic Pauline effort "to use the gospel of the exalted Christ as the kerygmatic key for understanding the Hebrew scriptures."[48] This is an idea woven throughout the entire apostolic witness, going as far back as the early credal fragment affirming that

46. Noble, *Canonical Approach,* 305.

47. *Biblical Theology,* 244; Childs also returns here to the existence of a two-Testament canon as a crucial factor distinguishing the situation of later Christians from the apostolic church.

48. *Biblical Theology,* 381; Childs makes a similar point about the centrality of the Christ-event as the lens through which the NT reads Scripture in several other places (*Biblical Theology,* 264, 459, 477, etc.).

these things happened "in fulfillment of the Scriptures" (1 Cor 15.3–4), with no sign whatsoever of doubt or contradiction. Childs seems to recognize the problem that this represents; to the familiar idea that the two-Testament canon decisively alters the situation, he adds what amounts to a total exemption for apostolic eisegesis. The apostles had "unmediated access to God's revelation" (which seemingly enables them to ride roughshod over historical or theological constraints), but we do not.[49] The post-apostolic community must instead turn to their authoritative witness embodied in Scripture, which rules out "any direct imitation of the New Testament's hermeneutical practice" (*Biblical Theology,* 381).

The question at this point is simple but telling. It is absolutely central to Childs's entire approach that the witness of Scripture is granted primacy. As he says, it is "scripture itself which remains the sole vehicle from which the gospel is preached to the church and world."[50] Is it possible to accept the apostolic witness to the Gospel and at the same time deny one of its most consistent elements? It is difficult to see how one should receive the substance of that witness as authoritative, and yet dismiss its attitude to Scripture as a "time-conditioned feature" or a unique apostolic privilege. Moreover, it may be that the reception of the OT is part of that substance or one of its necessary conditions. Here one can draw a parallel with the empty tomb: as commentators have noted, though modern theologians may devise ways to maintain their faith without affirming that Jesus' tomb was empty, it is impossible to believe that apostolic Christians did not think it was or that their faith would have survived proof that Jesus' dead body remained in the tomb to rot.[51] Similarly, though Childs has attempted to show how post-apostolic Christians might receive the OT in a Christian mode without following the lead

49. *Biblical Theology,* 381; this notion of unmediated access is left without explanation or expansion.

50. *Biblical Theology,* 50; though this caps a historical discussion of Calvin, Childs is speaking in his own voice.

51. See Gordon D. Fee, *The First Epistle to the Corinthians* (Grand Rapids: Eerdmans, 1987), 725–26, in commenting on 15.3–4: "one may scarcely on good historical grounds deny that they so believed [that the tomb was empty]."

of the NT,[52] one cannot imagine that the apostolic church would have endured if forced to admit that they were seriously astray in reading the Scriptures. To cite an important study of Pauline hermeneutics, "there is no possibility of accepting Paul's message while simultaneously rejecting the legitimacy of the scriptural interpretation that sustains it."[53] Here as elsewhere Childs has failed to take up the full theological consequences implied by the canonical approach.

Intention and inspiration

The distinction between source and witness on which Childs lays so much stress leads him to focus on the final form of the biblical text within a canonical context. It is this text in that context that most fully represents the testimony of Israel or of the early Church to their encounter with God and transmits it to future generations of the believing community. The canonical process shapes the text to that end through "the multilayering activity of tradents who were continually at work in the individual testaments bringing the authoritative writings into conformity with a larger canonical intentionality" (*Biblical Theology,* 75). "Canonical intentionality" is a mysterious phrase; Childs is too skilled a scholar to deny the existence of unintentional factors influencing particular texts, yet

> irrespective of intentionality the effect of the canonical process was to render the tradition accessible to the future generation by means of a "canonical intentionality," which is coextensive with the meaning of the biblical text.[54]

The notion of canonical intentionality appears to be a postulate, designed to guarantee meaning within the final form of the text. (Childs cannot adopt a postmodern lack of concern for intended

52. An attempt that, as seen earlier, offers only the most vague and impressionistic suggestions.

53. Richard B. Hays, *Echoes of Scripture in the Letters of Paul* (New Haven: Yale University Press, 1989), 182. Hays does not directly engage Childs's view of apostolic exegetical practice, surprising since both were Yale faculty at the time.

54. *OT as Scripture,* 79.

meaning, given his insistence that the mission of exegesis is to hear the Bible as the witness of Israel and the apostolic church to the divine reality.)

This concept of canonical intentionality is peculiar to Childs, as is the use to which he puts it. Classic theologians would have taken divine inspiration as the final guarantor for the existence of meaning within the biblical text.[55] It is a striking feature of his work that even the word "inspiration" is rarely associated with the composition of the Bible. When the word is used, it is always connected with the "traditional" understanding, which he rejects due to its inadequate grasp of history and canonical process.[56] The term seems to be implicitly understood in a flat and verbal fashion, after the artistic image of the Holy Spirit dictating in the ear of the biblical writers, and in separation from the community as a whole. The neglect of current theologies of inspiration with their social focus and the turn toward more nuanced views of authorship and composition is surprising. As Childs's most perceptive critic notes, "granted a suitable doctrine of inspiration, the rest of C's programme flows naturally from it."[57] One could speculate as to why Childs fails to develop such a doctrine, but without a more explicit discussion of the topic on his part, the effort would be fruitless.

If canonical intentionality rather than inspiration is the foundation of biblical meaning, that intentionality itself is founded on the fact that the biblical text is the product of the canonical process. However, acceptance of that process and its resultant canon "as normative does not function initially as a derivative of reasoned argument."[58] The canon is a given, which one receives as an integral part of membership in the religious community because the community finds its authoritative norm "in the literature itself" (*Biblical Theology,*

55. Cf. the discussion of Origen and Aquinas in the first chapter.

56. *OT as Scripture,* 51; *NT as Canon,* 6; *Biblical Theology,* 64.

57. Noble, *Canonical Approach,* 31. More modern ideas of inspiration are discussed in the concluding chapter, as well as in the treatments of Segundo and de Lubac; see also Karl Rahner, *Inspiration in the Bible,* trans. Charles H. Henkey (New York: Herder and Herder, 1961).

58. Childs, "Response," 56; cf. *Biblical Theology,* 70–71.

71). It is a matter of faith. But here the emphasis on canonical process and the community's shaping and reception of its traditions falls short.

> Childs would rely on the canonical process, but one should rely on the God who supervises that process. Childs would trust in the believing community's faithfulness to revelation, but one should rely on the revealer. . . . Childs is correct in his assertion that the canon must be taken as a given. One must, however, receive it explicitly as a gift (truly a given) from the Giver.[59]

Failure to engage the traditional idea of inspiration leaves a crippling gap in Childs's attempt to sanctify the canonical process as the source of meaning, and bare insistence on (his idea of) canon as a constituent part of Christian identity does nothing to fill it. The systematic theological justification for the move is simply lacking.

Conclusion

The seriousness and learning with which Childs engages in his effort to turn modern exegesis away from what he perceives as the deeply flawed but still predominant historical-critical outlook and toward an explicitly theological concern with the canonical Bible are undeniable. He raises important questions about the value of an exegesis aimed at probing farther and farther behind the text, which neglects to return and illuminate the canonical Scripture with the results of those probes. In a more global way, his work forces "every committed reader to confront his or her own method for using scripture in theology, his or her own implicit or announced biblical theology."[60] Yet as often happens when shifting from opposition to construction, Childs's positive account of his own approach falters.

Earlier we noted that the important role accorded historical studies sets the canonical approach apart from pre-critical or anti-critical modes of interpretation, while the emphasis on canonical Scripture

59. Dale A. Brueggeman, "Brevard Childs's Canon Criticism: An Example of Post-critical Naïveté," *Journal of the Evangelical Theological Society* 32 (1989): 319. Indebted as my argument at this point is to Brueggeman's article, I could not better his phrasing of this conclusion.

60. Timothy F. Lull, "Why Does Childs Matter?," *Dialog* 33 (1994): 88.

as the primary context of exegetical work and theological concern sets it apart from classic historical-critical scholarship. The examination here has shown that both these supporting pillars suffer from significant difficulties. Childs accepts the employment of historical tools, but this becomes an integral part of interpretation only to the extent that these tools are focused upon the history of the biblical text rather than biblical events. His emphasis on reading Scripture as witness rather than source overshadows questions of historical truth or falsehood. More troubling, however, is the lack of a complete and systematic foundation for his idea of canon as the central tool for biblical exegesis. The actual development of the canon is forced to fit his ideals of canonical process, while the views animating the Christians who completed that process are overlooked. Interpretive techniques and principles that the NT writers employ in dealing with the OT, which Childs recognizes as an important element of their witness, are rejected as models for later Christian practice with little more explanation than "they were Apostles, we are not." And finally, when he sets up "canonical intentionality" as the guarantor of meaning within the biblical text in lieu of the classic idea of inspiration, he completely fails to address the theological shift involved in moving from a Bible whose meaning is inspired by God to one whose meaning is the result of the canonical process of Israel and the Church.

This consistent lack of attention to important theological issues raised by his own thought can only bring the entire structure into question. Unlike Brown, whose aim was to secure the place of historical biblical study, Childs attempts to recast contemporary approaches to the Bible and then to present his approach as an absolute requirement if the biblical text is to be taken seriously as Christian Scripture. That is a demanding task and one ill-served by the boundaries that specialized training imposes on the subdisciplines of theology. Yet while it may be neither entirely fair nor entirely reasonable to expect someone to be exegete and systematic theologian in equal measure, it is not unreasonable to require foundations capable of bearing the load placed upon them.

One must conclude, with regret, that Childs offers little to our broader project. Though his focus on the canonical text as the primary context of exegesis is in itself welcome, the reasons given to support the canonical approach and guide its practice do not withstand investigation. The main service performed by this exploration of his views is a cautionary one, as it illustrates the intrinsic difficulty of developing an interpretive framework capable of doing justice to historical studies and yet affirming the unique status and character of the Bible.

CHAPTER FOUR

JUAN LUIS SEGUNDO

Unlike Brown and Childs, Juan Luis Segundo was not a biblical scholar by profession, and his work includes a strong critique of contemporary academic exegesis and theology as being isolated from the concrete circumstances of the present day as a result of "the naive belief that the word of God is applied to human realities inside some antiseptic laboratory."[1] This resistance to any separation between theology and praxis is, of course, characteristic of Latin American liberation theology in general. What causes Segundo to stand out among his colleagues are the extent and depth of his methodological reflections on the problem of applying the Word of God to human realities in all their concrete particularity. Not content with the more popular and more naive tendency to make a certain reading of Exodus the primary interpretive guide to the whole Bible, he instead lays out a complex vision regarding the role of faith and ideologies in human life that grounds an approach to Scripture as teacher of liberative practice rather than depository of theological data.[2]

1. Juan Luis Segundo, *The Liberation of Theology,* trans. John Drury (Maryknoll: Orbis Books, 1976), 7.

2. For criticism of a monistic reliance on Exodus, see *Liberation,* 112. Anthony J. Tambasco, *The Bible for Ethics: Juan Luis Segundo and First-World Ethics* (College Park, Md.: University Press of America, 1981), 139, recognizes Segundo's superiority in this regard; see also Alfred T. Hennelly, *Theologies in Conflict: the Challenge of Juan Luis Segundo* (Maryknoll: Orbis Books, 1979). Later discussions of Segundo's hermeneutics largely follow them. The recent article of Peter Phan, "Method in Liberation Theologies," *Theological Studies* 61 (2000): 40–63, speaks of Segundo only in relation to the hermeneutic circle, with no mention of these subsequent works. The article takes as representative of Latin American liberation theology Clodovis Boff, who calls his approach to Scripture the correspondence of relationship model: "the Christian writings offer us not a *what,* but a *how*—a manner, a style, a spirit whereby we may act in our context as Jesus acted in his" (56). We will see below that this is also Segundo's focus and so, *mutatis mutandis,* much of what is said here may be applied to other liberation theologians.

When these methodological statements are combined with his discussion of the historical Jesus, one can examine his approach to the Bible in some detail. Such an examination is missing from prior treatments of Segundo's biblical thought, which were based upon earlier material and could not take into account the more developed presentation offered as part of his Christology.[3]

We begin with his assessment of biblical scholarship and theology in their present situation. Though this is not so central an aspect of his thought as it is with Childs, he does identify serious flaws in both classical and modern approaches to Scripture. His own understanding of "hermeneutic circle" offers a means by which individuals can avoid those flaws and come to see the Bible in a new and liberative perspective. However, the hermeneutic circle appears mainly as a pedagogical tool for bringing people to that new perspective. Its utility is more *quoad nos* than *quoad se,* to use terms from a different milieu. Segundo's substantive opinions begin with the idea of faith as a constant and constituent factor in human living, prior to and apart from any specific religious commitment, together with the essential role of ideology in bringing faith to concrete expression in a given context; he then describes the distinguishing characteristics of religious faith. With this general framework in place, we can discuss the ways in which Segundo uses it to explain the role of the Bible in Christian religious faith and set up the witness of the historical Jesus as the touchstone of that faith. The chapter concludes by raising both historical and theological questions regarding Segundo's engagement with the biblical text. As his use of the term "historical Jesus" indicates, the most significant question concerns the precise status of the Bible itself.

ASSESSMENT OF THE PRESENT SITUATION

The state of contemporary scholarship is hardly Segundo's primary concern, and he spends less time discussing it than either

3. Juan Luis Segundo, *Jesus of Nazareth Yesterday and Today,* trans. and ed. John Drury, 5 vols. (Maryknoll: Orbis Books, 1984–88). There are significant expansions on related topics in *The Liberation of Dogma: Faith, Revelation, and Dogmatic Teaching Authority,* trans. Phillip Berryman (Maryknoll: Orbis Books, 1992).

Brown or Childs does. Yet his concern to set out methodological foundations for liberation theology obliges him to give some account of what it is that liberation theology seeks to supplant. That account takes shape within the explanation of the hermeneutic circle in the opening chapter of *Liberation of Theology;* the circle is not only a hermeneutic device but also a pedagogical one intended to lead people to a new and liberative perspective. Consequently he takes care to be clear in stating the critical differences that distinguish liberation theology from classical or academic theology.[4]

It is noteworthy that the value of historical study is not among those differences. Theology and exegesis are properly engaged with all "the sciences which help to understand the past," and recovering the variety of historical situations underlying diverse biblical texts is of "decisive importance."[5] Academic exegesis and theology fall short, not in looking to history, but in being so focused on retrieval of what is past that they overlook and neglect the present. An uncritical belief in their own objectivity bars many exegetes and theologians from accepting what Segundo sees as an essential starting point: the suspicion that "anything and everything involving ideas, including theology, is intimately bound up with the existing social situation in at least an unconscious way" (*Liberation,* 8). Without this suspicion, scholars are unlikely ever to see the ways in which the structure of their society (and their own position within it) are continuously "shaping our theology so as to uproot it from its base in divine revelation and place it in the service of social interests" (*Liberation,* 47). An energetic study of the present that reveals those social interests and their distorting influence is a necessary condition if historical work is to have any real independence or effect. This is not to say that Segundo sees all traditional theologies as mere supports of the *status quo;* however, without sustained study of the extant situation in its own right, such theologies do not have accurate criteria for whatever evaluations they

4. One should note that Segundo is moving at a rather high level of abstraction throughout this discussion, without much mention of specific theologies or theologians, due to the fundamental nature of his observations.

5. *Liberation of Theology,* 7, 108; parenthetical references in this and the two subsequent paragraphs are to this work.

make of it. Whether those evaluations are negative or positive is irrelevant. And so,

> the fundamental difference between the traditional academic theologian and the liberation theologian is that the latter feels compelled at every step to combine the disciplines that open up the past with the disciplines that help to explain the present. (*Liberation,* 8)

Only if due attention is given to both past and present can one begin to formulate a theology that expresses what the Word of God has to say here and now.

Segundo offers a specific method for bringing these dual concerns into harmony, which he calls "the hermeneutic circle." The term itself is hardly new, as he acknowledges, but the precise explanation that he gives is all his own. The circle refers to the continuous process of change in biblical interpretation generated by shifting factors in the present circumstances (individual or collective) of the interpreters. The process is continuous because one must constantly bring real situations and the biblical texts into contact: "each new reality obliges us to reinterpret the word of God afresh, to change reality accordingly, and then to go back and reinterpret the word of God again, and so on" (*Liberation,* 8). But before one can embark on the hermeneutic circle, two essential prerequisites must be satisfied. The first is directed to the situation of the would-be interpreter. That situation must evoke basic and profound questions regarding the entire set of values and beliefs imbued in us by the broader society. As Segundo sees it, only a deep and abiding suspicion that the world is not as we have thought it to be can "force theology to come back to reality and ask itself new and decisive questions" (*Liberation,* 9). The second prerequisite is related to the first; such new theological questions must also provoke (or at least be capable of provoking) a new interpretation of Scripture. Otherwise, even if theology should be taking account of real circumstances, its attempts to address them will be founded on exegetical frameworks and results developed within a different milieu as responses to different questions. These prerequisites guarantee an antecedent willingness on the part of the interpreter to engage the really extant situation and, in turn, to let the situation truly engage one's theology. In the absence of this willingness, theology is too easily incorporated into a society's dominant preconceptions or ideologies.

Keeping these preconditions firmly in mind, Segundo goes on to set up four distinct stages within the hermeneutic circle. First is the change in one's outlook, based on a recognition of oppression and injustice inherent in the contemporary environment, that results in "a pretheological human commitment to change and improve the world" (*Liberation,* 39). From this comes an ideological suspicion that the customary ideas taught and accepted in society are, consciously or unconsciously, in whole or in part, means used by dominant groups to maintain and strengthen their own power at the expense of others. In the second stage of the circle, one applies this suspicion to a critical analysis of these ruling beliefs, with particular regard for theology lest it "remain the unwitting spokesman of the experiences and ideas of the ruling factions" (*Liberation,* 39). The positive consequence of critical analysis is a new understanding of theological realities, as instruments of liberation rather than oppression, that leads to the next stage; here the suspicion turns toward biblical exegesis in the conviction that it too has been distorted and important scriptural data has been obscured. The fourth and final step of the circle is the beginning of a larger task, where one puts into action "our new way of interpreting the fountainhead of our faith (i.e. Scripture) with the new elements at our disposal" (*Liberation,* 9).

The way that Segundo reserves the main work of biblical interpretation to this last stage shows the limitations of the hermeneutic circle for a discussion of his approach to Scripture. The circle seems instead to describe the process by which an interpreter moves away from the distortions imposed upon theology and exegesis by dominant ideologies and toward a new and liberative perspective. The emphasis on ideological suspicion and critical analysis further reveals the essentially remedial concerns animating the circle in practice. The circle clearly reveals the shortcomings of contemporary theology and exegesis and also the fundamental commitment that interpreters should bring to their work. Though far from unimportant, given Segundo's desire to bring a real concern for present as well as past into the practice of theology, this discussion does not constitute a substantive treatment of the Bible and its function in Christian belief and practice.[6] For that, one needs to examine Segundo's analysis of faith and ideology and then move on to the key role he allots for Scripture in specifically Christian faith and ideology.

FAITH AND IDEOLOGY

All humans find themselves faced with the necessity of choosing a form of life—not merely a job or career, but the fundamental values and convictions that provide structure and coherence to their existence. The motivation driving this choice is the common desire for happiness. Regardless of the concrete option an individual adopts, everyone does choose the path that seems to them to have the best chance of securing lasting and stable happiness. The difficulty that arises here is that, given the limitations of human life, reason and personal experience cannot be the deciding factors in our selection. To choose one option is to close off all others; with only one life to live, there is no way to acquire direct knowledge of the diverse satisfactions presented by different ways of life. Instead,

> experiences of effectively realized values are conveyed to us by our fellow human beings. Before we have these experiences ourselves, we perceive their value and their possibilities for satisfaction in and through the experience of others.[7]

The main factor influencing the values that individuals adopt is the conviction, based on the witness provided by the lives of others, that a life dedicated to a given value is superior (i.e., more conducive to happiness or ultimate satisfaction).

According to Segundo, "faith" in the broad sense refers to this ac-

6. Nor is it intended as such, I think. One could also consider the fact that in this earlier work Segundo was very much concerned with distinguishing liberation theology from traditional first-world theologies and so naturally stressed the circle's role. By the time that *Jesus of Nazareth* is written, that concern has diminished.

7. *Jesus of Nazareth,* vol. 1, *Faith and Ideologies,* 6. One is reminded here of Lonergan's idea of incarnate meaning; Bernard J. F. Lonergan, *Method in Theology* (Toronto: University of Toronto Press, 1990), 73.

ceptance of specific "referential witnesses" and their testimony about a given value as the ground for one's basic choice of life. This sort of faith is a universal component of human being, since everyone has need of such referential witnesses, and so Segundo will habitually refer to it as "anthropological faith." The decisive characteristic of anthropological faith is that it lends order and structure to an individual's life by setting up one such value (be it material wealth, honor, the creation of a more just society, etc.) as absolute for that particular individual. This both structures the realm of values as a whole, by subordinating all others to this absolute, and "enables people to classify happenings and events . . . in accordance with the values they have accepted."[8]

Once such a framework is chosen, one is faced with the task of making it actual. Faith does not operate in a vacuum; although it determines the values at work in human actions, it does not control the situations in which individuals try to live them out. The counter factor providing the objective data that must be taken into account is "the structure of reality itself, which holds true for all and which is neutral vis-a-vis the values we want it to serve."[9] The main concern here is utilitarian and pragmatic, as inquiry seeks to learn "what will happen in the face of certain conditions or circumstances . . . or the conditions one must satisfy if one wants certain results."[10] Without a clear knowledge of the means that are or could be effective in a given situation, the commitment to goals and values made in anthropological faith (whatever those values may be) would remain an empty fantasy.

Segundo employs the term "ideology" to refer to any such body of knowledge regarding the means used to achieve some end.[11] It

8. *Faith and Ideologies*, 25.

9. *Faith and Ideologies*, 26.

10. *Faith and Ideologies*, 27.

11. *Faith and Ideologies*, 16 and passim. Segundo is at pains to distinguish his usage of ideology as a universal and neutral factor from the more negative meaning Marx gives it as the view of life supporting the dominant class in society (though he is not always consistent in practice). As Harold Wells observes, this understanding "makes him an exception among liberation theologians"; Harold Wells, "The Question of Ideological Determination in Liberation Theology," *Toronto Journal of Theology* 3 (1987): 214.

constitutes another universal dimension of human living that is complementary and subordinate to faith. Although a faith without ideology is impotent, an ideology without faith would be inert. The energy that drives (without determining) the development and then the use of an ideology is always provided by the antecedent choice made in and through faith to pursue a specific set of values. Properly understood, ideology and faith are not in opposition to one another. Segundo criticizes in particular the tendency to speak of Christianity as a faith with no need of ideology, which he sees as imprecise and obscure. One can hardly speak of Christian faith as real if it must exist "without methods conditioned by the changing reality of history that are designed to implement certain values which are judged to be essential to the Christian."[12] An ideological component of this sort is essential if one is to offer any Christian guidance beyond such purely formal statements as "love your neighbor as yourself." Important though this is, even the first and greatest commandment risks becoming an empty platitude if one does not go on to discuss what this love may require in the situation at hand.

One phrase in the passage cited above, "methods conditioned by the changing reality of history," is worth expansion. Segundo sees ideologies as radically particular, bound closely to the circumstances in which they originated. Efficacy in promoting a given end is the primary concern of any ideology, and the precise configuration of means changes in response to historical conditions. Care for the poor, for example, is a central element of Christian faith that finds active expression in the importance the Gospels place on almsgiving. Yet the effectiveness of individual acts of charity is much reduced in modern societies with their complex economic structures. The selfsame care for the poor today is expressed in "the payment of just taxes" in support of society's corporate efforts on behalf of the disadvantaged.[13] An insistence on almsgiving strictly along the evangelical

12. *Faith and Ideologies,* 20. There is expansion on the same point in *Faith and Ideologies,* 120, 128.

13. The example is Segundo's (*Faith and Ideologies,* 123), following Vatican II (*Gaudium et Spes* 30).

lines would overlook the vast differences between first-century Palestine and the present.

Segundo is highly sensitive to the dangers involved in absolutizing an ideology, through either historical insensitivity or the mistaken notion that the commitment of faith can be implemented in only one way. Such missteps can imprison faith in an outdated or unsuitable ideology, and so render it ineffectual. The sole criterion for evaluating an ideology is its efficacy in bringing one's faith to bear on the contemporary situation. "All ideologies are in and of themselves neither good, nor bad, but indifferent."[14] The character and content of an individual's basic faith may be open to moral critique, but the ideology used to implement it may not.

Though the example was drawn from Christian ideas, the description of faith and ideology has so far been entirely concerned with anthropological faith. The adoption of a set of fundamental values and the need for ideology to realize them are universal human phenomena irrespective of religious affiliation. Segundo presents an account of specifically religious faith as a further determination of anthropological faith. Attempts to separate religious and anthropological faith on the ground that anthropological faith is derived from human testimony but religious faith relies on divine revelation and *auctoritas Dei revelantis* are rejected as simplistic. Any such revelation is necessarily given and transmitted through human beings, and those who commit themselves to the values expressed therein are no less dependent on human testimony than anyone else. Instead, religious faith is initially distinguished by an affirmation that a particular human witness or group of witnesses was "the vehicle for a revelation about God, about the values that God himself was elevating to the level of the absolute."[15] However, that affirmation says less about reli-

14. Bernard J. Verkamp, "On Doing the Truth: Orthopraxis and the Theologian," *Theological Studies* 49 (1988): 9; cf. *Faith and Ideologies,* 45, where Segundo says "an act of adultery does not consist in some specific or specifiable use of sexual relations in itself, but rather in the result of a person's intended project. Only that project gives the act its moral dimension of adultery."

15. *Faith and Ideologies,* 64; further arguments regarding the essential role of human witness in religious faith are found in *Faith and Ideologies,* 79–81.

gious faith itself and more about the authority that people ascribe to it. The discussion moves quickly to an objective description more concerned with functional characteristics.

Segundo identifies two factors that must be present if an anthropological faith is to become religious faith: a body of transcendent data and a tradition of witnesses from which one acquires such data. The notion of transcendent data refers to particular statements about the ultimate constitution of the universe and of human beings. Such statements are transcendent because they concern reality as a whole, and "the total possibilities of reality exceed the limits of direct experience and verification."[16] Without being veils for personal or scientific ignorance, such data serve a vital function by asserting a basic correspondence between the structure of the world and values chosen in faith; a given set of transcendent data establishes the conditions of possibility for pursuing a given set of values. A prime example of a transcendent datum within Christianity is the Resurrection:

> The fact that the Father raised Jesus from the dead also makes certain things worthwhile. It would be foolish to maintain that particular meaning-structure if the "datum" were wrong. As Paul put it, we would be "of all men most to be pitied." (1 Cor 15.19)[17]

It is unclear whether an individual's acceptance of transcendent data precedes or follows the onset of faith. At some times Segundo speaks of transcendent data as decisive in the actual choice of specific values, and at other times he suggests that the choice of values determines what transcendent data are accepted. The relationship seems to be one of mutual influence.[18] Yet the presence of transcendent data is not sufficient in itself to constitute a religion. While an explicit religious faith may highlight such data or possess a greater store of

16. *Faith and Ideologies,* 73.

17. *Faith and Ideologies,* 73.

18. The uncertainty appears clearly in *Faith and Ideologies,* 70–83 and 152–55. Segundo's interest falls more on "what values or what meaning-structures those transcendent data support, correct, develop, or deepen"; i.e., their effect on an extant faith (*Faith and Ideologies,* 74). One also finds that values can have corrective effects upon transcendent data, as his treatment of dogma (which he takes to represent transcendent data) indicates (*Faith and Ideologies,* 76–77).

them, there is no instance of anthropological faith without at least some transcendent datum (be it only a basic confidence that working to realize one's values will not prove futile in the long run). "The transcendence to be found in any and every anthropological faith vis-à-vis the limits of human existence does not make such faith 'religious.'"[19]

The truly decisive factor in constituting religious faith is the existence of a tradition of witnesses, spanning a variety of historical situations, while remaining united in anthropological faith. Testimony to a set of values offered by only a single witness is too easily confused with the particular ideology, limited by specific circumstances, that the witness employs. A changed situation not only can invalidate the ideology but also can lead the careless to abandon the underlying values. Focus upon a multitude of witnesses lends depth and texture. By making their experiences one's own, which is central to Segundo's idea of adherence to a tradition, one acquires the skill of "learning how to learn."[20] This is a matter of reading the present environment, with all its particularity, in light of the common values transmitted by the tradition. One can then begin to discern appropriate ideologies and actions. What is crucial "is not the 'divine' nature of what is being transmitted but rather the importance of the witnesses."[21] Learning how to learn in this fashion is more art than science; it depends on immersion in a stream of living experiences held in suspension, as it were, by tradition. And so, as an observer rightly notes,

> the "religious" tradition which defines Christianity should be understood as the trail of the more or less winding movement described by the anthropological faith at work in the people of Israel, then in the apostolic community, before being recovered in the Church, within perpetually new situations.[22]

19. *Faith and Ideologies*, 82.
20. *Faith and Ideologies*, 70–78.
21. *Faith and Ideologies*, 76.
22. René Marlé, "Foi, idéologie, religion chez J.-L. Segundo," *Recherches de sciences religeuses* 76 (1988): 270.

BIBLICAL APPLICATIONS

Segundo gives no indication that Scripture is less than central to Christian faith, and he regards attempts to displace or disregard it with puzzlement.[23] The Bible plays an indispensable role because it is there that we find the tradition of witnesses, and the transcendent data to which it points, that constitutes Christian faith. However, this function has often been obscured by abstract or careless application of the familiar affirmation that Scripture is the Word of God, and so Segundo attempts to understand Scripture as a work of divine pedagogy rather than divine inspiration.

Inspiration versus pedagogy

His criticism of the classical idea of inspiration is clear and unequivocal. That idea is founded upon an abstract theological deduction: the Bible is the Word of God, therefore God is the true author of both Old Testament and New Testament, with human writers serving merely as instruments. One might even do better to substitute the word "stenographers" in place of the word "writers," since God's action in producing the Scriptures is consistently referred to as "dictation."[24] The absolute truth of each and every statement or affirmation made in the biblical text is then guaranteed by the authority of their divine source. While he finds no logical flaw in this chain of reasoning, Segundo shows that it becomes untenable as soon as one considers the Bible in its historical reality. Many if not most biblical writers show no apparent awareness of their inspired status, and one

23. *Liberation of Theology,* 37 n. 55; as Phan recognizes ("Method," 56), Segundo did "not apply the hermeneutics of suspicion to the Bible itself."

24. *Dogma,* 40–41, 73, 77. Segundo's understanding of inspiration in its traditional form is notably flat. Not only does he make a straw man of pre-modern ideas, but there is no consideration at all of contemporary theological reflection on the topic. See Raymond F. Collins, "Inspiration," 1031–33, for a brief summary of that reflection, which includes a significant Catholic contribution that Segundo ought to have at least acknowledged. Rahner's social notion of inspiration could have been helpful to him, inasmuch as it stresses the ongoing use of Scripture in the community; cf. Karl Rahner, *Foundations of Christian Faith,* trans. William V. Dych (New York: Crossroad, 1978), 374–78, or *Inspiration in the Bible.*

can find serious contradictions within the texts themselves. One example that he favors is the consistent denial or rejection of an afterlife in nearly all of the OT as opposed to the unanimous affirmation found in the NT.[25]

Segundo focuses more intently on disagreements of this sort because they expose an internal incoherence. On the one hand, genuine problems arise if Christians read the OT in its own right. It is difficult to see the Father of Jesus in a God who endorses sentiments such as "Happy those who seize your children and smash them against a rock" (Ps 137.9). On the other hand, there is a tendency to neglect the OT or bind it within a gilded cage of allegories and so reduce it to "a prolegomenon that might make the contents of the 'New' Testament possible, understandable, and plausible."[26] Each of these alternatives, in practice if not in theory, diminishes or denies the OT's place in the Bible and its status as divine revelation. Rather than join Marcion in rejecting the OT as incompatible with Christian teaching, or destroy the integrity of the text through interpretive artifice, Segundo abandons the ideas of divine authorship and inspiration as inadequate to the reality of Scripture.

The Bible is better understood as a work of divine pedagogy, where God is the director of a long educational process that is recorded and set forth in the biblical texts. The basis for this is taken from Vatican II's Constitution on Divine Revelation *(Dei Verbum):*

> "the books of the Old Testament, in accordance with the state of mankind before the time of salvation established by Christ . . . though they *contain some things which are incomplete and temporary,* nevertheless show us a *true divine pedagogy.*" (DV 15; emphasis his)[27]

Segundo takes this as an implicit rejection of the older notion of inspiration; if the human writers were no more than scribes taking dic-

25. *Dogma,* 244 (where Segundo also brings up the polygamy of the patriarchs and Mosaic permission of divorce as direct contradictions of Jesus' sayings on marriage). With respect to a personal afterlife, he does not distinguish between an active rejection and a simple failure to develop such an idea due to the OT focus on communal immortality through descendants and nation.

26. *Dogma,* 64.

27. *Dogma,* 75

tation from God, it would be impossible to speak of God as giving "incomplete and temporary" information. The open acknowledgment of the incomplete and temporary within the biblical text is due to the recognition that the humans involved in the composition of Scripture are true authors with different skills, different interests, and different limitations imposed by their cultural and historical circumstances.[28] We find in the texts they produced not a sheer mass of revealed data, but instances of faith finding expression through diverse ideologies. This is a common feature of human existence, and taken individually, each part of the Bible does no more than illustrate it. But Scripture taken as whole displays a series of witnesses to faith, a tradition in Segundo's terms, in which the basic values and "transcendent data offered by God penetrate into the corresponding questions that arise within the whole of human experience."[29] At the core of this tradition is the conviction that God's will and desire is liberation, the release of the human race from all the conditions of oppression and servitude that impede and obstruct its full development. Understanding Scripture as a record of the ways in which these values and data are communicated and extended, under God's guidance, leads Segundo to embrace the notion of divine pedagogy. That pedagogy as the Bible presents it is the proper object of inspiration; no biblical text by itself is more than one (limited) stage of an ongoing process.

One notable objection to this account flows from the same quotation that he uses as a foundation. *Dei Verbum* is referring to the OT, "before the time of salvation established by Christ"; that would be a simpler and more natural cause for limited or incomplete features of the text. Segundo's adoption of divine pedagogy as the primary category for understanding biblical revelation may be an extreme response despite its agreement with his broader analysis of faith and ideology. One does find an answer to this objection in his text, although he does not seem to take it seriously in itself. The suggestion

28. Segundo sees the first sign of this in the 1943 encyclical *Divino Afflante Spiritu*, with its emphasis on the intended meaning of the human writer, and further confirmation in *Dei Verbum* (*Dogma*, 73–74).

29. *Dogma*, 92.

that the OT is, as revelation, lacking in comparison to the NT is something we have already seen him reject. Though the obligation is not always fulfilled, it is incumbent on Christians to "believe in God's 'revelation' in the Old Testament in the same fashion and for the same reason that they believe in it in the New."[30] Any limitations found in the one must also be found in the other. This much he takes almost for granted; his main concern with the NT at this point is different (though related).

Segundo wishes to show that the divine pedagogical process begun in the OT does not change its fundamental character with the advent of the NT. Although he grants that *Dei Verbum* as well as the normal teaching of the Church incline in that direction, it is an error to assume that the revelation of God in Christ presents us with "perfect and invariable" explanations. Real education does not culminate in the ceremonial delivery of a "Teacher's Edition" with neatly arranged answers, and the NT itself indicates that we must go beyond the letter of its statements. Segundo twice highlights the promise of the Paraclete in Jesus' farewell discourse (Jn 16.12–13): "If I do not go away, the Paraclete will not come to you. I should be able to tell you many other things, as well, but you could not manage them now. When the Spirit of Truth comes, he will guide you to the whole truth."[31] A major aim of any pedagogy is to do away with the need for a pedagogue, not by exhausting the stock of information to convey, but by rendering the students capable of learning on their own. They can then apply values and concepts appropriated during their education to whatever new and different situations may arise in their own lives. Only in this way can we speak of the NT as the conclusion or fulfillment of the divine pedagogy. Each subsequent generation, formed by the biblical witness and under the continuing guidance of the Spirit, "is thrust toward a more perfect maturity, and toward a new, deeper, and richer truth."[32]

30. *Dogma,* 244. Segundo's insistence on the essential parity of OT and NT is oddly reminiscent of Childs, and the same difficulties raised in our discussion of Childs apply here.

31. *Dogma,* 119–20, 245–46, citing Jn 16.7, 12–13.

32. *Dogma,* 246.

The witness of Jesus

Segundo maintains a focus on the particular example and witness of Jesus within this pedagogical process. Without minimizing other stages, the whole divine pedagogy "culminates in the direct witnesses to Jesus, in whom is concentrated the totality of faith."[33] We as Christians take our bearings from the faith and values expressed in Jesus' life and mission and through the specific ideologies that he employed in his own historical environment. In this there is no difference between the Christian and anyone else; as we have seen, faith in the anthropological sense begins almost always from the lived example of another human. What does distinguish Jesus, not only from witnesses to different forms of faith but also from other witnesses within the biblical tradition, is the transcendent datum of the resurrection. For Segundo, this serves as answer "to the question of the ultimate fate of the values taught and practiced by Jesus."[34] The recognition that "God has made him both Lord and Messiah, this Jesus whom you crucified" (Acts 2.36) offers verification to the disciples that a life lived in commitment to delivering others from servitude and oppression, to announcing "the reign of God" in which this is the dominant concern, is not futile. Where others must take the transcendent data needed to support their faith on trust, in the hope that the values to which they have given themselves are in harmony with reality, witnesses to the resurrection (together with those who accept their testimony) know and can be sure that this is the case.[35]

Though the resurrection confirms the values and mission of Jesus, Segundo also sees it as simultaneously obscuring or concealing them. The total reversal of normal expectations represented by the resurrection, and its essential role in justifying the continued existence of

33. *Jesus of Nazareth,* vol. 2, *The Historical Jesus of the Synoptics,* 6.

34. *Historical Jesus,* 175.

35. Though Segundo understands the limitation of appearances to those who were pre-paschal disciples to show that "pursuit of the same values that Jesus held dear is an indispensable prerequisite for being able to 'see' and recognize the risen one," this is taken as a sign of necessary continuity (albeit within difference) between the pre-paschal and post-paschal Jesus (*Historical Jesus,* 171).

the community, naturally centers "attention and preaching . . . on a point other than the one that was central for Jesus himself."[36] Where Jesus focused on the liberative message of the kingdom in opposition to the oppressive religious structures dominating Palestinian society, the early church is concerned with the message of Jesus as Messiah.[37] The ways in which different figures within the NT express that message may have a lesser or greater relationship with the preaching of Jesus, but all of them are unavoidably distinct from the original concerns at work in Jesus' ministry. However, though important, this distinction should not be overstated: "it is not that the message of Jesus was *lost;* the Gospels themselves are the best proof that it was not. But the fact is that we can get to it only *indirectly* [emphases his]."[38]

The Gospels are not histories in the modern style, nor are they much concerned with reproducing the *ipsissima verba* of Jesus. Each of the four evangelists presents an account of Jesus shaped in light of the resurrection and aimed at the concerns facing the community for which he wrote. In John's phrasing (20.31), "these things are written that you may believe that Jesus is the Messiah, the Son of God, and that through this belief you may have life in his name." To approach Jesus from the start with that belief, as every witness within the NT does, is to be working "from above." Segundo prefers to begin from the historical words and deeds of Jesus of Nazareth, "from below," while not entirely condemning the other path.[39] Without adopting the interpretations of the evangelists, which are adjusted and conditioned by their own circumstances, he wishes to "rescue the data

36. *Historical Jesus,* 185.

37. This contrast depends on Segundo's account of the historical Jesus, as set out in *Historical Jesus,* 45–165. There he presents Jesus as a rebel not against Rome but against an oppressive religious structure within Judaism itself (and the Pharisees as prime representatives of that structure). The precise details are not a direct concern here; the issue is more the function of the historical Jesus within his overall framework.

38. *Historical Jesus,* 186. The point is made at more length in *Jesus of Nazareth,* vol. 4, *The Christ of the Ignatian Exercises,* 19–21.

39. "There is no good reason why a christology 'from above' has to contradict or oppose a christology 'from below.' Ordinarily they should dovetail with each other and ultimately complement one another" (*Jesus of Nazareth,* vol. 3, *The Humanist Christology of Paul,* 91–92).

about the 'historical' Jesus from this overall picture in which they are presented to us already interpreted."[40] This makes it possible to distinguish between the faith that impelled Jesus to action and the ideologies used to implement it, to recognize that "the significance of Jesus of Nazareth was made manifest in a specific historical context of tasks, motivations, and interests."[41] Those who would call themselves Christians must then express and live out the same basic faith displayed by Jesus in their own quite different historical contexts. This is

> the ongoing task of creating gospels that are truly good news for our contemporaries, while still continuing to verify their *coherence* [emphasis his] with the gospel that was preached in history by Jesus of Nazareth.[42]

This does not at all diminish the value of the canonical gospels or the other NT witnesses. They play an important role that goes beyond providing data for historical investigation. Study of the historical Jesus makes it possible to discern the creative work of the evangelists, Paul, and other writers as they bring their own interests to what they know of Jesus and interpret him to and for their contemporaries. They provide an essential example for later Christians, who face exactly the same task as they attempt to make Jesus speak to their situations. This is what Segundo means by saying that

> the only valid approach to Jesus of Nazareth is that of the New Testament. It entails a process of successive readings that start out from the concrete historical interest he aroused in his own time and place and move on to the human problems of later times and our own present day.[43]

While the specific readings given by the NT authors may no longer be appropriate ideologies for different circumstances, the way that they came to those solutions continues to be instructive.

40. *Christ of the Ignatian Exercises,* 66; Segundo lays out a standard account of the methodology to be employed in historical Jesus research in *Historical Jesus,* 45–70, though he does not attempt to justify his own historical conclusions in a detailed fashion because that would be "alien to the aim" of the book (*Historical Jesus,* 198 n. 22). In general, he falls firmly within the so-called Second Quest of the historical Jesus inaugurated by Ernst Kasemann; cf. N. T. Wright, *Jesus and the Victory of God* (Minneapolis: Fortress Press, 1996), 3–25.

41. *Historical Jesus,* 27.

42. *Historical Jesus,* 40.

43. *Historical Jesus,* 39.

EVALUATION AND COMMENT

That a first-world theologian should offer commentary upon work originating in a third-world context almost requires a disclaimer. One cannot stress enough that criticizing a theology is not the same as endorsing the situation the theology seeks to change: "if one member suffers, all suffer together with it" (1 Cor 12.26). This fact of Christian life nonetheless finds itself accompanied by the obligation of "speaking the truth in love" (Eph 4.15). The following observations attempt to do justice to both Pauline sayings.

We begin with a subordinate issue, one less concerned with what Segundo does than with the way he does it. He emphasizes the historical circumstances of both biblical events and the biblical texts, but in practice he displays a "lack of familiarity with recent biblical scholarship."[44] This is particularly clear with regard to his treatment of the historical Jesus. As John Meier has shown, Segundo's portrayal of Jesus as a political activist engaged in an attempt to overthrow the oppressive religious structures of first-century Judaism distorts both exegetical and historical evidence.[45] The most significant of those distortions is the presentation of first-century Judaism itself, whose traditions and authorities Segundo identifies as Jesus' primary enemies. Drawing more or less directly from the four Gospels, without attention to recent studies that stress the complexity of Jewish religious life at the time, he considers it historically accurate to say that the Pharisees dominated the religious establishment and were "the enemies *par excellence* of the God that Jesus reveals."[46] One finds here an insensitivity to the potential dangers of anti-Semitism that is striking (though clearly unintentional) in a modern Catholic theologian.

44. John P. Galvin, Review of *The Humanist Christology of Paul* by Juan Luis Segundo, in *Heythrop Journal of Theology* 30 (1989): 357.

45. John P. Meier, "The Bible as a Source for Theology," in *Proceedings of the Catholic Theological Society of America* 43 (1988): 1–14.

46. *Historical Jesus,* 99, and more broadly in 86–103. We point again to E. P. Sanders, *Paul and Palestinian Judaism,* as the seminal work in reconsidering older scholarly views of first-century Judaism, and to *Judaism: Practice and Belief* for a more recent statement.

This is but one of the examples that Meier selects; he finds in general that Segundo consistently allows "his desire to draw parallels between the political oppression of Jesus' day and political oppression in Latin America today" to produce questionable and even improbable conclusions.[47] Given the important role that Segundo allots to historical study, and the historical Jesus in particular, his maladroit use of biblical studies is disturbing.[48]

More significant than any of Segundo's particular conclusions, though, is the way that he views the Bible as historical source and exemplar rather than authoritative witness. One sees this in his wish to "rescue" the historical Jesus from the NT and its post-paschal perspective. It is that rescued and reconstructed Jesus that he considers primary. The value of the NT lies in its ability to provide us with the raw material for historical work and in the example that it gives of Christians translating and adapting the original message of Jesus. The NT itself takes a secondary position. "We thus put ourselves, without further pretensions, in the same situation as the evangelists," faced with the same problem of making the historical Jesus speak to our own circumstances.[49] We may learn from their example, but the concrete answers that we reach inevitably differ just as our historical situation does.

One sees a similar shift of emphasis elsewhere:

47. Meier, "Bible as Source," 10. Meier's critique has drawn two responses, those of Jon Nilson, "A Response to John Meier," in *Proceedings of the Catholic Theological Society of America* 43 (1988): 15–18, and Arthur F. McGovern, *Liberation Theology and Its Critics* (Maryknoll: Orbis Books, 1989), 80–82. Neither does more than insist on the perspectival nature of history, and the limitations of historical method, without engaging Meier's specific exegetical or historical arguments. They also fail to address Segundo's apparent belief that his conclusions do follow accepted criteria of historical Jesus research and meet the standards of biblical scholarship (see *Historical Jesus,* 45–70).

48. Segundo could perhaps appeal to John Dominic Crossan, Marcus Borg, and others who identify a substantial political component in Jesus' ministry (summarized in Wright, *Jesus,* 28–82). However, Brown's masterful distinction between an essentially quiet political environment in Judea and Galilee from A.D. 6–41 and the turmoil of A.D. 43–66 does much to reduce the force of the appeal; cf. *Death,* 676–93.

49. *Historical Jesus,* 192 n. 13, quoting Leonardo Boff as an expansion and confirmation of Segundo's own thought.

With regard to a christology "from *below,*" i.e. one fashioned out of the very *history* of Jesus, we could say that we find no written example of such a christology in the New Testament. . . . [None of it] really starts off from below, from the history of Jesus uninterpreted by the witnesses (if that is possible).[50]

In founding his own thought upon just such a Christology from below, which he acknowledges to be entirely absent from the NT, Segundo implies that the biblical witness lacks any claim to be authoritative even in a matter central to Christian belief. "The history of Jesus" alone is sufficient.[51]

Segundo's development of the notion of divine pedagogy, as a replacement for inspiration, displays the same tendency to move authority away from Scripture. The keystone of his argument is the citation of *Dei Verbum:* notwithstanding the document's own references to the NT as final and complete, Segundo extends its recognition of incomplete and temporary aspects within the OT to the Bible as a whole.[52] The Johannine promise of the Paraclete, "who will lead you into all truth" (16.13) is taken as an indication that the NT itself is simply a stage of the divine pedagogy, whose particular content will be surpassed in the ongoing process. However, this is another instance of Segundo's failings as an exegete. Taken in the context of

50. *Christ of the Ignatian Exercises,* 65; as one reviewer notes, this seems to reduce Christology from below "to the status of 'pure nature,' an inaccessible figment" (Joseph A. Munitiz, Review of *Christ of the Ignatian Exercises* by Juan Luis Segundo, *Heythrop Journal of Theology* 30 [1989]: 359).

51. Although not directly concerned with Segundo, William Loewe indicates some of the dangers inherent in such a move. The wide and resurgent pluralism of historical judgments renders the substantive history of Jesus a far less univocal notion than it was at the height of the Second Quest; cf. "From the Humanity of Christ to the Historical Jesus," *Theological Studies* 61 (2000): 314–31.

52. *Dei Verbum* 4, and also 17–20, make the document's meaning clear. It is not a question of merely "inclining" against Segundo's position. The same point is made in a 2001 document of the Pontifical Biblical Commission, *The Jewish People and Their Sacred Scriptures in the Christian Bible,* which stresses the complex and dialectical relationship of the two Testaments (§ II). One simply cannot act as though this does not matter. Francis Guibal, "Existence, sens, Écriture(s): La théologie fondamentale d'un théologien de la libération (J.-L. Segundo)," *Études théologiques et religieuses* 74 (1999): 505–22, blurs the subject by writing as though Segundo's approach were confined mainly to the OT (518–22).

John as a whole, "the 'truth' in which the Paraclete guides the community must have the same sense as 'truth' elsewhere in the Gospel: belief in Jesus as the sole revelation of God and the one who speaks the words of God (e.g., 3.20,33;8.40,47)."[53] It is not a matter of providing entirely new or different material, but of illuminating and elucidating a reality already fully present in Jesus. *Dei Verbum* itself sees the gift of the Paraclete at work in the inspiration of the NT, enabling its writers to

> firmly establish those matters which concern Christ the Lord, formulate more and more precisely his authentic teaching, preach the saving power of Christ's divine work and foretell its glorious consummation.[54]

There are no grounds for employing the Paraclete in a way that diminishes the importance of the biblical revelation as final and authoritative; nor is saying that this revelation is final and authoritative inconsistent with accepting, as we must, that our understanding of it has developed and will continue to do so under the guidance of the Spirit (cf. *Dei Verbum* 21–25, esp. 24).

One could go on to discuss Segundo's caricature of the idea of divine inspiration, or the way in which he too quickly assumes the essential parity of OT and NT, but that would not be to the point. Our main concern is with his approach to Scripture, and the preceding observations are all that are needed.[55] In his efforts to find a place for Scripture within his broader analysis of faith and ideology in human life, he has treated the Bible as an essentially human artifact. He sees it as the record of a historical process, transmitting a tradition of witnesses to certain values and being necessary to any who would follow that tradition, but not as authoritative in itself. To borrow a phrase from Childs, Segundo transforms Scripture from witness in its own right to a source requiring excavation. The locus of authority becomes the historical mission and preaching of Jesus (together with

53. Pheme Perkins, "The Gospel according to John," *New Jerome,* 977.

54. *Dei Verbum* 20, which closes with an explicit reference to Jn 16.13.

55. His concern with the application of Scripture to the interpreter's present situation, though admirable, does not outweigh the flaws pointed out above. As we will see in the next two chapters, the same concern may be met in other ways.

a certain manner of responding to them) as recovered from the Gospels rather than the kerygmatic presentations of the Gospels themselves (together with the rest of the NT). Be the historical work involved accurate or inaccurate, this shift represents an understanding of the Bible that cannot be reconciled with Christian tradition. While Segundo's acceptance of modern biblical studies is clear and unfeigned, he lacks the other prerequisite of our investigations: one cannot say that, for him, the words of Scripture are also the Word of God, or at least linked with it, in a way that nothing else is.

CHAPTER FIVE

HENRI DE LUBAC

Though belonging to an earlier generation, Henri de Lubac addressed many of the same topics as the other figures under review. He consistently displayed a strong interest in exegesis and the role of the Bible within the Church. The sixth chapter of *Catholicisme* (1938), on the interpretation of Scripture, contains in germ all that he would later expand and develop in *Histoire et Esprit* (1950) and *Exégèse médiévale* (1959–64).[1] These volumes have two related aims, one historical and the other constructive. The historical aim was "to disentangle the complex of false ideas long entertained by most historians" in his day regarding patristic and medieval Christian exegesis, and in this he was largely successful.[2] The standard English treat-

1. *Catholicisme: Les aspects sociaux du dogme chrétien* 4th ed., (Paris: Cerf, 1947), cited here from *Catholicism: Christ and the Common Destiny of Man,* trans. Lancelot C. Sheppard and Elizabeth Englund (San Francisco: Ignatius, 1988); *Histoire et Esprit: l'Intelligence de l'Écriture d'après Origène* (Paris: Aubier, 1950); *Exégèse médiévale: Les quatre sens de l'Écriture,* 4 vols. (Paris: Éditions Montaigne, 1959–64). All citations in this chapter without an author are de Lubac's work. The interpretation put forth here, while different in its organization and purpose, is indebted to Marcellino G. D'Ambrosio, "Henri de Lubac and the Recovery of the Traditional Hermeneutic" (Ph.D. diss., The Catholic University of America, 1991), which is by far the most complete and comprehensive account in English. The work of Susan K. Wood, *Spiritual Exegesis and the Church in the Theology of Henri de Lubac* (Grand Rapids: Eerdmans, 1998), is better seen as a treatment of de Lubac's ecclesiology than of his exegesis; the clear and competent "synthetic exposition of the principles of spiritual exegesis" (51) serves as a springboard for tracing links with his theology of Church and sacrament, in order to demonstrate the organic unity of his thought. In keeping with that design, there is little engagement with issues particular to biblical hermeneutics. (This is not to criticize Wood but only to note that her purpose is different.)

2. *At the Service of the Church: Henri de Lubac Reflects on the Circumstances That Occasioned His Writings,* trans. Anne Elizabeth Englund (San Francisco: Ignatius, 1993), 83.

ment of medieval exegesis acknowledges his demonstration of the central role played by allegorical or spiritual exposition in making "the sacred writings Christ-centred, unifying them and turning them into a history of salvation and guide to right living and mysticism," and an introduction to patristic exegesis sees his work as the main catalyst of a new scholarly consensus on the principles of traditional exegesis.[3] De Lubac's constructive aim, however, was frustrated or left undeveloped. He hoped that a substantive understanding of classical Christian exegesis would lead to a new and productive collaboration among systematicians, exegetes, and spiritual directors. While the differentiation of theological disciplines was a positive and necessary development, the diverse areas had become not only distinct but separated from one another. The older exegesis offered a way of integrating the full resources of Christian teaching around the understanding and application of Scripture, if the tradition could be retrieved and reformulated to fit the modern situation as well as the present state of exegetical and theological knowledge.[4]

This practical concern was not the only motivation behind de Lubac's efforts. He considered the traditional Christocentric focus at work in classic exegesis, or at least its core elements, "an exegetical doctrine directly linked with the very essence of the Christian Faith."[5] Although classic exegesis was influenced by Hellenistic techniques, the main impetus came from the practices of the first apostolic generation found, above all, in Paul's letters. When Origen, Thomas, or others sought to justify their approach to the Bible, they relied on

3. Smalley, *Study,* preface to 3rd ed. (Oxford: Blackwell, 1983), viii; Joseph W. Trigg, "Patristic Biblical Interpretation," in *Biblical Interpretation,* ed. Joseph W. Trigg (Wilmington, Del.: Michael Glazier, 1988), 31.

4. The importance of this latter proviso cannot be stressed enough; he always vigorously disclaimed "any sort of archaism, any sort of desire to arrest time or stem its flow" (*Exégèse médiévale,* vol. 1, p. 19). Subsequent references to *Exégèse médiévale* in this chapter will be given by volume and page number alone. Translations are either my own or those of the Eerdmans partial translation cited in the bibliography.

5. "Hellenistic and Christian Allegory," in *Theological Fragments,* trans. Rebecca Howell Balinski (San Francisco: Ignatius, 1989), 173.

Paul to express the fact that only "when one turns to the Lord" is the whole meaning of the biblical text unveiled (2 Cor 3.16). This is the root to which de Lubac traced the framework of spiritual exegesis. It becomes a basic part of Christian belief in the NT's affirmation that the death and resurrection of Christ occurred "according to the Scriptures" (1 Cor 15.3), or as the Nicene Creed has it, "in fulfillment of the Scriptures." In a striking contrast with Philo's arbitrary and contingent applications of Hellenistic allegory to the biblical text, the extended senses of Christian exegesis proper rely on a single presupposition: that the God of Israel has spoken a final and definitive Word in the Incarnation of Christ, which provides context and perspective for understanding everything else God wishes to express (I.204).

De Lubac was not a highly organized thinker, as he himself acknowledged; a less systematic systematician is difficult to imagine. This exposition attempts to distill his characteristic ideas but does not mirror any particular structure found in his work. We begin with his assessment of modern biblical exegesis, together with modern views of ancient exegesis. Both topics elicit cautionary observations, but he gives no hint of any idea that problems with modern perspectives can be resolved by a simple return to patristic and medieval practices. Such a restoration would ignore the genuine flaws in the older tradition, particularly with regard to history, and also would fail to recognize the necessary specialization of theology that began in the medieval period.

Next is the substantive core that constitutes Christian exegesis per se, which turns around two poles. First and most important is Christ himself. The incarnation, passion, and resurrection of Jesus reveal the culmination of God's redemptive design and work a genuine transformation on all prior understanding of the divine acts and purposes. The relationship between the Christian Gospel and the Scriptures of Israel is more than an inheritance of history and themes. Both the reader and the text read differently due to the light of Easter and the influence of the Spirit; only as a result of this can one say that "All Scripture is one book, and that one book is Christ, because all Scripture is fulfilled in Christ."[6] The second pole of Christian exegesis concerns the way that difference is understood and further developed. The fundamental Pauline distinction between letter and spirit grew into the fourfold sense of Scripture, which is less a doctrine than a single dynamic movement of spiritual understanding at work in a differentiated appropriation of Christian realities from the biblical text, where the *allegoria, tropologia,* and *anagogia* of the tradition represent the various elements of that appropriation.

DIAGNOSTIC REFLECTIONS

Accurately understanding de Lubac's purpose in these lengthy studies of exegetical procedures held in disdain by most scholars at the time of his writing requires some review of the initial situation as he understood it. Without restating the history of twentieth-century theology, the best approach is to consider three particular factors that influence the context of his substantive thought: modern exegesis, modern views of ancient exegesis, and his own reservations regarding the traditional practices.

Modern exegesis

Prior to the publication of either *Histoire et Esprit* or *Exégèse médiévale,* de Lubac was forced to clarify his position regarding modern biblical studies, or "scientific exegesis" as he normally referred to it. In a letter to his colleagues at Lyons, he expressed some bemusement at the need to establish his bona fides in this regard. In addition to naming a number of exegetes in the Lyons faculty whose work he had praised, he went on to say that "since the beginning of my theological studies, I have not ceased to educate myself through series such as the *Revue Biblique* and the *Études Bibliques.*"[7] No reasonable

6. *Histoire et Esprit,* 403, citing Hugh of St. Victor, *De arca Noe morali,* II.8; cf. also I.323.

7. *Service of the Church,* 312; the footnotes of his major writings show a familiarity with leading French biblical scholars of his day, which reveals this to be more than sheer rhetoric. As a sample, the conclusion to *Histoire et Esprit* refers to M.-J. Lagrange, Lucien Cerfaux, Celestin Charlier, Jean Levie, and M.-E. Boismard among others.

evaluation can portray de Lubac as either opposing or dismissing scholarship directed toward the literal and historical sense of the biblical text. Even a critical reviewer acknowledges that "there is never any question of literal exegesis *giving way* to spiritual exegesis; and he is sincerely convinced that spiritual exegesis is without value, even dangerous, unless it is founded on scientific exegesis."[8]

De Lubac's endorsement of modern exegesis is rooted in this scientific, or better, this historical character. Concern for history is one of the distinguishing features of Christian belief, which not only justifies but requires the full employment of whatever tools and methods are at hand. The Hellenistic world approached its myths and religious stories as veils over different cosmic and universal truths; "it is not as if these things really happened."[9] From a Christian perspective, however, "religion is first of all a historical fact."[10] God has acted in history, through given deeds and individuals in the world around us, as part of a purposeful set of objectives. Presenting the story of these actions, and the range of human responses to them, is what is first and foremost in the Bible. Modern techniques of philology and critical history thus represent "an instance of enormous progress" in our attempts to grasp the circumstances and meaning of the biblical texts that goes far beyond the resources of earlier exegesis (I.20). With their aid,

> the historian's entire effort should allow him to become an intimate of God's witness [i.e., the biblical author], to know his particular language, the style which expresses his soul, to know his habits and his interior life, the rites which he observed, his tastes, and the flavor of his meditation.[11]

This requires a radical faithfulness to the text on the part of the exegete, and the result of this effort and fidelity is "the religious mean-

8. John L. McKenzie, "A Chapter in the History of Spiritual Exegesis: De Lubac's *Histoire et Esprit*," *Theological Studies* 12 (1951): 378.

9. *Catholicism*, 166.

10. "On an Old Distich: the Doctrine of the 'Fourfold Sense' in Scripture," in *Theological Fragments*, 114.

11. *Histoire et Esprit*, 398 n. 71, adopting a description of the exegete's task given by Jean Steinmann. Allowing for a more poetic style, this explanation has much in common with Brown's understanding.

ing of the Bible"; the understanding and beliefs animating the religious consciousness expressed in the biblical text, achieved through historical reconstruction just as one might recapture the spirit of any past era.

De Lubac adds one main caution to this fundamentally positive assessment. Though historical exegesis is utterly necessary, it does not exhaust the potential or define the limits of biblical exegesis per se. If one were to regard the Bible in an exclusively historical way, as a document or set of documents used mainly to instruct us about the past (even with the recognition that the words and beliefs of that past continue to be ours today), "such an attitude inevitably remains essentially objective and impersonal. It is correct, but it is also incomplete."[12] At a time when historical investigation of Scripture was struggling to find acceptance, the natural tendency was to focus on history as though that were the whole of exegesis. This tendency was also useful in a tactical sense, since a significant portion of the opposition to biblical studies was due to the belief that exegesis and dogmatic theology contradicted one another. Defining exegesis in an exclusively historical way helped to assuage that belief and insulate exegetical practice from theological disputes.[13] However, the movement of exegesis is not finished until understanding of the past is joined with application to the present. Scripture has an ongoing role in the community, which does not receive it solely as a word spoken long ago, but as a present and active voice: "let us not imagine that this was not said *to us,* because at the time we were not there."[14] De Lubac's work on spiritual exegesis represents an attempt to recover the traditional approach used to appropriate the Bible as a present discourse, without minimizing the role of history.

12. *Histoire et Esprit,* 436; de Lubac is thinking mainly of the OT, but the point also encompasses the NT.

13. This observation has been made earlier regarding facets of Brown's work.

14. II.485 quoting Augustine, *In Ioh.* 30.7; this concern for present application, if not the way de Lubac pursues it, is reminiscent of Segundo.

Modern views of ancient exegesis

From the initial days of de Lubac's interest in the topic, the overwhelming weight of scholarly opinion set up an obstacle. The older tradition of exegesis with its focus on allegory and spiritual understanding, far from being a source of help or a worthwhile area of investigation, seemed little more than a relic of obscurantism inherited from an era unconcerned with history if not opposed to it. The best that could be said for it was that "allegorical exegesis did yeoman service in maintaining the Bible in a very pure and very high sphere of ideas and sentiments, until men's minds became mature enough to embark on a knowledge of the past and a direct application of texts" (I.13).

Classical Christian exegesis had been led astray by an attitude found in Hellenistic interpretive techniques and mediated largely through Philo of Alexandria. Pagan scholars found themselves faced with a variety of mythological tales, most authoritatively expressed in the Homeric epics, which seemed to express all sorts of unsuitable things regarding the gods, their interactions with one another, and their interactions with the world. Rather than reject Homer, as Plato had advised in the *Republic,* the scholars developed instead symbolic explanations that saw allegories of ethics or physics behind the myths of divine activities.

> Myths distribute throughout time and separate from each other beings who are not separated in reality . . . ; they cause to be born what was never begun, they divide it, thus teaching what they can and leaving to the one who understands the task of recomposition.[15]

Zeus, Apollo, and the rest lacked any meaning or significance beyond their service as poetical wrappings placed around these higher teachings.

Philo was to modify some of this technique as he employed it upon the Torah, but the essentials remained. Though he did not

15. II.391 citing Plotinus, *Enneads* 3.5.9; cf. David Dawson, *Allegorical Readers and Cultural Revision in Ancient Alexandria* (Berkeley: University of California Press, 1992), on philosophical allegory.

deny the historical character of Moses or the patriarchs, much of their value lay in the way that their actions symbolized physical or ethical doctrines. The results of the actions themselves need not possess any intrinsic relationship to the doctrines drawn from them, normally a set of abstract and timeless truths. "The formal principle of the exegesis . . . was an arbitrary principle, not resting on any plausible given of the biblical text or even of revelation in general."[16] This is the aspect of allegorical exegesis, derived from an aversion to history, that the scholarship de Lubac knew regarded as a cancer on the body of exegesis. Allegory diverted energy and resources away from more productive activities by hindering the development of an objective knowledge of the texts rooted in their historical circumstances and significance. However useful in adapting Christianity to the environment of late antiquity, its lack of controls or criteria rendered the Bible completely plastic in the interpreter's hands.[17]

De Lubac shares this same view of Philo and his Hellenistic predecessors, but criticizes prior scholarship for failing to perceive the differences between Philonian and Christian exegesis. Though there are "reflections of a Philonian nature" to be found in the tradition, part of the natural influence exerted by the surrounding culture, these tend to involve particular details of this or that passage and make little impact on the underlying principles used in Christian allegory.[18] The most important of those principles is a very different approach to history. Neither a fable nor merely the occasion for imaginative reflections, the history and events related in the biblical text were matters of vital interest. "The Christian exegetes were essentially concerned to show how biblical history bears witness to Christ and how, in return, in the light of Christ, . . . it takes on an entirely Christian significance."[19] The narrative of God's dealings with humans and with the world assumes added depth and perspective once the deci-

16. I.204, cf. II.373–78, 514, and *Histoire et Esprit,* 150–66.

17. The best brief account of the older scholarly position in de Lubac is the essay "Hellenistic and Christian Allegory," 174–79.

18. I.207; cf. II.521–22 on the pragmatic usage of Hellenistic allegories among the Fathers.

19. "Hellenistic and Christian Allegory," 193.

sive goal and climax of those dealings is known and the ways in which what had gone before served to prepare and anticipate the conclusion become clear. Yet this takes away nothing from the reality of those earlier dealings, or their importance in their own right. No Christian writer could make their own what de Lubac regarded as the emblematic attitude of pagan allegory: "It is not that these things ever happened."[20]

Neglect of this distinctive Christian approach to allegory led to another gap in scholarly understanding, inasmuch as the intrinsic biblical roots of the practice were overlooked. "There is a preoccupation only with the links that it has with Philo—when, that is, it is not linked with the pagan Cornutus and those of his ilk" (I.13). Those links did exist, but they were not formative for Christian tradition. Instead, "both the word and the idea of Christian allegory come from St. Paul."[21] One finds the word, of course, used with reference to Sarah and Hagar as representing the old and new covenants (Gal 4.24). The idea is more clearly expressed elsewhere, in terms of a distinction between the letter and the spirit of the biblical text, when Paul speaks of a veil over the minds of those who approach Scripture that is set aside "only in Christ" (2 Cor 3.14–16). It is these passages, together with other NT witnesses, that provided the materials later used to develop the structure of Christian allegory.[22]

Reservations

Critical reflection upon aspects of modern exegesis and scholarship does not lead de Lubac to antiquarianism or thoughtless nostalgia for something long gone. The practices of traditional exegesis cannot be "repristinated" as though the last several hundred years were an illusion to be dispelled. Those centuries have produced in us a vastly increased knowledge of history, which pertains as much to the Bible as to anything else. Theology itself, in a process beginning even earlier, grew into diverse areas of study. Dogmatics, exegesis,

20. *Catholicism,* 166, and also I.388, II.514.
21. "Hellenistic and Christian Allegory," 165–66; cf. *Histoire et Esprit,* 69–76.
22. Cf. Hays, *Echoes of Scripture.*

and spirituality (to follow de Lubac's standard division) have their own procedures and standards of judgment. Both of these developments are praiseworthy, even necessary. If their flaws were to lead us to admire "the ancient constructs so much that we longed to make them our permanent dwelling . . . we would be abandoning the present without being able to find refuge in the past."[23]

There is no refuge in the past because classic exegesis has its own imperfections. The most important concerns the tendency, in practice, to deal lightly with history. Notwithstanding the differences noted earlier, Hellenistic allegory was not completely without effect on Christian exegetes such as Origen. Their movement toward spiritual understanding was often hasty; "historical data are frequently given short shrift, and serve as springboards rather than as terms for thought."[24] This trait is exacerbated by an idea of biblical inspiration that looked almost exclusively to divine agency in the formation of Scripture, with less attention to the role of human authors with their own particular characteristics and limitations. Each biblical text had to bear some profound meaning, down even to small details, or at least one that was not unworthy of God.[25] The result is a great deal of poor exegesis; for example, ignorance of Hebrew parallelism led to a search for subtle distinctions where only synonymous phrases existed. The same lack of attention to the human elements of Scripture forbade recognition of genuine contradictions or discrepancies among different biblical witnesses. Difficulties that could not be resolved on the basis of a literal interpretation were often dealt with by shifting the terms of discussion and employing allegorical solutions; that is, careful allocation of some passages to literal interpretation and others to spiritual might harmonize diverse Gospel accounts.[26]

The rise of distinct areas of study within theology is another ma-

23. *Histoire et Esprit,* 375.

24. *Histoire et Esprit,* 376.

25. *Histoire et Esprit,* 304, and also IV.75–76; de Lubac portrays this principle as an inheritance from Jewish exegetical tradition, and so part of the cultural environment rather than intrinsic to the uniquely Christian perspective he is trying to outline.

26. *Histoire et Esprit,* 203–5.

jor factor preventing an antiquarian revival. Traditional exegesis originated at a time when theology, from a methodological point of view, formed an undifferentiated whole. Exegesis, dogmatics, and spirituality did not function as elements of a larger discipline, distributed among a range of specialists trained in subjects and standards appropriate for each particular area. Instead, exegesis in the ancient Christian sense was a broader enterprise that organized "all of revelation around a concrete center, which is fixed in time and space by the Cross of Jesus Christ. It is itself a complete and completely unified dogmatic and spiritual theology" operating on the idea that all theology, the whole of Christian wisdom, is embraced in the interpretation of Scripture.[27] Topics that later theology would treat as different areas were presented as aspects of the biblical text thanks to the fourfold structure of multiple senses.

When this sense of unity began to break up, much of the rationale and inner logic of Christian allegory went with it. The final volume of *Exégèse médiévale* follows the transition, as allegorical interpretation decayed into a game of words on the periphery of theology. Yet at the same time dogmatics, exegesis in the more narrow sense, and spirituality all profited from greater autonomy. The study of ancient modes of interpretation is not intended to reverse this differentiation, but to build upon it. "The declared inconveniences of a necessary fragmentation can indeed invite us to new efforts of synthesis: they should not arouse in us a romantic regret for past confusions" (III.424).

THE CHRISTIAN TRANSPOSITION

De Lubac's own effort of synthesis depends upon the basic principles at work in the traditional approach to the Bible, expressed as "spiritual understanding," and carefully retrieved from the host of witnesses assembled in his writings. Establishing this distinction between underlying principles and concrete applications is crucial, for the principles must be abstracted from the body of the tradition as a

27. I.13; the title of *magister in sacra pagina* held by scholastic masters such as Aquinas reflects this same idea at work.

whole in order to filter out cultural or personal idiosyncrasies of given authors.[28] Yet it may not be appropriate to speak of principles in the plural; the root lies in the recognition that

> Scripture has two meanings. The most general name for these two meanings is the literal meaning and the spiritual ("pneumatic") meaning, and these two meanings have the same kind of relationship to each other as do the Old and New Testaments to each other. (I.306)

Whatever misapplication or neglect may have occurred in the course of history, de Lubac takes this idea as an invariant and unique element of Christian belief.

The act of Christ

The existence of a dual meaning within the Bible is not based on any general theory of interpretation, but on an insight into the reality of Christ that transforms the understanding of the biblical text. The sole justification lies in "the all-powerful and unprecedented intervention of Him who is Himself at once the Alpha and Omega, the First and the Last" (I.320). Christ manifests the redemptive design of God in a new and definitive way. This is less a commitment to a specific soteriology than to a Christocentric perspective on God's action in the world; the full expression of God's character and the completion of God's purpose is achieved in Jesus. As a result, the prior understanding of God's relationship with the world in general and Israel in particular is reconstituted as one of prelude and preparation, just as a complex detective story comes into focus only after the solution to the mystery is revealed and an array of data suddenly fits into a new and intelligible configuration.

Yet unlike the detective story, where all necessary clues are present beforehand and resolving the mystery is an exercise in deduction, the

28. "He is sensible of the havoc that could be played with his presentation by presenting all the authors in detail"; Walter Burghardt, "On Early Christian Exegesis," *Theological Studies* 11 (1950): 105. There is also a polemical need on de Lubac's part to sink the foundations of Christian allegory so deep that they could not be questioned; he rejects the notion of periodic repressions of a more historically focused exegesis consciously opposed to allegory (as mentioned in the discussion of Brown).

Christian story depends on the introduction of an entirely new element. The Christian reading of the Scriptures of Israel is not based on those texts alone, nor is it plain to any reader of good will and perception, no matter how perfect one's grasp of the history and situation of the various writings. "If the fact of Christ had not occurred . . . all the exegesis which 'spiritual understanding' or related terms suggest within Christianity would be pure phantasmagoria."[29] The tendency of later tradition to speak of the older Scripture as foreshadowing the Christian gospel, based upon such references as Colossians 2.17 ("These are shadows of things to come; the reality belongs to Christ") or Hebrews 10.1 ("The law has only a shadow of the good things to come") implies as much. To be a shadow necessarily involves being the shadow of something, but a silhouette on the wall may be due to a bird or a clever puppeteer. Without some perception of the object casting it, a shadow is not fully seen *qua* shadow.[30] Without prior awareness of Jesus, the earlier words and deeds recounted in the Bible do not reveal an orientation beyond themselves.

This awareness of Jesus as the one in whom God's promises are fulfilled is not something gained simply by measuring the narrative embodied in the apostolic preaching against the biblical text, as though one were verifying a news report. The transformation in the context and meaning of Scripture that takes place once the incarnation, death, and resurrection of the Son reveal "the plan of the mystery hidden for ages" (Eph 3.9) requires a parallel transformation in us. A key passage for de Lubac as for the tradition he follows is 2 Corinthians 3, especially verses 15–17: "whenever Moses is read, a veil lies over their minds; but when one turns to the Lord the veil is removed. Now the Lord is the Spirit, and where the Spirit of the Lord is, there is freedom." The same words are read, whether the veil is present or absent, but the text is fully understood only through adherence to Christ and the resulting participation in the Spirit. This participation makes it possible for the reader to acknowledge not

29. *Histoire et Esprit*, 395.
30. *Catholicism*, 172–73.

only the literal meaning of the biblical text but also the spiritual meaning, that is, its significance in the light of God's integral plan that culminates in Christ.[31]

De Lubac reserves the term "spiritual meaning" for this reading of Scripture from a full Christian perspective because the spiritual meaning is more closely and directly linked with the Holy Spirit. While the literal meaning of a passage is formed by the human author (though not apart from the Spirit's influence), the spiritual meaning "stems totally from the Spirit" inasmuch as it presupposes an entire grasp of the history of salvation as directed toward Jesus.[32] That sort of comprehensive overview is open only to God; even after the event, following the resurrection, a reading that finds Christian realities signified within the older Scripture derives less from study alone (though not without it) than from the gift of the Spirit causing us to share in the understanding of God's own intentions and goals.

The dialectic of old and new

For all the transforming impact that the event of Christ has on the understanding of Scripture, de Lubac also emphasizes that the relationship runs both ways. The gospel itself is unintelligible apart from the Scriptures of Israel. The messianic passage from Isaiah that the Lukan Jesus reads at the inception of his mission (Lk 4.16–21) and Paul's use of the cloud and the Red Sea to illuminate the meaning of baptism (1 Cor 10.1–5) are not mere embellishments. They are a constitutive factor at work in the formation of the Christian message, as are a host of other examples that one could select. "Thus, 'biblical images,' and the concrete facts behind them, furnish the thread, both historical and noetic, from which is woven the Christian mystery in all its newness and transcendence."[33]

The additional depth of meaning found in those images and facts when the Scriptures come to be read from an explicitly Christian perspective is a function of their prior role in setting the terms and syntax used to express the Gospel. That is what de Lubac means when

31. *Histoire et Esprit,* 315–16, 389–92. 32. *Histoire et Esprit,* 390.
33. *Histoire et Esprit,* 383.

he speaks of the dialectic of the Old and New Testaments: "the New Testament in its entirety is brought forth by the Old, while at the same time the Old Testament in its entirety is interpreted by the New."[34] Here the distinction of Old and New Testaments does not in the first instance refer to a subdivision of the Christian Bible but to two dispensations or covenants established by God. The goal of the prior covenant is to prepare for the later one, but that does not deprive the acts and persons involved of their own reality; otherwise, there could have been no true preparation. The constitution of Israel as a people by exodus and covenant, with their subsequent history and experience as related in the scriptures, is an intrinsic condition of the new covenant in Jesus. "The second arises from the first and does not repudiate it. The second does not destroy the first. In fulfilling it, it gives it new life and renews it."[35] The genuine differences between the old covenant and the new do not eliminate their common elements, any more than the common elements eliminate the differences.

De Lubac finds this dynamic relationship between the covenants well represented in the miracle of Cana. "Of all the symbols furnished by the Gospel, this is the one most often referred to in exegetical writings and in the liturgy."[36] There are two alterations presented within the narrative, each emphasized in different ways. First and more striking in itself is the miracle proper, the change of water into wine; to focus upon this is to stress the radical shift that Jesus works upon the plain water of the old covenant as it is taken up into the new. Yet the second alteration, the replacement of ordinary wine with better, should not be overlooked. The dramatic pacing of the story leads up to and emphasizes the steward's declaration that "you

34. *Histoire et Esprit,* 408, III.128–52.

35. I.310; de Lubac is aware, of course, that there is a tendency within the tradition to disparage the prior covenant in a way that seems to run contrary to this citation. He regards that as an inheritance from a "polemic stance" on Paul's part, directed against a refusal to recognize the old covenant *qua* old rather than the covenant itself (*Histoire et Esprit,* 398–400).

36. I.344; the story of Emmaus (Lk 24) is also an important passage for de Lubac's understanding, cf. I.323.

have kept the good wine until now." This is a question of qualitative change rather than complete transformation. Even though one wine is better than the other, both remain wine, and the same standard is used to evaluate them. The stress here is given to the fulfillment of the old covenant by the new, and also their continuity in that the latter meets and surpasses expectations set by the former.[37] The great merit of Cana as a symbol is that these aspects of transformation and fulfillment are both acknowledged without being separated.

The literature of the first Christian generations that makes up the written NT is in many ways a collective expression of the insight underlying the Cana narrative. The apostolic communities developed their own writings, involving a variety of genres and authors, but all woven from the prior times revealed in Scripture and their knowledge of Christ. On the one hand, the concepts, figures, and words of Israel's past constituted the language in which the significance of Jesus was understood and communicated to others; on the other hand, the experience of the risen Lord provided the lens through which the older Scripture was seen. However, "it may be that the mental operations of the New Testament authors transcend any such duality: simultaneously, they express the New Testament by the Old and spiritualize the Old by the New."[38] Though one can distinguish the individual phases within this dialectic, they can be described only with reference to one another.

This unity within difference of OT and NT is something that de Lubac sees as essential to any genuine understanding of Christian Scripture. Taken as a bare statement without further amplification, this would be a point of agreement with Childs. But where Childs takes this affirmation as a *brutum factum* that must be simply accepted, due to his unwillingness to discuss inspiration or the precise relationship between the two covenants, de Lubac bases it upon a unity

37. The fact that all this occurs at a banquet to which Jesus is called, one already provided with a steward and servants, offers other indications of continuity and "allows the historical preparation for the coming of Christ to be taken quite amply into account"; I.345.

38. *Histoire et Esprit,* 382 n. 12.

of subject within the biblical text. It is because "all of biblical history and all of biblical reality had Christ for its unique end" that both Testaments can be considered as one unified volume.

OMNIS SCRIPTURA DIVINA DE CHRISTO LOQUITUR

The unified volume is, however, far from uniform. This Christocentric focus also provides a theological warrant for additional dimensions of meaning within the biblical text. The distinction between the letter and the spirit drawn from Paul that de Lubac labels as the dialectic of Old and New Testaments is not exhausted by the institution of a uniquely Christian Scripture with its canonical division of OT and NT writings. Instead, it becomes the basis for a framework of multiple meanings. The "spirit" of the text, the sense borne by it in light of the event of Christ, finds expression in different ways corresponding to different dimensions or aspects of Christ himself: *"materia sacrae Scripturae totus Christus est, caput et membra"* [the substance of sacred Scripture is the whole Christ, head and members].[39] The several senses of Scripture developed by Christian tradition from Origen onward, to which de Lubac devoted so much study, owe their existence to this insight.

In this section we will consider de Lubac's account of the four classic senses of Scripture. This is more than a matter of simply defining them; the virtue of his presentation is the way they form parts of a single dynamic movement of understanding and application. The reappropriation of that movement in our day, *mutatis mutandis,* was always more central to his enterprise than a mere revival of ancient words or practices. Before embarking on this examination, however, we must give some attention to his emphasis on the four-sense schema over other options found in the tradition. His adoption of it is based not only on historical influence but also on a substantive theological judgment.

39. "Old Distich," 114.

Orders of understanding

The point from which *Exégèse médiévale* springs is "an old distich," composed by Augustine of Dacia and made popular by Nicholas of Lyra, which served as a mnemonic device:

> *littera gesta docet, quid credas allegoria,*
> *moralis quid agas, quo tendas anagogia*
>
> [the letter teaches events, allegory what you should believe, morality what you should do, anagogy where you should aim].[40]

While the structure set forth here is crucial to de Lubac's project, other frameworks that differed in substance, number, or order were well represented in the tradition. Some lists reached as many as six or seven, which he dismisses as aberrations of numerology that could scarcely provide any basis for an orderly exegesis (I.136–37). There is one division, though, that is too consistent to be dismissed. Some writers distinguished three senses: historical/literal, moral/tropological, and mystical/allegorical. Others preferred to make use of the four named in the verse above: literal, allegorical, moral, anagogical. The nature of the division is clouded by differences of vocabulary or usage, not infrequently within one and the same author, which can give the impression of a vast jumble. Despite the variations, however, there is an "overwhelming and persistent" difference that de Lubac singles out and uses to justify his focus upon the fourfold structure (I.144). The distinctive element is not the names of the different senses, or even their number, but the order in which they are found. Some frameworks place the moral sense directly after the literal, while others set allegory in the second place. This sets up a consistent and binary division that underlies other variations and bears significant theological import. One order is revealed "with origins in foreign regions," the other as "completely Christian in its structure" (III.415).

De Lubac sees formulae with moral interpretation in the second place to be derived ultimately from Philo and the Hellenistic tradi-

40. I.21; "springs" almost literally, for this is the first page of the introduction.

tion of interpretation. The threefold structure of literal, moral, and spiritual senses is the primary example of such a formula; its three senses are consciously drawn to parallel a tripartite anthropology that sees humans as composed of body, mind, and spirit. The revered text is then able to speak to every level of human existence, and it is the task of the exegete to make it do so. The use of this framework among Christians is traced back to Origen's account in *De principiis,* and de Lubac follows it out through later writers (III.410–11). Though this approach is not without virtues, particularly as a tool of spiritual pedagogy, there is one major drawback that requires him to set it aside.

As the link to Philo shows, such a mode of reading owes little to Christian belief. It operates on the basis of a specific philosophical anthropology and a conviction that the text read must reflect that anthropology. Neither of these elements has particular Christian content, and the framework itself can readily be applied to a variety of texts. Philo could employ it in commenting on the Septuagint, just as grammarians of Alexandria had done in reading Homer, and a Christian exegete could have no formal objections to raise. The substance and matter of interpretation would certainly be matters of dispute, but the framework itself has nothing to make it a Christian preserve or to restrict its use. In addition, as mentioned above, this use of a general anthropology to generate the multiple senses leaves only the loosest of links between the different levels of the text. There is an arbitrary element, based on the personal ideas and idiosyncrasies of the interpreter, and uncontrolled by any "plausible given of the biblical text or even of revelation in general" (I.204). The good that de Lubac often finds in his examination of writers who follow this tendency is due less to their stated interpretive theory than to their intrinsically Christian formation. Taken on its own, apart from such accidental factors, this ordering of senses must be seen as a cultural artifact embedded in the tradition, with little to offer a modern understanding of Scripture.

De Lubac's main focus falls upon the other sequence: "only the second of the two orders, the one that puts allegory right after history, expresses authentic doctrine in both its fullness and its purity" (I.169). Here as before, Origen is a crucial figure. The decisive factor, however, is not the explicitly theoretical treatment of *De principiis* but the actual practice retrieved from his homilies. One can trace in them a progression from a literal reading of the text to some facet of the reality of Christ and then an application of that reality to the situation, not of humanity or the individual in general, but of "the Christian soul."[41] This pattern is too consistent to be dismissed as some haphazard variation on *De principiis.* Instead, it represents an alternative approach with a much greater theological significance. When allegory (the significance of the biblical text vis-à-vis Christ) immediately follows upon a literal reading, further levels of meaning take form less as additions than as developments or specifications of that single shift. Interpretation then flows in a more or less continuous movement of understanding and application, in which the classic structure highlighted in *Exégèse médiévale* takes shape.[42]

At this point, it is important to recognize that the priority given to arrangements where allegory follows the literal reading has little to do with historical researches. Both the competing sequences are rooted in Origen, and well represented in the tradition as a whole.[43] What decides the issue is the singularly Christian foundation laid wherever allegory holds second place. Rather than an application of general anthropology, it is instead a development of the basic pattern discerned within the NT, where the event of Christ generates a new understanding of God's will and intention. The senses that follow allegory depend on that new understanding. As de Lubac says, "one must always return to the essential fact: the mystery of Christ, prefigured or rendered present in facts, interiorized by the individual soul and consummated in glory."[44] This emphasis on the one thing need-

41. I.203; cf. *Histoire et Esprit,* 139–50.

42. III.416; we will see below how de Lubac works this out to fit the fourfold structure; the point at hand is the emphasis given the sequence of senses.

43. Though Origen might take issue with the priority de Lubac gives his homiletical practice over *De principiis,* where he understood himself to be explaining and defending his approach in a methodical way.

44. "Old Distich," 118–19.

ful lies behind his tendency to speak of "spiritual exegesis" or "spiritual understanding" when describing the reappropriation of the classic approach that he hoped to foster. Without an awareness of their inner unity, the framework of multiple senses can become a straightjacket forced upon the biblical text (a process traced in the final volume of *Exégèse médiévale*).

Phases in movement

So long as the unity beneath the diversity is understood, however, de Lubac's endorsement of the fourfold schema is clear and strong. The "old distich" does grasp the essential moments in the movement of understanding and engagement that is integral to a Christian use of Scripture. The second volume of *Exégèse Médiévale* sets out at length his understanding of the different senses and their mutual relationships, with some care devoted to disentangling modern preconceptions that contribute to the genuine lack of clarity in traditional practice. Here even more than elsewhere we will be forced to condense a great deal as we go through each of the various senses according to de Lubac, with the main emphasis falling on points of specific utility for our present purpose: the description given each sense, its characteristic focus understood as part of his larger Christocentric perspective on the whole of the Bible, and any particular problems it may present.

Littera gesta docet

One surprising difficulty at the outset, in explaining the literal sense, is that none of the other senses can be understood in so many different ways. Much of the confusion is due to a change within the classic tradition itself. The literal sense did not at first include figures of speech, but referred to the immediate signification of the words as they stood. This is the basis for statements by Origen and others that some passages of the Bible did not have a literal sense; if the prima facie meaning of the words was clearly unsuitable (e.g., references to "God's arm" understood as though God were corporeal), no literal sense existed. Later figures in the tradition expanded the literal sense to include metaphor and other figures, as the focus of interpretation turned toward the writer's intention. The shift in meaning is clear, and de Lubac scores those who see the earlier usage as a denigration of the literal sense per se for a lack of understanding.[45]

De Lubac's own practice may lend itself to such confusion, though he would see it as clarifying the presuppositions of the classic practice. Notwithstanding his use of the old distich as the structural basis for *Exégèse médiévale,* he normally refers to the first of the four senses not as literal but as historical. "The word *letter* is doubtlessly called for by the meter of the verse . . . It is in every case synonymous with *history,* taken in a large sense" (II.425). A forest of references are adduced, where the word is applied to many passages not normally thought of as historical. De Lubac takes it as illustrative of the historical character of the whole Bible. "It recounts a series of happenings, which are really past, and it is essential that they are really past. . . . There is nothing untemporal" (II.429). While there are whole books of Scripture that may seem lacking in specific historical focus, such as Psalms or Proverbs, this does not prevent them from being temporal insofar as they take shape in response to God's actions in history.

The stress on the role of history goes beyond questions of medieval terminology or the distinguishing characteristics of Christian exegesis. Far from being confined to revelation and the means of its transmission through Scripture, history is an essential element of Christian faith.

> For if the salvation offered by God is in fact the salvation of the human race, since this human race lives and develops in time, any account of this salvation will naturally take a historical form—it will be the history of the penetration of humanity by Christ.[46]

History, for de Lubac, is a process that reveals its meaning only from the perspective of the Incarnation; apart from that, it remains either an endless recurrence or a formless sea of particularity without significance.[47] The importance of the historical sense, the *gesta* recounted

45. II.448; cf. the development vis-à-vis Origen and Aquinas in the first chapter.

46. *Catholicism,* 141; cf. II.470–71.

47. Though familiar with alternative attempts to find meaning in history, he does not regard them as germane due to their dependence on extra-historical

in the *littera,* is based on this. Only through Scripture is it possible for humans to discern the central movement within the historical flux. The emphasis on the necessary historicity of biblical revelation helps to explain his distress when the classic tradition is accused of denying or diminishing the role of the historical literal sense for interpretation. Though historical work was not always done well in the patristic and medieval period, and de Lubac acknowledges that modern research has vastly increased our knowledge of the biblical circumstances and situations, that is a far cry from saying that history was insignificant or irrelevant.

The literal sense, and the narrative that it expresses, is always received as the sine qua non of engagement with the biblical text. "God has chosen a people for himself, he has intervened in human history: the first thing to do is to learn, from the book where the Holy Spirit has committed it, the result of his interventions."[48] A reading on this level bears its own significant value and utility. Through it one comes to know God's actions and the corresponding range of human response within Israel, the apostolic memory of Christ and the word of the kingdom, along with the initial effects of the Gospel in the world. In addition to this rather pragmatic observation, de Lubac also offers a more lofty and theologically substantive point.

The analogy between Christ as the Word of God incarnate and the Word of God expressed in Scripture is ancient. Though the analogy is a disproportionate one, since the Word is not "inscribed" in the text as he is incarnate in Jesus of Nazareth, for de Lubac it offers the clearest way to assess the value of the literal sense both in itself and in relation to the other senses. "It is basically one and the same Word of God—his own unique utterance—who descends, in order to conceal and reveal himself all at once, in the letter of the Scripture and in the flesh of our humanity, in that flesh 'infirm and without beauty'" (II.454). Just as attempts to minimize or dismiss the reality of Jesus'

philosophical foundations. Indeed, this serves as a proof for his assertion that history alone does not reveal its own meaning.

48. II.429; he does not take up the degree to which the biblical presentation is already an interpreted if not idealized history.

humanity are rejected as docetism of one stripe or another, so also should any notion of dispensing with or avoiding the literal sense be rejected. It is only in the humanity of Christ that we perceive the divinity, and it is only through the humanity that the divinity is revealed; it is only in and through the historically conditioned expressions of the literal sense that we come to find additional levels of meaning. This serves as a theological and intrinsically Christian rationale behind the traditional insistence on the importance of the literal sense for any further biblical understanding.

These analogies may remain unsatisfying, however, for those more accustomed to current perspectives. For all the emphasis on history and the literal sense as a foundation, the practice of history seems to be pursued less for its own sake than as a necessary prequel for engagement with the other more "spiritual" senses. The analogy of the foundation itself indicates as much; humans build foundations for their houses, but only so that they may live in the upper stories. We saw earlier that de Lubac does criticize patristic and medieval interpretation for showing a tendency in practice to skip lightly over the literal and historical level. Yet the words "in practice" are significant, for de Lubac sees this mainly as a failure to be self-consistent that was often made worse by a lack of historical knowledge and tools. To take it for more represents a failure to see that the historical understanding did have its own value and worth for classic interpreters, although not in the same way that it does for modern figures.

Much of the contemporary emphasis on history stems from the Romantic revival, and the eruption of history into philosophy, which began and flourished in the nineteenth century. Interest centered on knowing and appreciating each event or period in its unique singularity. For de Lubac, this represents a shift in the idea of history. The goal that had animated historical study, from Herodotus until this change, was quite different. Rather than focus on the particular, the ancient and medieval approach to history was concerned with the universal element. "History was a moral science, which one studied with a view to improving behavior. That was at least its essential goal" (II.467). The happenings and individuals of the past were studied and remembered with an eye toward the lessons that could be learned now or in the future. This does provide a genuine motive for historical study in its own right; for us to dismiss it as inferior or unworthy represents a lack of historical appreciation that demands to measure the past by the standards of the present.

Another difficulty comes from within the tradition itself. This positive assessment of the literal sense's worth appears to run contrary to Paul's vigorous polemic against "the letter that kills" (2 Cor 3.6), a polemic taken up and maintained by later writers. De Lubac recognizes the force of the criticism, but denies that it is directed against the literal sense as intended here. The killing letter was not "the historic reality: it was . . . the 'Judaic' interpretation of the Scriptures."[49] That interpretation was rejected by Paul and his successors, not because it was historical, but because it was restricted in scope. It failed to acknowledge the inner potential that would find its actuality in the Gospel and, explicitly or implicitly, denied the affirmation that would later be integrated into the Creed: that these things happened in fulfillment of the Scriptures.

'Quid credas allegoria'

Allegoria as used in the old mnemonic represents a restriction of a broader usage. In the grammatical sense, an allegory is a continued metaphor where "one thing sounds in the words, while another is signified in the mind" (IV.136). Among Christians the word was quickly transferred to the symbolic recasting of OT realities in the light of Christ. There allegory became one of several labels (such as

49. II.439. Scripture here primarily refers to the OT, as the reference to Judaic interpretation indicates, though it is not inherently impossible to read the NT in an analogous way. De Lubac uses stronger terms elsewhere, saying that the killing letter "was, in other terms, the sterilized letter. This letter kills because it is itself dead" (II.446). His record in the French Resistance as a steadfast opponent of both Nazism and anti-Semitism makes it difficult for any but the most critical to take this as more than vivid language; cf. Joseph A. Komonchak, "Theology and Culture at Mid-Century: The Example of Henri de Lubac," *Theological Studies* 51 (1990): 579–602. One should also recognize that the greater energy of the traditional polemic was aimed not so much at Jewish interpreters as at those Christians who (rightly or wrongly) were seen as supporters of an exclusively Judaic reading.

mystical or spiritual) that were "frequently mingled in diverse combinations" and applied to any interpretation extending beyond the literal sense (II.403). As the tradition developed, though, the general term acquired a specific function within the interpretive structure.

Allegory in this precise meaning refers to the way in which the narrative within Scripture foreshadows or prefigures matters pertaining to the work and salvific activity of Christ. This Christian employment of the term can be distinguished from strictly grammatical allegory in several ways. The most significant is that this allegory is not a matter of texts and words, as though one were reading an allegorical poem or romance and seeking to place all the references. De Lubac makes a very strong distinction between *allegoria facti,* allegory of deeds, and *allegoria verbi (vel dicti),* allegory of words; the former is unique to Christian use of Scripture, while the latter is a feature of many literary traditions (not excluding the Christian one). The basis of Christian allegory is taken from events, because "these events all contribute, more or less, to prepare the great event on which the salvation of the world depends."[50]

As the citation indicates, this allegory not only proceeds from events, but also terminates in an event. The physical or philosophical doctrines characteristic of pre-Christian allegory have no place in it; one finds instead connections within a series of actions directed to a common end. "Everything culminates in a great Deed, which in its unique singularity, has multiple repercussions; which dominates history and is the bearer of all enlightenment and all spiritual fruitfulness: the Deed of Christ."[51] However, those prior happenings are not considered solely in their preparatory role; if that were the case, allegory would be a historical endeavor akin to tracing the links between, for example, the Reformation and the Thirty Years War. The events of the past have a genuine value as signs, as intentional bearers

50. II.433; those events are recounted in a text, of course, but the interpretive focus of allegory is turned toward the event. De Lubac insists on this point, seeing it as central to the larger issue of Christianity's historical character.

51. II.515; the question of allegory as an interpretive tool within the NT will be discussed shortly.

of meaning, quite apart from any causal efficacy. God is entirely capable of arranging matters in the world in meaningful patterns open to our exploration, even though we ourselves are restricted to syllables and letters for our own communications.[52] In either case, under the preparatory aspect or the revelatory aspect, the crucial element rests in the linkage between events and event, between what had gone before in Israel and what has now occurred in Christ.

Although always Christocentric, this does not entail a flat way of reading confined to one-to-one correspondences between the OT and the Gospel narratives. De Lubac stresses that one must look to the whole Christ, whose activity neither begins with the Nativity nor ends with the Resurrection, but reaches as far as the creation, redemption, and eschatological fulfillment of the world (IV.114). More important, however, than understanding the whole work of Christ as a basis for allegory is understanding the whole person of Christ as its focus. Drawing on a tradition that finds its earliest clear expression with Tyconius and Augustine, de Lubac establishes the strongest possible bond between Christ and the Church:

> The Church is in truth the 'body' of Christ; it is his 'flesh'; it forms with him 'one single person.' . . . If one considers the whole group of texts, it is a matter of the total Christ, inseparable from his Church: "the substance of sacred Scripture is the whole Christ, head and members." (II.502–3)

He denies that this constitutes an expansion of the Church at the expense of Christ: "the more importance is given to the one, the more the grandeur of the other is exalted. All the mystery of the Church, all its life, depends on the fact of the Incarnation" (II.511 n. 7). The Christ foreshadowed through Scripture is the Christ united with the Church his body, so much so that to speak of the one implies the other. This opens a wide range of avenues, where the interpreter is free to employ allegory as a way of engaging multiple dimensions of both the experience preserved in the OT and the complex reality of Christ.

52. II.496–98; the same point is made above in considering Aquinas, though de Lubac here refers to earlier writers.

So far allegory has been presented exclusively with regard to the reading of OT events and figures in light of Christ. Yet the tradition de Lubac was engaged in retrieving does include allegorical interpretations of the NT. This presents a question regarding the adequacy of his explanation that is worth exploration.

De Lubac insists that allegory in the strict sense, where Christian realities would prepare and foreshadow something beyond themselves, has no place within the NT. An allegorization of the NT would imply that the covenant established in the dying and rising of Christ will one day be surpassed in the same way that the Mosaic covenant of Sinai was surpassed. "One should therefore say . . . that the NT 'stands for itself as it reads; there is no allegory; it does not signify another Christ.' . . . Outside of Jesus Christ, we have nothing more to hope for" (IV.110). The use of an allegorical approach for some parts of the NT still remains, though, and de Lubac makes no attempt to deny it. What his account tries instead to establish is that, although a valid aspect of the tradition, NT allegory serves only to explore further dimensions of one and the same Christ represented upon the surface of the text. "Everything which remains hidden in the NT still makes up part of the NT" (IV.111).

This assertion relies on the recognition that not all of Jesus' activity as recounted in the Gospels bears an equal relation to the central act of passion, resurrection, and ascension that stands as the charter for Christian allegory. "The events related by the evangelists before these great saving deeds are not only therefore *exterior* to this Mystery; they are equally *anterior*" (IV.119). The NT, as we have seen above, is for de Lubac not primarily a set of writings but a New Covenant (to hark back to an original meaning of *testamentum*) fully established only through the paschal event. Just as one can allegorize the events and personages of the OT insofar as they bear some relation to that event, so also can one find further significance in the Gospels, which constitute its immediate antecedents. This sort of reading is especially common with respect to parable or miracle; for example, "the healing of the paralytic at the pool of Bethsaida can be considered as an allegory of baptism, just as much as the old episode of the rock of Horeb" (IV.116). The significant difference between Bethsaida and Horeb, though, is that the former incident leads one to understand more deeply the same Christ who is at work in the story itself rather than pointing toward a different figure.

Another feature of de Lubac's account of allegory is a relative scarcity of sustained examples of the allegorical sense in action. An innumerable host of instances are drawn from figures of the past, which is in keeping with the historical nature of the project, but little of this is in direct voice. Most of his concern is focused on ensuring an understanding of what the tradition was trying to achieve, or on establishing the transformation worked on the OT through the event of Christ. This does not seem to be due only to the historical nature of *Exégèse médiévale* and his other works. Something in his approach toward allegory as a topic leads him away from detailed commentary, even though it would have blunted some criticisms and advanced his overall project.

The contributing factor appears to be the belief that, so long as the overall principle of allegory is understood and accepted as an integral aspect of the Christian relationship with Scripture, many of the various ways that it comes to be expressed in readings of specific texts can be viewed as *adiaphora*. Some will of course be better founded than others, and de Lubac does value the wider knowledge of biblical events and circumstances available now as a help in pruning the excesses of the past. Nonetheless, the status of particular readings is not a major question:

> *Allegoriae* are never more than the small change of the main *allegoria* that the believer has presented initially with all the vigor of his faith, and he is well aware that the work he is doing with the *allegoriae* is less assured. Taken one by one, the *allegoriae* that he discovers can be rather subjective. . . . But the principle that they should highlight, the major *allegoria* of Scripture, is always objective.[53]

However subjective a given interpretation may be, so long as there is linkage with that major *allegoria* (explained above as "the Christian

53. "Old Distich," 122.

transposition"), the interpretation is not without basis. Here the ancient idea of analogy of faith is brought in as a support; de Lubac sees this as the recognition of a substantive unity, defined by its Christocentric focus, not only within Scripture but also between Scripture and the Church's ongoing tradition of teaching. "When the commentator's work is brought forth within the Church, it never completely lacks a certain kind of objectivity, because Scripture is indeed a real whole and the Church has intuition of this whole" (IV.91).

This conviction has significant repercussions for de Lubac's overall understanding of allegory; the effect is not confined only to propping up unstable or overly subjective uses of it. We have seen him make a major distinction between the *allegoria facti* peculiar to Christianity, which relies on connections of causality or meaning between the realities portrayed in the OT and the realities brought into being by the paschal work of Christ, and the more common *allegoria verbi,* which relies on literary symbolism and wordplay. As a result, the immediate explanation of allegory here has so far been focused exclusively on *allegoria facti;* however, once the principle of analogy of faith has been deployed to make the soundness of individual *allegoriae facti* a distinctly minor concern, the door is opened wide for the acceptance of *allegoria verbi* as a valid part of interpretation.

This latter form of allegory takes its start from the words and verbal images of the biblical text rather than the events and persons represented there. Instead of looking to Joshua or David, the *Akedah* or the crossing of the Red Sea, *allegoria verbi* takes up such common words as "rock," "lamb," or "vine" (among a host of others). Wherever they appear, the traditional reader finds an opportunity for some Christian significance within the verbal linkage. One can find the different types of allegory side by side, in a variety of authors, with no apparent sense of incompatibility. De Lubac embraces this aspect of the tradition wholeheartedly, yet without altering his stress on the theological importance of *allegoria facti;* the ability of the tradition to encompass the most varied uses of verbal allegory is itself made possible by clearly distinguishing the two allegories from one another.

The most important example of all, and perfectly clear, is that of the Song of Songs: from one end to the other, in the traditional interpretation, the work is an *allegoria dicti;* but it deals throughout with the total Object of revelation; it constantly directs the reader to the reality at once historic and spiritual that is the union of the Word of God and humanity, the union of Christ and his Church. (IV.149)

The overarching goal is to ensure that this reality is recognized, together with its transforming effect upon the letter of Scripture, which directly generates *allegoria facti* and indirectly validates *allegoria verbi.* Once that recognition is in place, de Lubac leaves the specific applications of it that may be drawn from the biblical text to the insight and perception of the interpreter. So long as the applications illuminate and remain faithful to their inspiration, even if sometimes stretched or overly imaginative, he sees no harm in them.

'Moralis quid agas'

Of the two senses remaining in the mnemonic verse, the moral or tropological is perhaps the more straightforward.[54] Yet it may be something of an error to speak of senses in the plural. The moral and anagogical senses appear less as separate ways of interpretation than as a further development of the shift from literal to allegorical. De Lubac directs much of his energy toward establishing a Christocentric principle at the root of that shift, as we have seen. Once it is in place, no further principle is introduced; that is part of his disagreement with allegory à la Philo, where metaphysics and ethics appeared to function separately in producing various levels of reading. He depends instead on the differing aspects of the complex reality of Christ to generate the different senses found in the tradition, so that "after the historical sense, all those that one can enumerate still form part of one and the same spiritual sense" (II.549).

The distinguishing characteristic of the moral sense rests in the fact that the Christian reality is not confined solely to the realm of abstract or speculative knowledge. The *gesta* recounted in the literal

54. "Moral" here should be taken as broadly as possible, indicating a whole way of life as with the Latin *mores,* and not in the narrow sense of obligatory or forbidden behavior.

sense and the *credenda* explored by way of allegory raise the question of *facienda*. The focus of the moral sense rests on the sort of actions that either advance or hinder the progressive development of the Christian life, rather than some generalized ethics or vision of the good. "If it is true that nothing rises above the Mystery of Christ, one ought not to forget that this Mystery, which was figured in the Old Testament, is still realized, is actualized, is completed in the Christian soul" (II.557). We will expand upon this in a moment. First, though, there is an important clarification to make. The moral sense that forms a part of the fourfold structure is every bit as extra-literal as allegory. It has little to do with those portions of Scripture that are, at the narrative level, concerned with guiding human action in the world; in Proverbs, the parable of the Good Samaritan, or the Sermon on the Mount, the literal sense has itself a moral aim. In the words of the tradition de Lubac is following, texts of this sort present *moralitas simplex* as they stand. The moral sense as understood here begins from the *res,* the deeds and persons of the Bible, and tries to draw out additional meaning for the situation of the present. A treatment of Jacob, for example, would begin less with any personal qualities shown in his story than with the fact that he had two sisters as wives and their maidservants as concubines (cf. Richard of St. Victor's *Twelve Patriarchs*). This presents a parallel between allegory, where "through one fact another is understood," and the moral sense, where "through one fact something else to be done is shown" (II.553).

Yet while allegory involves a transformed understanding of the biblical witness in light of Christ's saving action, tropology involves the personal appropriation of what has been understood. This is not a matter of drawing examples from narratives of the past; such a notion would be too extrinsic. De Lubac sees an inner drive within allegory that remains unsatisfied without a movement of concrete application; "far from constituting a negligible appendage, [this] is essential to the full understanding of Scripture" (II.556). The same paschal act that generates allegory also lies at the source of Christian existence, and to the extent that the life of Christians is sustained by a real participation in the risen Christ, change and growth in understanding of the latter cannot take place without repercussions for the former.

The traditional exegesis of the Song of Songs offers a fine example. Read on the level of allegory, the Song was from the earliest times seen in terms of the union between Christ and the Church. Equally ancient, however, is an interpretation that portrays the Song in terms of Christ and the individual; writers easily shift between them or employ both at once. De Lubac takes this as an illustration of the reciprocal balance of the tropological and allegorical senses. On one hand, the relationship of Christ and the individual requires the prior bond between Christ and the whole Church as its ground and context. On the other hand, the union of Christ and the Church is void or lacking without concrete expression in the lives and circumstances of individuals. This sort of existential element forms for de Lubac an inescapable part of any Christian approach to the Bible (though it may sometimes be minimized). When brought to the fore, the moral sense takes shape as the instrument by which the interpreter attempts to make the reality discerned through the texts active in the present. Only then "is Scripture fully *for us* the Word of God, this Word which is addressed to each, *here and now,* as well as to the whole Church, and saying to each 'what concerns his life'" (II.566).

'Quo tendas anagogia'

The final element of the mnemonic is the least distinct. While the initial senses can be discerned almost from the beginning, anagogy develops its own identity more slowly. (*Anagogia* as found in the verse is an improvisation to fit the rhyme, reworking the Greek *anagoge,* which means ascent or leading up.) The patristic period for the most part treats anagogy and allegory as synonyms, taking this ascent as the ascent from the literal to the spiritual. Gradually, however, anagogy acquires its more specialized meaning where the ascent in question is the progress from earthly to heavenly realities. "One is in the presence of an anagogical sense 'when through one thing another is understood, which is to be desired, namely, the eternal happiness of the blessed'" (II.623).

In keeping with his Christological perspective, de Lubac brings in the idea of multiple Advents in order to clarify the relationship between anagogy, allegory, and tropology. Each of these spiritual senses is engaged in drawing Christ forth from the letter of Scripture, but does so with regard to a different phase of his action:

> The first coming . . . achieves the work of redemption which is continued in the Church and its sacraments: it is the object of allegory properly speaking. The second coming . . . takes place in the soul of each disciple, and it is tropology which explains it. The third coming is reserved for the "consummation of the age," when Christ will appear in his glory and seek out his own to be with him: this is the object of anagogy. (II.621)

The tension between what is already here and a consummation not yet present provides the distinguishing characteristic of anagogy. For all his focus on the paschal act of Christ, de Lubac consistently stresses that the central goal of this action is the redemption of all creation into the trinitarian communion of God; the life of the Church serves as a guarantee and anticipation of this greater reality. Consequently the biblical *res* that illuminate present aspects of Christ and Christian existence are also capable of representing the world to come with "the new people in the new Jerusalem" (II.627). This is less a matter of genuinely different senses than of understanding one and the same object in related stages of a single process. To borrow medieval terminology, it is a question of whether the reader is seeking within the text to grasp the situation of Christ *in via* or the situation of Christ *in patria*. The latter is the concern of anagogy, while allegory and tropology are occupied with the former.

There is a certain complication with anagogy, though, which is absent from the other senses. It stems from a division within anagogical interpretation, which de Lubac traces to a duality within its subject matter. Looking toward the consummation of Christ's action in the world, eschatology is in the foreground of its vision. The last things may be seen from different perspectives, however, and each of those perspectives generates a different type of anagogy. One considers the substance of salvation, as expressed for example in Isaiah's vision of the peaceable kingdom, and this he calls doctrinal anagogy.

Here the aim is to enhance understanding of "what eye has not seen and ear has not heard" by moving from the experience of earthly realities to their promised fulfillment. Another examines the manner of salvation, so to speak, by tracing out a route for those in search of it; its objective is less understanding than to foster a real perception, however limited, of "what God has prepared for those who love him," and this de Lubac calls practical anagogy. Each type is equally focused on the eschatological summit of redemption in Christ, but they employ different means to explore it: "in modern language, the one is speculative, the other contemplative" (II.625).

Maintaining a balance between these two concerns in the practice of anagogy depends on continued awareness of eschatology as a concrete element within the history of salvation. When this fades, so that the anticipated consummation is no longer seen in terms of the saving event that establishes it, anagogy breaks down into its component parts. De Lubac attributes this to the influence of Pseudo-Dionysius's focus on the transition from earthly plurality to heavenly unity, as expressed in the abstractions of later Neoplatonism. Anagogy then "tends to become, on one side, a process of natural mysticism, and, on the other, a chapter of natural theology" (II.642).

Highlighting the eschatological unity of speculation and contemplation within anagogy allows de Lubac to present this last sense of the four as not only final but also complete. Allegory's drive toward grasping the significance borne by events and persons in the light of Christ reaches a natural term in doctrinal anagogy, revealing inter alia both Israel and the Church as reflections of Jerusalem on high, while tropology's search for concrete manifestations of biblical meaning in the present life of the reader finds its resolution in practical anagogy, offering a foretaste of the world to come. As a result, anagogy "forms the total and definitive sense. It sees, in the eternal, the fusion of mystery and mysticism. Alternatively, the eschatological reality attained by anagogy is the eternal reality in which every other has its consummation" (II.633).

Neither glossary nor method

De Lubac's enterprise requires not only an understanding of the four-sense framework but also an understanding of what that framework is not. He is quite concerned to ward off misconceptions regarding the general role and function of classical exegesis, even when they stem in part from those who would normally be considered his allies, for mistakes of that sort run the risk of nullifying his entire project to recover the traditional ways of reading. It does no good to retrieve a buried tool for one who does not know how to go about using it.

A particularly significant question has to do with terminology. De Lubac was far from the only person with an active interest in retrieving ancient modes of interpretation, and this led to a wide range of approaches and vocabulary. A number of writers eventually came together in making use of a distinction between allegory (understood as a symbolic and ahistorical focus in interpretation) and typology (understood as a focus on intrinsic connections between historically related events) to distinguish between pagan and Christian exegesis. Though this distinction corresponds in substance to the one drawn above between Philonian and Christian allegory, de Lubac does not see it as an indifferent matter of labels; instead, he rejects it with some firmness. This is partly due to his historical/linguistic observation that the distinction is without foundation; the term "allegory" is in common use by a host of Christian writers, with few apparent qualms, whereas typology "is neither scriptural or truly traditional."[55] The main part of his opposition, however, comes from a more substantive difficulty.

The essence of typology lies in establishing "a correspondence between historic realities at different moments in the history of salva-

55. "Typology and Allegorization," in *Theological Fragments,* 129, which makes the linguistic point in some depth, even though this requires him to take issue with his brother Jesuit and theological associate Jean Danielou. This is all the more striking, and reveals some of the importance he sees in the subject, when one considers that the essay first appeared in the midst of the *nouvelle théologie* controversy. The same criticism appears in IV.130.

tion"; beyond this it does not go (I.353). This restriction in scope appears to be the major failure that makes it impossible for him to accept typology as an adequate description for Christian exegesis. To simply recognize the parallel between baptism and the passage through the Red Sea, or between Easter and Passover, is not sufficient. Genuine parallels though they are, typology regards them from an extrinsic perspective that remains purely descriptive without going on to the explanation of their causal or revelatory significance within the larger framework. Typological exegesis could in theory come to an end with the complete collection of all these parallels and correspondences, as though one were assembling a glossary of artistic motifs and symbols. "It has the drawback of referring solely to a result, without alluding to the spirit or basic thrust of the process which produces that result."[56] Another facet of the same flaw is the lack of engagement with the need for personal appropriation. A typology that is passive and bound to links within history has little or no ability to make the transition from the past to the present, much less the future, that occurs in the moral and anagogical senses of traditional exegesis.

The need for an improved vocabulary that underlies the attempted shift toward typology remains, however, and de Lubac acknowledges it. For better or worse, allegory is not satisfactory in the modern context; the effort of verbal retraining is not worth it. Generations of scholarly disdain have had their effect, not to mention the equivocations left encrusted upon the word by the sheer accumulation of time and tradition. There would be a constant need to distinguish the different forms of allegory: Philonian or Christian, the broad meaning that takes in all of traditional exegesis or the narrow one that refers to one sense among others. He recommends instead a return "to the most traditional and the most general expression of all, and . . . to speak once again, quite simply of 'spiritual meaning' [or] 'spiritual understanding.'"[57]

This usage avoids the problems of typology and allegory while of-

56. *Histoire et Esprit,* 388.
57. *Histoire et Esprit,* 388.

fering advantages of its own. One lies in the very broadness of the phrase; de Lubac can make use of this latitude to stress the differing senses as elements within a larger whole, so that they do not come to be understood in isolation from one another. If the traditional exegesis is to have an intrinsically Christian character, as we have seen above, its multiple senses must be traced back to a common source in the impact of Christ upon the letter of the text. (It is otherwise too easy for such an exegesis to fall back upon philosophical abstractions in the manner of Philo.) "Unity of source, and unity of convergence: through them, Richard of St. Victor says, *Scriptura multa nobis in unum loquitur*" [Scripture says to us many things in one] (II.650). An apt example can be drawn from Aquinas:

> For when I say "let there be light" in a literal way concerning bodily light, it pertains to the literal sense. If "let there be light" is understood as Christ born in the Church, it pertains to the allegorical sense. If "let there be light" is understood as through Christ we are led to glory, it pertains to the anagogical sense. But if "let there be light" is understood as through Christ we are illuminated in mind and set afire in feeling, it pertains to the moral sense.[58]

Adopting spiritual understanding as the primary descriptive term also helps forestall mechanical applications of the four-sense framework, as though one could draw all four in equal proportion from any and every given text. This represents a related failure to grasp the unity of classic exegesis that de Lubac attributes to an atomistic habit more common today than in the past. The present tendency is to perceive the Bible as a series of self-contained texts where our predecessors "recognized rather an assured truth hidden within the whole mass of the text and manifested more or less in each passage." The traditional illustration of the point is furnished by a lyre with its many strings; the whole instrument is directed toward the production of sound, and each string contributes its note, yet the resultant melody resides in no single component.[59]

58. II.644 citing Aquinas, *In Gal.* V.7.

59. IV.76 for the quotation; the example of the lyre is discussed in "Old Distich," 120.

There remains a positive benefit in speaking of spiritual understanding; this is the explicit integration of the Spirit's role into the formulation. We saw above that de Lubac finds this element crucial to Christian exegesis. His concern with the Holy Spirit's relationship to Scripture bears little resemblance to the doctrine of inspiration, though, at least as that teaching was presented at the time of his writing. The standard notion of inspiration, whether in Catholic or Protestant form, devoted its attention almost entirely to the inspiration of the biblical writers. The work of the Spirit appeared to reach an end with the production of the text, which was then treated as a perfect and inerrant linguistic artifact. This represents a constricted focus upon a single aspect of an older and broader view.

> It is not only the sacred writers who were inspired one fine day. The sacred books themselves are and remain inspired. It can and must be said of them, with especially good reason, what Saint Augustine said of all the beings of creation: "God did not create them and then depart from the scene. They come from him and exist in him."[60]

An adequate understanding of inspiration for de Lubac includes the continued and continual action of the Holy Spirit through the medium of Scripture, extending past its production and into its reception and application. It would be only a slight exaggeration to see here a lesser and derivative Pentecost, working not through a rushing wind and tongues of fire but in the course of exegesis. This side of his thought may also help to explain the absence of an explicit method for spiritual interpretation in his writings. Typology can be conducted by way of a method, with the attendant recurrent series of operations and progressive increase in results, because it stands outside the past events whose connections it explores. Spiritual understanding, while not without a methodical component in knowledge of the text and the ways Christ may be revealed in it, requires an element of personal participation that cannot be reduced to schematic procedure.

60. I.128 citing *Confessions* IV.12; cf. also *Histoire et Esprit,* 428 and IV.76, 144. While de Lubac does attribute some of the faults in classic exegesis to an exaggerated idea of biblical perfection and inerrancy, such ideas increased their influence over time.

That personal element is what enables the interpreter to engage varying dimensions of meaning within the text, in response to the concrete circumstances of community or individual, with the confidence that the Spirit by whom Scripture was given continues to make the gift effective.

> The Spirit communicates to the sacred text a limitless potentiality, which therefore entails degrees of profundity which can go on and on. No more than this world was Scripture, that other world, created once for all: the Spirit "creates" it still, as if every day, to the extent that he "opens" it.[61]

One can see from this how spiritual interpretation overcomes the passivity woven into the structure of typology. The shift to present application by way of moral and anagogical readings takes place less as a matter of subjective caprice and more as a matter of pneumatic appropriation of the Bible in the present situation, following the pattern set by the fundamental transition from the narrative of the *littera* to the understanding of Christ. One and the same Spirit is at work throughout, lighting up varied aspects of the reality of Christ in various situations, and de Lubac sees in this an assurance that the developed framework of the four senses attains spiritual understanding rather than spiritual fantasy.

EVALUATION AND COMMENT

This treatment can only be seen as a sketch of the argument and research that de Lubac laid out at such length, yet the limits of time and space require a shift from exposition to evaluation. As we will see, not only the achievements but also the failings of his effort have something to offer. The clearest of those achievements lies with the history of exegesis. Despite a certain degree of abstraction and uniformity imposed by his desire to draw on as many witnesses as possible, present scholarship continues to follow his broad outline of classical exegesis. Its rules and operational integrity are recognized, so

61. II.654; the study devoted to Origen is apparent, as de Lubac falls in with the Alexandrian's view of interpretation as an activity with both scholarly and pneumatic aspects.

that one can no longer simply dismiss traditional practice as nothing more a formless twisting of the text. It appears instead as rooted in aspects of the NT and developing on the basis of a specific and widely shared theological understanding of Scripture and its role. Without overlooking genuine imperfections, de Lubac does succeed in showing the central role played by this exegetical approach for more than a millennium of Christian reflection on the Bible; later attempts at building up a theological framework for exegesis must take both its positive and its negative elements into account.

De Lubac's success with these researches is far less clear when one moves beyond questions of historical theology to constructive impact on the present. His effect on biblical exegetes, especially those outside France, was at best negligible. He seems to attribute this in part to the vicissitudes of the 1950s, and later, the tumult associated with Vatican II acting to overshadow or block the reception of his work, and in part to the "formless" and "unmethodical" character of *Exégèse médiévale.*[62] These points are somewhat extrinsic, though, and one finds little attention to potential flaws in his own arguments. The criticisms to which he responded were for the most part historical in nature, where he would act to defend his understanding of the tradition.[63] What makes this regrettable is that much of his lack of effect may be traced to a single cause, namely, the doubts regarding the depth and reality of his commitment to the role of history in biblical interpretation that are raised by aspects of his thought. It is no accident that a serious critique by a practicing North American exegete centered on this very point.[64]

De Lubac's focus on what may be called the objective character of

62. *Service of the Church,* 85.

63. For example, the essay "Hellenistic and Christian Allegory." There is also the possibility that the relative lack of engagement with the present in his own voice led others to engage him mainly on historical grounds; cf. Burghardt's review article, which treats de Lubac only vis-à-vis Origen and finds a partner for general discussion of spiritual exegesis in Danielou.

64. McKenzie, "Chapter in the History of Spiritual Exegesis." He does not clearly distinguish between the general role of history and the application to specific passages, but this is a fault of phrasing more than thought.

inspiration, inhering in the Bible itself as much or more than in its writers, did enable him to open an avenue for the ongoing role of the Spirit in interpretation. This preference for the broader context has a secondary effect, which he seems to have neither intended nor explicitly stated. As one magnifies the importance of the overall biblical gestalt as the object of God's intention and a primary medium of the Spirit, so the significance of what the human authors of individual books intended to convey diminishes. Their intention, as with any human effort, is part of a particular historical context that is now gone; it must pale to some degree when contrasted with an opportunity to discern the movement of the divine plan borne by the Spirit. It is not clear whether de Lubac is aware of this hazard, but nothing in his work poses an effective counter. Reserving a special place for "the religious meaning of the Bible" as the goal of historical research is not enough; the concept is too general to be useful, and stands at some remove from exegesis. Historical study of Scripture does hold an honored place, because to reject it is to reject the fundamentally historical character of Christian revelation, "but he has not shown the function of exegesis in the rigorous sense" in relation to spiritual understanding.[65] These two are juxtaposed without being integrated.

Another factor is the tolerance de Lubac shows toward *allegoria verbi*. The distinctiveness of Christian allegory in his presentation depends on its historical character, where the deeds, places, and persons that constitute the *res* of Scripture serve as the basis for allegory rather than the verbal symbolisms explored by Hellenistic allegory. *Allegoria facti* requires a real foundation in the knowledge of the *res,* while *allegoria verbi* is a purely literary phenomenon. Yet after devoting considerable attention to this point, he restores *allegoria verbi* to an accepted though subordinate role in interpretation. So long as *allegoria facti* is given first place, and the theological principles that establish its validity granted, he regards the use of verbal allegory as a matter of indifference. An interpreter may use it or not, depending

65. McKenzie, "Chapter in the History of Spiritual Exegesis," 378–79; he also notes that grasping the religious meaning of the Bible is "the work of biblical theology" rather than exegesis proper (380).

on tastes and circumstances. Here as before, the specific contours of the discussion weaken his arguments for the importance of history to the extent that his practice allows what his theory would seem to exclude. Even if the theory proves robust enough to accommodate *allegoria verbi,* which one may or may not grant, some loss of force and credibility occurs.

When these points are joined with the lack of any sustained example of spiritual interpretation in his own voice, doubts regarding de Lubac's real engagement with modern historical study of the Bible cannot be avoided. Unequivocal though his statements in support of it are, the interpretive structure that he lays out does not offer intrinsic points of practical interaction between historical and spiritual exegesis. History seems to resemble an honored guest being conducted on a tour of some factory; all proper courtesy is shown, and no part of the establishment is excluded from view, but one does not expect the guest to lend a hand in the work. At the end of the day, even though theology requires that an account of "salvation will naturally take a historical form," exegesis is for de Lubac a fundamentally theological enterprise rather than a historical one.[66] The consequence is that the actual value of history and a literal sense linked with it become problematic.

Focus on this defect, however, can be taken too far. It is a distinct overstatement to say that there are "no methods and principles which secure spiritual interpretation against fancy."[67] While the principles de Lubac employs are theological rather than historical in nature, they nonetheless present a safeguard against the wholesale embrace of caprice. As shown at length above, the structure of spiritual senses is generated by a Christocentric approach to Scripture that establishes some standard of evaluation for particular readings. De Lubac goes on to set spiritual exegesis within the global context of Chris-

66. *Catholicism,* 141; it is theology that lends meaning and importance to history as a result of the Incarnation, working "from above" as it were, rather than history possessing an importance that is then taken up into theology.

67. John L. McKenzie, "The Significance of the Old Testament for Christian Faith in Roman Catholicism," in *The Old Testament and Christian Faith,* ed. Bernhard Anderson (New York: Herder and Herder, 1969), 104.

tian belief as expressed in the teaching of the community, and so provides additional guidance (IV.90–92). A wide scope is left open for individual ingenuity, but he accepts this as a sign of strength whereby the Spirit makes it possible for the biblical text to speak to a variety of individual or collective situations.

This is where the value of de Lubac's work lies for the project at hand. In strong contrast with both Segundo and Childs, he offers a way of exploring broader dimensions within Scripture and engaging contemporary circumstances that is intrinsically Christian in substance and well grounded in the tradition as a whole. It does fall short of the mark by a significant margin with regard to the function of history, but as we will see, the defect is far from irreparable.

CHAPTER SIX

UTRAQUE UNUM

At this point we should remember that neither de Lubac nor any of the other figures considered were examined for their own sake, but rather for an underlying purpose that was constructive and synthetic. Now we must offer, with the resources available from those prior analyses, some resolution to the issue with which the investigation began. The traditional Christian approach to Scripture involves one set of affirmations, and the characteristic modern approach a quite different set. This clash poses no difficulty for those content to adopt one approach in toto and completely reject the other, but that is more easily said than done.

Only fideism can fail to recognize the human factors and historical conditions at work in the Bible; only lack of faith can fail to acknowledge God as the unifying authority and unique source of the Bible. The substantive problem lies in finding a way that allows classic and modern approaches to function together. Modern biblical study, as seen in the first chapter regarding Spinoza, came to exist in large part as an effort to undermine and replace older ways of reading founded on theological commitments. Even today, one need not go far to find those consciously pursuing a similar project in the name of scholarship and reason. The resultant mistrust of historical-critical methods, though reduced, has not been eliminated by pointing out the large number of practitioners who function within the mainstream Christian community; the practical demonstration all too often fails to be supported by theoretical justification.[1] A mirror image of this diffi-

1. A recent and popular effort to emulate Spinoza would be Robert Funk, *Honest to Jesus.* As we saw with Brown and Crossan, disputes on the basis of history do little to resolve an issue stemming from differences of horizon.

culty arises when theological views of Scripture are required to incorporate historical perspectives. The abstract value of those perspectives may be affirmed without any real notice being taken of them, leaving theology itself almost untouched and exegetical work an academic pursuit in the worse sense of the term. We have seen this objection raised against de Lubac, not without some justice, and a similar concern seems active in more contemporary disputes.[2] In light of these tensions, simply affirming the mutual compatibility of the two approaches does little good. There must be an explanation that accounts for their coexistence and assigns real tasks of mutual value to each.

Crafting such an explanation involves sifting necessary prerequisites from habitual presuppositions. As the first chapter illustrated, there are deep rifts between the biblical understanding of an Origen or Aquinas and historical study of the Bible carried on à la Spinoza or Troeltsch. Whether those rifts taken in their pure state may be bridged is at best a doubtful enterprise; however, the central affirmations of the opposed sides can be shaped into a concise set of criteria. Those requirements that stem from theological roots may be identified as unified medium of revelation and consonance with tradition. "Unified medium of revelation" includes recognition of the following points: that the Bible is a privileged arena of divine revelation, offering not only information about God but God's own self present and active, and that the Bible is as we have it, with these particular books gathered into two Testaments, as a deliberate result of God's providential action in the world. Without becoming lost among competing theologies, these affirmations express the irreducible minimum necessary for receiving the biblical text as Scripture. "Consonance with tradition" involves an application of the broader theological principle, and requires that any proposed account be capable of explaining and incorporating the approach to the Bible shown in the

2. It is certainly present in William S. Kurz and Kevin E. Miller, "The Use of Scripture in the *Catechism of the Catholic Church*," *Communio* 23 (1996): 480–507, or Joseph A. Fitzmyer, "Concerning the Interpretation of the Bible in the Church," *Josephinum Journal of Theology* 6 (1999): 5–20.

writings of the New Testament. To the extent that any particular view of Scripture and its role served as a constitutive element of apostolic faith and teaching, subsequent Christian reflection cannot overlook or dismiss it.[3] Modern biblical perspectives add but a single factor, which may be called historicity. As understood here, "historicity" requires that one acknowledge historical situation and circumstance as intrinsic factors that condition all human expressions of meaning, including biblical meaning, with the consequence that the application of all available means of historical study to the Bible is not only useful but necessary. The grasp of history as a structural element of human existence is a central achievement of modernity, whatever the disruption brought in its wake.[4]

The features of these criteria may be traced with more detail in the first chapter. Their brief expression here is meant to recall the standard operating in the consideration of representative modern figures and to indicate what each of them has to offer. This proves to be a substantial amount with respect to Brown and de Lubac, *mutatis mutandis,* but much less vis-à-vis Childs and Segundo. While Childs's intense focus on the canon as theological principle appears to satisfy the criterion of unified medium of revelation, the lack of substantive justification for this stance apart from assertive rhetoric undermines what he is able to draw from it. His expression of the canonical principle also runs contrary to tradition in that he explicitly rejects any role for the type of biblical understanding displayed in the NT despite its importance in molding the actual formation of the Christian Bible. There is more depth in his application of historical tools, befitting his vocation as an OT scholar, but the relationship between the

3. Let the reader also note that consonance differs from identity. One could say, for example, that Einstein's physics is consonant with Newton's inasmuch as it includes the main elements of Newton's thought within a broader explanatory framework.

4. Cf. Lonergan, *Method,* 175–96; it is interesting that history is the only one of his functional specialties that requires two chapters for its explanation, indicative of its importance. A CDF declaration of 1973, *Mysterium ecclesiae,* offers an illustration of the disruption with respect to the historical understanding of dogmatic statements (§ 5).

biblical witness and the history of Israel or the Church is labeled as dialectical and put aside without apparent effect on his practice. Taken on the whole, only in the most prima facie way does his thought measure up to the requirements of our project. Segundo, on the other hand, presents a mixture of positive and negative aspects. One finds an acknowledgment of human historicity and a sensitivity to resultant questions of horizon that go beyond any of the other figures examined (though in practice his historical judgments tend to be inaccurate and drawn from rather dated scholarship). On the theological front, however, there is a crippling flaw in the presentation of the Bible as a tool of divine pedagogy whose goal is to inform us with the values pursued by Jesus and endorsed by the God he called Father. The values themselves are to be excavated from the Bible by historical work, and the Jesus reconstructed by that investigation is primary. Consequently, Segundo portrays Scripture as a human artifact recording a historical process of witness to certain values; once the values have been grasped, their scriptural wrappings become *adiaphora*. Although backed up by a substantial analysis of faith and ideology as constitutive factors of human existence, which also provides the basis for the stress on historicity, his outlook directly conflicts with traditional views of the Bible as an authoritative and unsurpassable medium of revelation.

What sets Brown and de Lubac apart from these others is not so much that they meet the requirements better, since each taken on his own fails to do so. The distinguishing feature is that neither sets his thought on any active rejection of the standards of revelation, tradition, and history. Furthermore, the arguments they deploy around their central affirmations are open to productive development and interaction. Brown provides an explanation of the exegete's task that allows for the full range of historical investigation and is justified by the need to preserve the apostolic character of Christian teaching. It is in moving beyond the immediate work of exegesis that he loses focus, as the argument shifts toward wider theological questions. De Lubac, on the other hand, is at his best with the general Christian approach to the Bible and the traditional framework used to draw out and elaborate biblical meaning in that context. The faults in his understanding appear when it becomes necessary to take up specifics, not only for individual texts, but also with respect to the role and fruitfulness of historical studies.

There is a clear reciprocal character in these strengths and weaknesses, as Brown measures up to the criterion of history yet falls short of the others and de Lubac in turn misses the mark vis-à-vis history. One may therefore think that a simple juxtaposition of the two will create a theologically coherent combination of modern and classical exegetical approaches. This would be a mistake, however, because it overlooks necessary adjustments and corrections to be made on each side. Brown's account of exegesis must be opened to a more explicit contact with theology, while de Lubac's theology needs to incorporate a genuine role for history that preserves the ability of Scripture to challenge the present.

The twin buoys to which our attempt at a synthesis is anchored are the ideas of intentionality and application.[5] In the first place, with respect to intentionality, there are sound reasons that require both a focus on authorial intention as a primary goal of exegesis and the recognition of a dual aspect within it. One can then present the literal sense in a way more open to broad theological context without breaking the connection to historical circumstances. In the second place, with respect to application, other sound reasons indicate the value of a Christocentric framework as a guide for present engagement with the biblical text in a variety of situations. Highlighting the role of explicit faith in the origin and use of that framework both forestalls certain difficulties and agrees better with the fundamental apostolic practices incorporated into the NT.

5. Because of a certain ambiguity in the term “actualization,” I will be speaking instead in terms of “application,” despite the current prevalence of the former term. As Peter S. Williamson sees, actualization has “a broad sense, as the present meaning of biblical text (its religious meaning for Christian faith today), or more narrowly, as a particular application of a text to a contemporary question or circumstance” (*Catholic Principles,* 291). The broad sense corresponds to matters discussed here in terms of divine intention, subject to certain qualifications made below, and the narrower sense is better and more simply understood in terms of application.

DUAL INTENTIONALITY

The role that an author's intent should play in interpretation has long been a subject of controversy. For many philosophers and literary critics, authorial intention is counted as the equivalent of phlogiston and dismissed as one of the discarded concepts that litter the history of ideas. Others, working from a range of perspectives, have sought to defend its value and usefulness.[6] Nothing here should be taken as a direct attempt to settle the issue one way or the other; this is not an investigation in either philosophy or literary criticism. It remains an exercise in Christian theology, however, and that theology does tend to work in favor of a focus on authorial intention.

The tendency is driven less by a specific understanding of how written texts function than by a desire for continuity. The point is made well in Brown's work, albeit it serves there more to establish the need for historical studies. Christians do not ordinarily turn to the Bible as though to "a classic," drawn by the literary power with which it presents alternative perspectives on the human condition.[7] They turn to it for the sake of what it conveys, the memory and experience of God and God's actions within Israel and the church, seeking to recover the memory and participate in the experience as "a Christian heir to the people of Israel and the people of the early church, and not independent of them."[8] This involves a willingness to hear the words of, for example, Jeremiah to Jerusalem and Paul to Corinth as words that make sense in those environments; it also implies the existence of a stable core that remains accessible to those who are not sixth-century Hebrews or first-century Corinthians.

The simplest way of accommodating these features is to adopt the conventional view: authors write with the intention of communicat-

6. There is a review of the topic from a postmodern perspective in Stephen E. Fowl, "The Role of Authorial Intention in the Theological Interpretation of Scripture," in *Between Two Horizons: Spanning New Testament Studies and Systematic Theology,* ed. Joel B. Green and Max Turner (Grand Rapids: Eerdmans, 2000), 71–87.

7. Even though the notion of the classic can be made to incorporate many aspects of their practice; cf. Schneiders, *Revelatory Text,* 132–56, especially 150–51.

8. Brown, *Biblical Interpretation,* 46, with much the same thought in *Death,* 7.

ing to an audience, and what they intend to communicate can be understood through what is written, even though differences of skill or knowledge on the part of author and audience influence the efficacy of the process. Taking this position need not preclude the accumulation of additional layers of meaning, as the text is read in later situations and develops its own history, but it does establish the meaning intended by the author as a foundation. This understanding is at work in mundane encounters with the written word, such as a business memorandum where staffers find the executive's plan for the next week, and one finds it also within theological accounts of the Bible. Our examination of Aquinas showed the preeminent place he allotted to authorial intention in an analysis stemming from Augustine's *De doctrina Christiana,* and one finds a similar emphasis in modern statements such as *Dei Verbum.* The PBC's *Interpretation of the Bible in the Church,* although influenced by contemporary doubts to avoid the term "intention" and define the literal sense as "that which has been expressed directly by the inspired human authors" (II.B.1), also stands in the same line of thinking and may be taken to express a majority consensus among Catholic biblical scholars.[9]

Yet given the prevalence of those contemporary doubts, it would be a worthwhile exercise to briefly go through an argument in favor of authors and their intended meaning as a central goal of interpretation. Such arguments are often drawn from contemporary analytic philosophy, with particular indebtedness to the speech-act theory inaugurated by J. L. Austin and continued by John Searle,[10] but the account employed here stems from Bernard Lonergan. Not only is Lonergan much closer to Catholic theological discourse, his more general discussion was later turned toward Scripture by Ben F. Mey-

9. As the analysis of Williamson (*Catholic Principles,* 165–66) makes clear, the Commission did not intend to abandon authorial intention but to ensure a focus on the text formed by the intention. As we are about to see, the relationship between text and intention marks a point where it is all too easy to become confused.

10. As mentioned before, Wolterstorff's *Divine Discourse* is thus far the signal achievement along this line but continues to be joined by others. See Vanhoozer, *Is There a Meaning,* 207–14, for a summary treatment of Searle's thought, together with the critique of this tendency in Fowl, "Role of Authorial Intention," 76–82.

er.[11] Our aim, it must be remembered, is not to settle the question: it is to show that interpretation for authorial meaning is not unreasonable and that theological predispositions to such interpretation are not without support. The best way to do that is to address what many consider the central difficulty with regard to authorial intention. As one writer puts it,

> it is simply impossible to arrive at (or at least to establish that one has arrived at) the meaning intended by the author. The subjective intellectual state of an ancient writer (to say nothing of the increased complexity in regard to texts redacted by numerous authors over hundreds of years) is simply no longer accessible to us no matter how sophisticated our methodology.[12]

While there is more to it than that, this statement reveals a common confusion of terms that makes a significant contribution to the problem.

The intention sought by interpretation has no immediate connection with the subjective awareness of a writer, which is indeed inaccessible apart from personal interrogation or telepathic probe. To imagine that it has such a connection is to lose sight of "the fundamental distinction between intention and the textual realization of intention."[13] At the heart of writing is the ability to transmit meaning

11. Lonergan's main treatment of the topic is *Method* and its chapter on interpretation as a functional specialty, which provides the framework that Meyer explicitly applies to biblical hermeneutics with "The Primacy of the Intended Sense of Texts," in *Lonergan's Hermeneutics,* ed. Ben F. Meyer and Sean E. McEvenue (Washington: The Catholic University of America Press, 1989), later joined by *Reality and Illusion in New Testament Scholarship* (Collegeville, Minn.: Liturgical, 1994). "Primacy" is the more detailed and specific account, being written for a more specialized audience.

12. Schneiders, *Revelatory Text,* xxxi; she goes on to say that authorial intention is not even a desirable goal because that would be to shut out the reader's active engagement in the generation of meaning and deny the possibility of multiple valid interpretations. Stephen Fowl would acknowledge that "it is possible to speak in a coherent if constrained way about an author's intention," but he also finds it undesirable to do so if that would necessarily "accord privilege to the intentions of a scriptural text's human author" ("Role of Authorial Intention," 73).

13. Meyer, "Primacy," 106; as an indication of how widespread the error is, in the cited passage Meyer is criticizing a prominent supporter of authorial interpretation (E. D. Hirsch) for it.

to others without being physically present to them, and so being left unable to clear up gaps or misunderstandings. This produces the peculiar burden and labor of writing, which is to shape one's communication in such a way that it not only expresses meaning but also anticipates potential difficulties for the reader. And so,

> in writing, the transmission is a "text," that is, a written word sequence encoding the message of the writer. The "message" is whatever the writer intends to encode and succeeds in encoding. The writer, then, expresses a message in a text and the reader construes a text with a view to receiving its message. . . . "Intention" or "intended meaning" is thus not only in the writer; it is also intrinsic to the text insofar as the text objectifies or incorporates or encodes or expresses the writer's message.[14]

Just as the composer's score or the architect's blueprint enables the trained musician or contractor to follow out the signs and produce an ordered sequence of sounds or a physical structure, so it is with a written text.[15] The author shapes a series of signs aimed at eliciting the reader's reception of a particular message, and after that shaping is completed with the end of composition and the release of a text to its audience, the intention is fixed within the text much as the form imposed upon clay is fixed by the kiln. From this point of view, the object of interpretation is "the sense that the author both intended and managed to encode or express in the text."[16] Other senses may coalesce around this one as a text moves through history (the root of Brown's distinction between what a text meant and what it means), but while those additional meanings are not a priori inferior, accuracy and fidelity to the history of a text's reception require that they be distinguished from the author's sense.

14. Meyer, "Primacy," 83.

15. It is in some ways unfortunate that silent reading became habitual, for if reading aloud had continued, we might well be more attentive to the active role of the reader in recovering meaning from texts. There is at least as much activity in that as there is in either example; we simply notice it less, and this helps generate the prima facie illusion of reading and interpretation as purely passive acts of reception.

16. Meyer, "Primacy," 107; while one may read with other purposes in mind, as when the social historian studies *A Christmas Carol* and *The Pickwick Papers* to illuminate the impact of Dickens upon modern ideas of Christmas, that is analysis rather than interpretation.

The circumstances of the biblical text do, however, generate some additional difficulties in speaking of authors and intentions. One problem is due to the equivocal way the term "author" can be used with respect to Scripture. An individual may be known as the source of a biblical text in any of several modes: writing with his own hand, dictating, providing a summary of ideas to an associate who then produces a complete text, being a revered figure whose disciples write under the guidance of his thought, or being the archetype for a particular genre (cf. Solomon's role in the wisdom literature). However, this represents little more than an argument about words generated by the more specific modern usage that restricts the definition of author to "the original writer of a literary work." The real equivocation, and one already noted above, stems from what one may call the distributed character of biblical authorship. Many portions of the Bible were composed over a considerable length of time, extending to centuries in some cases, which makes an issue of the relationship between earlier writers and later redactors. Such an amorphous situation can make it difficult to determine which author or whose intention is to be sought.

Adopting a concern for authorial intent raises a more serious difficulty when one considers that biblical authorship is necessarily multiplex from a theological perspective. We saw above, in Origen and Aquinas, the bedrock Christian conviction that Scripture reveals and makes known to us what God wishes to be known. Although this can be understood and developed in different ways, at a minimum it seems to require a dual agency at work. In addition to the communicative intention of the human or humans involved in the writing of a given text, we must also acknowledge the communicative intention of God. How these two intentions are related to one another is far from clear, but there is a prima facie case to be made that they are not simply identical. As one writer states the point,

> How was a French parish priest in 1150 to understand Psalm 137, which bemoans captivity in Babylon, makes rude remarks about Edomites, expresses an ineradicable longing for a glimpse of Jerusalem, and pronounces a blessing on anyone who avenges the destruction of the temple by dashing Babylonian children against a rock? The priest lives in Con-

cale, not Babylon, has no personal quarrel with Edomites, cherishes no ambitions to visit Jerusalem (though he might fancy a holiday in Paris), and is expressly forbidden by Jesus to avenge himself on his enemies.[17]

And yet this French priest, together with a multitude of Christians in a variety of situations, receives Psalm 137 as divine revelation: "useful for teaching, for refutation, for correction, and for training in righteousness" (2 Tm 3.16). What God wishes to communicate must somehow go beyond the passionate grief and anger woven into an Israelite poet's lament, lending it additional significance without destroying its character as an expression of human meaning. In the balance of this section, we will attempt a more detailed account of this dual intentionality.

Human intention

Brown understood the literal sense "as the sense which the human author directly intended and which the written words conveyed."[18] Though the second clause may appear redundant, it ensures a focus upon the text at hand as well as some concern for the text's reception by its initial audience. The definition's broader function for his thought is as an anchor, which fixes the primary meaning of a given passage within a historical setting open to investigation and sets the parameters of possible interpretation. This serves in part as a safeguard against attempts to minimize the role of historical methods in exegesis. Both personal experience and pastoral concern led him to a concern for the security of modern biblical studies within Catholic thought and practice that is a consistent feature of his methodological discussions.

For present purposes, however, it is the definition itself that is of interest. Incorporating an express role for the written words as bearers of intentional meaning helps to explain why the problems in-

17. David C. Steinmetz, "The Superiority of Precritical Exegesis," in *The Theological Interpretation of Scripture*, ed. Stephen E. Fowl (Oxford: Blackwell, 1997), 28; the modern response to this difficulty by the simple redaction of the text, expressed inter alia in the present Liturgy of the Hours (Tuesday Vespers in Week IV of the Psalter), is little more than bowdlerization.

18. Cf. the discussion of Brown above.

volved in referring to the human author of a biblical text are less than they seem. No matter how widely the process of formation may be distributed over time or among individuals, the work of a particular writer or redactor eventually brought it to an end. The one whose intention governs the final stage and integrates the prior work into a completed whole is the author in the strict sense of the term.[19] Recognizing this need not diminish the importance of that prior work, however, nor release an exegete from the necessity of exploring it. The way that available resources were employed, and with what modifications, can shed a great deal of light on the intended meaning. The Synoptic Gospels present an excellent example; much of the success enjoyed by the Two-Source theory of their origins stems from its explanatory power. Matthew's or Luke's intention and their literary means of expressing it appear more clearly in comparison with Mark and the reconstructed Q document, enabling the interpreter to reach a more full and nuanced grasp of the evangelists' theologies. While this may be considered a special case, due to the advantage of possessing Mark's actual work rather than depending upon hypothetical reconstructions, the difference is only one of degree. There is no reason to abandon a helpful instrument simply because its utility varies according to circumstances.

Adopting this concern for the intention presented by the text nonetheless does shift the primary aim of historical investigation. As both Childs and Brown observe, it is possible to become entangled in source criticism and the search for events "as they really happened."[20] This runs the risk of reducing the one component that is truly present, the biblical text itself, to a simple point of departure. An explicit focus upon the meaning intended by the author within a particular historical context as the goal of interpretation helps to forestall confusion by ensuring that one not only begins from but re-

19. Putting aside the issues raised by individual texts with a complex history of transmission (e.g., the Western form of Acts) as exceptions that prove the rule; difficulty in determining the form of the text naturally leads to difficulties in other aspects of interpretation.

20. Childs is peculiarly sensitive to this, perhaps due to his involvement with Pentateuchal studies.

turns to the text. The document then places controls upon historical hypotheses, which can be tested against the text for explanatory power, and history sets limits to potential interpretations, which can be tested for plausibility against the historical situation.[21] There is a pragmatic advantage worth notice in this move, as it avoids some of the difficulties associated with making historical judgments. The problems displayed in arguments that stem from differing horizons tend to turn less around exegesis proper than around the historicity of events. To take but one example, disputes over wonders performed during Jesus' active ministry do not usually involve reading John without reference to Jesus' signs or Mark without reference to deeds of power. They instead take up competing definitions of "miracle" in light of modern natural science, the validity of Troeltsch's principle of analogy, or similar points. These are matters of horizons and history rather history alone, for as a recent writer notes, "if the miracle tradition from Jesus' public ministry were to be rejected *in toto* as unhistorical, so should every other Gospel tradition about him."[22] While there is much work to be done on ways to address conflicting horizons, or the impact of the Incarnation and the presence of God in time, one need not wait for resolution of these questions

21. The prior mention of the Two-Source theory of Gospel origins is an example of history being tested against the text, while an example where historical knowledge should limit the range of interpretation may be found in Jerome Murphy-O'Connor's reading of 1 Corinthians 7.32–34 (*New Jerome,* 805). One cannot seriously present the unmarried man anxious only to please God and the married man anxious to please both God and his wife as equivalent instances of excessive concern when Paul explicitly regrets that the married man "is divided" (7.34a); the negative weight of the latter term in the ancient context is simply too high to permit it. Cf. Fee, *Corinthians,* 343.

22. Meier, *Marginal Jew,* vol. 2, 630; one advantage of Meier's famous "unpapal conclave," where four hypothetical scholars of differing backgrounds must agree on the historical conclusions put forth about Jesus—despite the shortcomings discussed in Roc Kereszty, "Historical Research, Theological Inquiry, and the Reality of Jesus: Reflections on the Method of J. Meier," *Communio* 19 (1992): 576–600, and elsewhere—is precisely that it helps to highlight the importance of horizons. The lack of attention to the problem helps to generate a situation where there are, in the words of Luke Timothy Johnson, "more versions of 'the historical Jesus' and of 'early Christianity' than are compatible with the perception of history as a scientific discipline" (*Future,* 14–15).

in order to pursue exegetical ends.[23] The role played by historical investigation, though necessary and vital, is better directed toward the understanding of texts rather than the progress of events; in this way, it serves as an instrument of exegesis and not a goal in its own right.

Understanding the function of history in this way may appear Spinozist to some extent in that the philosopher also emphasized authorial meaning as the main interpretive goal. However, Spinoza placed that meaning within a set of carefully designed definitions intended to remove most cognitive content from Scripture and portray it as little more than a collection of ancient histories intermixed with imaginative exhortations to moral behavior. The political aims and definitional structure conditioned his whole approach to the Bible, making any claim of priority on behalf of authorial intention only a matter of rhetoric. Absent Spinoza's theologico-political interests, there is no need to suspect the genuine primacy Brown would accord to the author's intention. The point that leads us to pursue some adjustment of his thought concerns the precise contours of the word "author."

Divine intention

The collaboration of multiple individuals in the production of a given biblical text poses little difficulty. As we have seen, focus upon the written words as bearers of authorial meaning allows this to be taken into account. Yet the definition with which Brown begins spoke of the human author and so alludes to the problem; Christians regularly affirm that humans are not the only agents involved in the formation of the Bible. Liturgical readings may begin by noting "the letter of Paul to the Galatians," for example, but they close by recognizing what has been read as "the word of the Lord." Credit for the existence of Scripture is ascribed both to God and to human writers,

23. There is a nice summary of the problem vis-à-vis history in Daley, "Patristic Exegesis," 190–91. The fine treatment of history and theology in N. T. Wright, *People of God,* 29–144, attempts to address both epistemological and theological difficulties, amplified as it is by the later discussion relating to history and the Resurrection in *The Resurrection of the Son of God* (Minneapolis: Fortress Press, 2003), 3–31 and 685–718.

which is one of the insights behind the theology of inspiration, and a way of expressing this that has in Catholic circles become traditional is to speak of a dual authorship. Such a duality, where one could refer equally to God and to humans as authors, establishes the prospect of two intentions at work in one and the same text.[24] Interpretive approaches focused on authorial intent as the defining characteristic of the literal sense should address this topic if they are to be theologically complete. Setting it aside from the outset through the structure of one's definition is not sufficient, for this begs the question.[25]

Aquinas's treatment of the literal sense does address the matter of dual intent, but in a way that offers little assistance. He focuses on the text as conveying its author's intended meaning through the "words or imagined similitudes" written upon the page, just as Brown does; that meaning is what constitutes the literal sense.[26] But because there are two genuine and distinct authors at work in the biblical words or similitudes, one divine and one human, he admits more than one literal sense to the same passage. Indeed, "more than one" is an understatement. When discussing biblical meaning outside the intention of the human writer, Aquinas ventures to say that "every truth which can be adapted to divine Scripture, keeping the circumstances of the letter, is its sense."[27] The whole range of those truths can exist within a single communicative purpose, inasmuch as God's infinite understanding includes the differing construals that

24. This is certainly the outlook of *Dei Verbum* 11–13; cf. Alois Grillmeier, "*Dei Verbum:* Chapter III," in *Commentary on the Documents of Vatican II,* vol. 3, ed. Herbert Vorgrimler (New York: Herder, 1969), 229–30, 238–44. There is also the more pointed analysis of Ignace de la Potterie, "Interpretation of Holy Scripture in the Spirit in Which It Was Written (*Dei Verbum* 12c)," in *Vatican II: Assessment and Perspectives: Twenty-Five Years After,* 3 vols., ed. René Latourelle (Mahwah: Paulist Press, 1988), 1:220–66.

25. It may be that Brown attempted to bring the question of God's authorial intention back in when he spoke of a canonical meaning, but that did not form a lasting part of his thought.

26. *Quodlibet* VII.16.

27. *De pot.* IV.1, cf. the discussion above; the restriction to truths is not insignificant, for in *De pot.* IV.1.ad5, Thomas rejects an interpretation on the grounds that its "contrary is proven well enough by evident reasons." See Boyle, "St. Thomas Aquinas," 96–97.

different audiences give to the words of the passage. This creates an indefinite number of literal meanings, as well as some unique benefits for the would-be interpreter of the Bible. Embracing a multiplicity of potential meanings helps to defend the biblical witness; if a particular interpretation should prove false or harmful, one can resort to another reading. The same multiplicity also enables a wide range of humans to approach Scripture, and develop understandings fitted to their capacities and situations, with some assurance that in doing so they attain the intention of the author rather than their own fantasy.

The difficulty with Thomas's approach lies in the decided finitude of human understanding. An indefinite plurality of meanings offers little guidance for interpretation. One recent writer takes this as a strength, opening the door to more pragmatic and pluralist ways of reading, which would no longer be subject to an overarching concern for authorial intention. "Ad hoc argumentation by interpreters guided by the virtue of prudence and by God's providence working through the Spirit" would serve to resolve disputes over the literal sense, in light of the goals of Christian life in particular communities and contexts.[28] In this line of thought, concern for God's intention would become an instrument for relativizing or dismissing the historical meaning of the human author. Such a move not only assimilates Thomas too closely to postmodern hermeneutics, making theological recognition of God's involvement in the Bible an interpretive carte blanche, but also overlooks an explicit reservation. However varied the range of potential meanings, there is a boundary set for them in "the circumstances of the letter." Although Aquinas leaves the precise contours of this boundary unspecified and unexplored, the reference does offer a starting point for reflection.

Explicit concern for the circumstances of the letter does not entirely resolve the difficulty, for many features of the text are not affected by considerations of dual authorship. The words remain the written expression of a particular human language, Hebrew or Greek, and require the same linguistic competence. So also do they

28. Fowl, "Authorial Intention," 84.

remain part of the larger context established by a particular book, such as Deuteronomy or Matthew, subject to the conventions of rhetoric, form, and genre employed within a given literary culture. At least initially, interpretive efforts directed toward the literal sense on these levels can find little help from consideration of divine intention, because the material with which they have to work is invariant and common to both divine and human authors.[29] True as it is that God's infinite understanding encompasses all the various readings humans may derive from a given passage, without some independent basis in the passage itself those readings cannot be justified as interpretations of a literal sense even if they should happen to express some truth. Augustine caught hold of a similar point when cautioning the would-be exegete:

> Anyone who understands in the Scriptures something other than that intended by them is deceived, . . . if he is deceived in an interpretation which builds up charity, he is deceived in the same way as a man who leaves a road by mistake but passes through a field to the same place toward which the road itself leads. But he is to be corrected and shown that it is more useful not to leave the road, lest the habit of deviating force him to take a crossroad or a perverse way.[30]

It may be that some such considerations or doubts about the real utility of multiple literal senses contribute to its scant treatment in Thomas's overall work. While abstract acceptance of the idea is evident, there seems to be little substantive impact upon his practice. De Lubac notes that the topic arises most clearly in *De potentia*, where it is a matter of reconciling conflicting authorities over the interpretation of Genesis, and that the whole discussion "has a rather pronounced pragmatist flavor."[31] Despite Thomas's clear recognition of dual authorship, the relative lack of specificity makes it difficult to

29. This may be a contributing factor in Joseph Fitzmyer's identification of the literal and the spiritual sense as one and the same; cf. *The Biblical Commission's Document "The Interpretation of the Bible in the Church": Text and Commentary* (Rome: Editrice Pontificio Istituto Biblico, 1995): 127–28, and also "Concerning the Interpretation," 16.

30. *De doctrina Christiana* I.36; translation from *On Christian Doctrine,* trans. D. W. Robertson Jr. (New York: Macmillan, 1958).

31. *Exégèse médiévale* IV.284.

derive a concrete procedure for distinguishing dual intentions within the literal sense.

Yet there is a single circumstance of the letter that does vary as the focus shifts from human to divine intention, and that is the Bible itself. A brief review of the history of the biblical canon shows that consolidation of the various books into one Bible with two Testaments came to pass long after the composition of even the most recent individual portion. None of the human writers involved could reasonably have been aware of the subsequent fate of their work as a biblical book in company with a specific set of other witnesses.[32] The continued acceptance of Scripture as a combined whole must be based either on simple acquiescence to the accidents of history or on the acknowledgment of God's deliberate purpose at work in the constitution of the Bible. While each of these alternatives is possible, only the latter measures up to the basic affirmations of Christian theology used to guide our investigation. The next task is to consider what implications this limited mode of access to the divine intention may hold.

Verba et res

To speak of God's purpose is of course dependent on faith, and that should be recognized from the outset. While one could grant a notional assent to the overall unity of the Bible for purposes of discussion, as perhaps takes place with Northrop Frye and other students of the Bible as literature, transforming the notional into the real requires a more substantive basis.[33] Brevard Childs was thus correct when he identified the biblical canon as an important theological

32. Note that to be aware of "Scripture" in general, as Paul and Luke certainly were, is far different from the specific understanding that one's own work will figure as a part of Scripture. Given the relatively late ranking of the apostolic writings as Scripture on par with the Old Testament, one could easily question whether even the compilers of Paul's letters had such an understanding; cf. *Anchor Bible Dictionary,* s.v. "Canon, New Testament." Apropos Aquinas, he also attributes the unity of the Bible to its divine authorship; cf. Boyle, "St. Thomas Aquinas," 93.

33. Cf. Frye's account in *The Great Code: the Bible and Literature* (New York: Harcourt Brace Jovanovich, 1982); another representative work would be Robert Alter, *The World of Biblical Literature* (New York: Basic Books, 1992).

reality in its own right, however ill-founded and inadequate his supporting arguments proved to be. When the unity of the canon is grounded in the communicative intention of God, and acknowledged as part of the divine project "to sum up all things in Christ, in heaven and on earth" (Eph 1.10), the interpreter is then able to consider the contribution and significance of individual passages within the larger whole.[34]

This new vantage point should not be thought to alter the immediate signification of words, as though some *testimonium internum* were giving witness to God's hidden purpose. The other circumstances of the letter remain what they are and continue to set limits on any attempt to disentangle human and divine elements. Recognition of the canon as a proper context for interpretation makes little direct contribution to a better understanding of, for example, Psalm 137 or Matthew's infancy narrative. Postulating equal knowledge of historical-critical tools and agreement on the results of their use, investigators should reach a common grasp of what a given text intends to communicate; that is the point of Brown's famous observation that there is "no reason why a Catholic's understanding of what Matthew and Luke meant in their infancy narratives should be different from a Protestant's."[35] The unification through faith of diverse volumes into a single Bible does not so much affect the *verba* taken as bearers of meaning as it extends or qualifies the exegete's knowledge of the *res* that are meant.

This distinction between *verba* and *res* inherited from Augustine was implicit in our earlier account of authorial intention as the goal of interpretation, but plays a sufficiently essential role at this point that a brief review becomes necessary. The *verba* involve the words themselves as communicative signs or expressions of meaning shaped to elicit specific acts of understanding in others; determining

34. Cf. Pontifical Biblical Commission, *Interpretation,* II.B.2: "The paschal event, the death and resurrection of Jesus, has established a radically new historical context, which sheds fresh light upon the ancient texts and causes them to undergo a change in meaning."

35. *Birth,* 8; note that the observation is limited to the understanding of texts. Judgments of history function differently.

their precise weight and significance depends in large part on our knowledge of language, situation, and literature. The *res* are best seen as the substance of what the writer intends to convey through those words, that which is to be understood concerning the subjects being discussed. With respect to biblical interpretation, the *verba* establish the literal sense and ground the necessity of historical-critical work. As expressions of meaning couched in specific human languages and contexts, they are open to the same interpretive tools as other human communications, regardless of whether one accepts or rejects the biblical canon. It is only through the relationship between *verba* and *res,* or better, between *res* and *verba,* that the canon begins to have an impact.

Acknowledgment of God's intention as the crucial factor unifying the biblical canon opens the way for a dual aspect to appear within the *res* understood. Just as the verse takes shape in light of the chapter and the chapter in light of the book, so also the meanings expressed in the various biblical books take shape in light of the whole Bible. The difference is that the latter step cannot be identified with the intention of the human writers, since it is due to the divine agency at work in the formation of Scripture.[36] The effects that the full canonical setting has upon the exegesis of individual texts should then be taken as genuine indicators of God's communicative purpose and allowed to influence the understanding of those texts in the same way as an understanding of, for example, the Gospel of Matthew will influence an interpretation of the Sermon on the Mount. Such a knowledge of the whole affects the part less by altering the immediate signification of the words than by conditioning the substantive meanings to be drawn from them due to a wider perspective on the subject or subjects involved. In the normal course of things this rela-

36. This need not, and should not, be taken to deny the historical and human process whereby that purpose came to completion; for the latter part of the process, see Metzger, *Canon of the New Testament.* The matter is similar to the rise of the monarchical episcopate, where a traceable period of development has not prevented later theology from seeing episcopacy as a constitutive element of the Church *de iure divino;* see Francis A. Sullivan, *From Apostles to Bishops: The Development of the Episcopacy in the Early Church* (New York: Paulist Press, 2001).

tionship of whole and part operates within a single authorial intention, or perhaps a single author's body of work, where the wider perspective arises naturally. The biblical situation is more complex, and so the point must be traced out further.

Approaches to the divine intention, especially when this intention may qualify or differ from that of the human writers, should keep certain considerations in the foreground. First and most significant is that discernment of what God means to communicate depends upon understanding the subject of a given passage in relation to the entire biblical witness on the matter at hand. Granting priority to some texts while excluding others—whether for historical reasons, as when Jeremiah's anticipation of a new covenant is confined to the context of the pre-exilic prophets, or for theological reasons, as when Romans is made the primary touchstone of belief—only sets human intentions against one another. God's intention becomes accessible to interpretation primarily at the canonical level, where the whole of Scripture may be taken into account. Another consideration directly implied by the first is that our knowledge of this divine intention is mediated through, and not apart from, the writers whose work is brought together. One cannot dismiss the human elements as simple chaff to be winnowed out in the process of uncovering the revelatory content, since what "God, for the sake of our salvation, wished to see confided to the sacred Scriptures" comes to us in specific writings whose meaning is expressed in historically and linguistically conditioned ways shared by all human communications.[37] Though not all human communications can be attributed to a dual divine and human authorship as Scripture is, for human readers the intention of the divine author nonetheless presents itself through the same expressive mechanism of words and substance, *verba* and *res;* consequently, it requires the same grasp of the words as instruments of meaning and involves the closest concern with the immediate setting of those words in the context of authorial circumstances, history, and language. Just as we can attend to the whole Bible only by acquiring

37. *Dei Verbum* 11, further illuminated by Grillmeier, *Dei Verbum,* 199–246.

a careful knowledge of the individual parts, so also we distinguish God's authorial intention only by understanding the human authors together as an ensemble.[38]

Without using historical sequence or theological preference alone to place one text above another, recognition of Scripture as a single communicative instrument established by deliberate divine action does allow the contours of the whole to provide some guidance in putting this ensemble together. The standard of relative importance by which to weigh the different biblical voices becomes less a matter of their particular history or theology, and more a matter of their role within the overarching structure. This can be determined partly by quantitative observations: it is not difficult to count Romans as more important than Jude, or to set James's statement that "faith without works is dead" (2.26) as a cautionary note aimed at misunderstandings of Paul, due to the sheer mass of the Pauline component in the Bible. Similar examples may stem from internal references, as when greater emphasis is given to Isaiah (or even to certain parts of Isaiah) due to its use among NT writers.[39] In the last analysis, however, role and significance are determined more by qualitative concerns than by the counting of verses or cross-references.

Theological affirmations of divine authorship imply a material as well as a formal unity within the canon, establishing it not merely as a whole but as a coherent whole, whose parts contribute to God's intention and may therefore be evaluated on the varying degrees of their contribution. As mentioned briefly above, and at greater length in the discussions of Childs and de Lubac, that intention must be seen as irreducibly Christocentric if continuity with the NT and Christian tradition is to be maintained. From Paul's inherited credal formula recalling that the death and resurrection of Christ took place according to the Scriptures (1 Cor 15) to the Nicene statement that

38. I do not wish to imply that God's intention or the influence of the Spirit are in themselves *(quoad se)* confined to the coalescence of individual texts into the biblical canon, only that we must begin with the whole canonical witness insofar as our investigations into the divine intention are concerned *(quoad nos)*.

39. An emphasis well illustrated by John F. A. Sawyer, *The Fifth Gospel: Isaiah in the History of Christianity* (New York: Cambridge University Press, 1996).

“he rose again in fulfillment of the Scriptures” to *Dei Verbum*’s recognition of Christ as “himself both the mediator and the sum total of Revelation” (2), there is a consistent emphasis that the biblical witness everywhere in some way leads toward or follows from the event of Christ as the primary action of God in the world.[40] This sets the Gospels in a central position, as the most direct and substantive biblical accounts of Jesus’ life, death, and resurrection, where they serve as a foundation with which the rest of Scripture must fit. Yet unlike physical structures, whose foundations are necessarily fixed and immobile, the interpretive foundation here remains somewhat open due to the preservation within the canon of four distinct Gospels with diverse perspectives.

According such an interpretive primacy of place to the Gospels does not require us to imagine that the evangelists dealt with all worthwhile topics, or blot out the significance of other parts of the Bible, but it does provide a starting point. The formal principle of the canon and the material principle of the centrality of Christ function as the main indicators of the divine intention within Scripture, where it can be distinguished from that of the human writers. The qualification is important, since in many instances the two intentions will run together indistinguishably. To take only the clearest case, “You shall love the Lord your God with all your heart, with all your soul, and with all your mind” (Dt 6.5, Mt 22.37 and parallels) presents the same meaning irrespective of divine or human authorship. In other instances, however, it will be possible and even necessary to

40. John of the Cross expresses the point well (*The Ascent of Mount Carmel,* II.22.3) “In giving us his Son, his only Word (for he possesses no other), God spoke everything to us at once in this sole Word”; translation from *The Collected Works of St. John of the Cross,* rev. ed., trans. Kieran Kavanaugh and Otilio Rodriguez, rev. Kieran Kavanaugh (Washington: Institute of Carmelite Studies, 1991). This same Christocentric focus finds related expression in the contemporary prevalence of the Franciscan view, where the motive for the Incarnation is understood as the perfection of creation, with redemption from sin as a concomitant effect, so that the incarnate Christ becomes central to all created being without being limited to a remedial role. Cf. John P. Galvin, “Jesus Christ,” in *Systematic Theology: Roman Catholic Perspectives,* vol. 1, ed. Francis Schüssler Fiorenza and John P. Galvin (Minneapolis: Fortress Press, 1991), 280.

disentangle the dual meanings. Returning to an earlier example, what of "Psalm 137, which . . . pronounces a blessing on anyone who avenges the destruction of the temple by dashing Babylonian children against a rock?" The psalmist's furious grief is unmistakable and the blessing likely to have been understood in the most literal way, yet we may scarcely take this as a meaning intended by the God who shines on just and unjust alike.

Here and in other cases the wider scriptural context helps to illuminate the passage and establish its role within the framework of God's intention. The Jerusalem for which the psalmist longs, which fuels his anger toward those responsible for the Exile, was not simply a cherished home. It was the city where God and the people of God existed as an ordered community, whose harmony made it possible for "the Lord's song" to be sung (Ps 137.4); and while the Jerusalem of memory is confined to a particular historical setting, the ordered harmony it continues to symbolize forms a constitutive part of God's salvific purpose. If the canon is to be taken as a significant factor in interpretation, it cannot be insignificant that the most sustained biblical description of accomplished salvation finds expression in the image of "the holy city, a new Jerusalem" (Rv 21.9–22.5).[41] The lament in exile from the old Jerusalem then takes shape as an echo of the groans with which creation awaits fulfillment (Rom 8.22–23), and the emotional charge in the words of the psalmist as an example of the sorrow our distance from that eventual redemption should evoke. But because the agent of that redemption is the same Jesus who turned himself and his followers away from vengeful retaliation, we have a legitimate basis to distinguish the psalmist's distress, in which God wishes us to share, from its manifestation in the blessing upon destroyers of Babylonian infants, which he does not. Similarly, when Hebrews denies the possibility of repentance and forgiveness for apostasy (6.4–8), the contrast with the Jesus who forgives the apostasy of Peter and requires an unlimited practice of forgiveness by others would tend to show that while the writer of Hebrews does well to take human sin

41. Cf. Wilfrid Harrington, *Revelation* (Collegeville, Minn.: Liturgical Press, 1993), 212–20.

and failure seriously, the conclusion that he draws is subject to qualification.[42]

One could devise additional examples, but these are intended only as illustrations of the main point: recognition of the canon in general and the Gospels in particular as legitimate guides to the purpose of God at work in the Bible makes it possible to discern the divine communicative intention in given instances where it may differ from the intention of the human writer. An explicit acknowledgment of this factor within frameworks of historical-critical interpretation would represent a significant advance, for God's authorial intent operating at the canonical level could provide a principled basis for integrating diverse biblical witnesses into a more coherent whole and so balance a tendency inherited from Spinoza to divide the Bible into ever smaller portions bound ever more tightly to the circumstances of the past. In addition, for reasons noted earlier, there is an inherent theological necessity for the community of faith to see some such divine involvement in the genesis of Scripture. If this need does not find a conscious formulation that safeguards the integrity of historical human writers whose intentions are expressed in the biblical texts, it will be likely to surface in other and less desirable ways. *Naturam expellas furca, tamen usque recurret* [You may drive nature out with a pitchfork, yet she will still return].[43]

GUIDED APPLICATION

These questions of authorial intention are directed to the understanding of Scripture, but understanding forms only a part of the full interpretive movement. It must be completed by application, by engagement with the concrete situation in which the interpreter is acting. Of the figures explored in this book, Juan Luis Segundo insists most strongly on this, and recent concerns for the actualization of the biblical text stem from the same root.[44] De Lubac, echoing Ori-

42. For Hebrews, cf. Harold W. Attridge, *The Epistle to the Hebrews: A Commentary on the Epistle to the Hebrews* (Minneapolis: Fortress Press, 1989), 168–73; he characterizes the denial of post-baptismal repentance as emphatic and unequivocal.

43. Horace, *Epistulae* I.10.24–25; translation my own.

44. Cf. above for Segundo; as for actualization, see Ugo Vanni, “Exegesis and

gen here as elsewhere, would tend to fall in by speaking of the Bible as an ever-present and ever-significant word. Even Brown's distinction between "what the Bible meant and what it means," though initially deployed to justify the possibility of agreement on the former, establishes the latter as its own area of investigation.

Yet while the need for application is widely recognized, there is a marked absence of consensus regarding the approach or procedure to employ in satisfying it. One finds a similar lack of consensus with respect to the role of historical understanding, extending from distant reserve to Segundo's use of history as a threshing fan to separate the wheat of faith from the chaff of ideology and finally to the portrayal of application as mere popularization of historical conclusions. Our effort in this section aims to offer some guidelines for application, consistent with earlier discussion, without pretending to reach so far as a method *sensu stricto* (to which the inherent variability of circumstance poses significant obstacles). Their substance will be drawn from de Lubac, but not without modification. Attention must be given in particular to the placement of his framework within the larger interpretive process of understanding and application, clearly delineating its relationship with historical interpretations focused upon authorial intent. It was precisely the lack of differentiation in that area that helped to confine the impact of his work to the history rather than the practice of interpretation.

Resources and adjustments

One may question the priority given de Lubac, considering that the topic at hand is less central to him than to Segundo. In addition to the greater theoretical emphasis present in the latter's work, the influence of the Latin American theology that he represents has been a major factor behind the increasing importance placed on genuine engagement between the present situation and the biblical writings. But however compellingly drawn the necessity of application may

---

Actualization in the Light of *Dei Verbum*," in *Vatican II: Assessment and Perspectives,* 1:344–63; Fitzmyer, *Biblical Commission's Document,* 170–76; and Williamson, *Catholic Principles,* 289–302.

be, or praiseworthy the practical consequences, flaws remain in the explanation used to ground the practice. Some have already been noted in reviewing Segundo's account, but one in particular assumes a higher profile at this stage: the incompatibility with even a moderate primacy for authorial intention. The value of Scripture for him lies in its transmission of certain transcendent values (faith) as they find categorical expression across a variety of socio-historical circumstances (ideology). The various authors and their texts, taken individually as human communications, present faith and ideology intertwined. Historical tools directed toward the situations in which the texts took shape allow the values to be sifted from their ideological expression, and then the contemporary adherent to the same transcendent values may find ideological means appropriate in the present to express the same values. The second step benefits less from the substance of the Bible than from its multiple examples of the transition from values to ideology; consequently, what the Bible does proves to be more significant than what it says. This puts the communicative intention of the author at some distance from the main areas of concern, holding at best a tertiary place. Such a move cannot be reconciled with the emphasis given above to authors' intentions as a primary objective in interpretation.[45]

De Lubac's approach proves to be a more productive resource because of its intrinsic connections with authorial meaning and the Christocentric perspective used to move toward engagement with the present. The former element would appear more clearly were it not for a stress on the continuing activity of the Spirit in and through Scripture that in practice overshadows the intentions of the biblical writers. Nonetheless, the need to grasp what those writers meant to communicate within their own situations is strongly affirmed; this serves as an indispensable starting point.[46] One also finds a primacy

45. To the extent that God's authorial role is also a feature of the present argument, Segundo's difficulties with Scripture as a unique and unsurpassable medium of revelation due to divine involvement represent another point of conflict.

46. This stress appears to be a corrective measure, to counter an over-focus on the mechanics of the writers' inspiration. By contrast, while the continuing activity of the Spirit is equally indispensable for Segundo, there the Bible starts as a source to be excavated rather than a foundation to be developed.

given to the kerygmatic presentations of the four Gospels, which fits well with the role outlined for them above as privileged indicators of divine intention. With regard to technique, the middle term in transitions from the literal sense to additional levels of meaning is always grounded in some facet of the reality of Christ. This is the key feature separating the Christian use of allegory from its Greek parallel, even though de Lubac is sometimes forced to distill greater unanimity from his sources on this point than they in fact possess. Its value here lies in the potential assistance provided to the movement of application by a structural guidance that goes deeper than individual caprice or ingenuity, and in its inherent links with the wider body of Christian teaching.

For this value to be realized, some adjustments are required. A certain lack of clarity in parts of de Lubac's account has to be cleared away if it is to function as part of a larger way of reading. At the outset, there is a question of terminology. The name applied to these extended meanings or to the process used to develop them varies between "spiritual sense," "spiritual understanding," and "spiritual exegesis."[47] This lacks significance in itself, as the variants are used interchangeably, but raises a problem. To speak of spiritual understanding or spiritual exegesis implicitly sets them in contrast with non-spiritual understanding and non-spiritual exegesis, to the effective detriment of the latter. In the context of the present discussion, where understanding refers mainly to the grasp of authorial intention as communicated in the biblical texts, the terms also generate confusion. Maintaining a clear distinction between the movements of understanding and application is essential, for while they should not be separated, neither should they be mixed. The best way to forestall difficulties and yet remain consistent with the older tradition is to restrict the usage to "spiritual sense," which carries overtones of meaning rather than procedure. Though continued use of "spiritual" as the qualifying adjective does leave a door open to implicit negative comparisons, that can be addressed without dropping an explicit

47. The same tendency continues in more recent work, such as Wilken, "In Defense of Allegory," 197–212, or Denis Farkasfalvy, "A Heritage in Search of Heirs: the Future of Ancient Christian Exegesis," *Communio* 25 (1998): 505–19.

connection with the Spirit by attention to the larger arena in which the spiritual sense operates.

As necessary as clarity of terms may be, the more important shift to de Lubac's account lies in the precise station allotted to the spiritual sense in the process of interpretation. Sequence matters here, because it determines both the resources at hand and the goals to which they are turned. The spiritual sense, with its extended meanings, functions as an instrument for applying or actualizing the biblical witness in the present setting of the interpreter and not as a privileged or alternative understanding of the witness itself. The traditional assertion that the spiritual sense depends on the *res* and not the *verba* catches only some of the point. The spiritual sense does begin from the substance of what is understood in the biblical texts (the dual communicative intention of its authors expressed in the words), but that is not sufficient without the immediate circumstances provided by a given interpretive environment. Much as a second point defines a specific line out of the infinite options established by a first point, so also does a specific set of circumstances make it possible to draw out further meaning from an understanding grasp of the biblical realities. This expands upon an observation made by Aquinas, taking the lion as an example; if we are to find particular significance beyond the author's intention in some biblical reference to such a beast, there must be an intervening factor that generates it. For Thomas, the factor in this case would have been knowledge of lions and their nature or the literal understanding of another part of Scripture. Yet that still leaves a great deal indeterminate inasmuch as both the zoology of lions and the literal sense of the Bible are wide areas of investigation. Consequently, for us the crucial factor is the setting of interpreter and audience as it presents a specific constellation of needs and interests, which guide the encounter with the biblical text by indicating which aspects of what has been understood are to be pursued. The pursuit takes place within a broadly Christocentric framework (to be outlined below), and its substantive results do involve the sort of knowledge that Thomas mentions, but the sine qua non lies in that immediate context of audience and interpreter.

When the effective function of the spiritual sense is portrayed in this way, as a bridge between past intention and present situation, some of the difficulties associated with the notion start to diminish. The point of departure lies in the passage or passages of Scripture at hand, viewed as instruments of communication shaped both by humans in a given socio-historical setting and by God as part of a larger canonical whole. A clear grasp of the literal meaning in all these particulars is indispensable; without it, there is no basis on which to work and no indication where to begin. As for the destination, it is established by the conjunction of the biblical text with an interpreter and audience in their socio-historical setting with its own specific needs. In contrast with the initial situation, which is at least in theory one and the same for all who pursue it even as dispute continues about the details, what we may call the immediate environment is by its nature varied and multiple. The latter's range can extend from the most general, as with a commentary or monograph intended for a wide public no better defined than "early-twenty-first-century North Americans," to the most specific, as with a conference given by one of their own to a stable parish or religious community. Yet the potential variation is finally reduced to concrete actuality in every individual case, providing the actual circumstances whose features must be understood if there is to be direction in the engagement with biblical meaning.[48] If we may step back from the details of transcendental philosophy, the need for a grasp of both past and present is well illustrated by a line from Kant: "Thoughts without content are empty; intuitions without concepts are blind."[49] Just as both elements are required for cognition in the First Critique, so here does productive use of the spiritual sense derive its foundation from authorial intent and its focus from present concerns.

When this is kept in the foreground, one can largely avoid the am-

48. Segundo's initial stress on combining "the disciplines that open up the past with the disciplines that help to explain the present" caught the point well; cf. *Liberation of Theology*, 8.

49. A51/B75; translation from *Critique of Pure Reason*, trans. Werner S. Pluhar (Indianapolis: Hackett, 1996).

biguity with regard to particular circumstances that mars modern attempts to revive the spiritual sense. A major impediment to the success of de Lubac's efforts was the lack of intrinsic connection between the literal and spiritual senses of a given passage, stemming from a tendency to see any specific interpretation as but the "small change" of the great allegory or transformation worked upon the meaning of Scripture by the event of Christ.[50] So long as that principle was secure, the success or failure of its individual uses was almost a matter of indifference. Links between the literal and the spiritual sense of the one and the same text could fend for themselves, if there were support for the extended meaning elsewhere on the literal level. Emphasis on an author's intentional communication conveyed through the words, taking into account the duality of biblical authorship, helps to reduce the problem by enhancing the importance of the text at hand. The words there are shaped as bearers of particular meaning within the literary structure of book and canon, and directed toward only a part of the larger whole that is the narrative of salvation, as a consequence of the author's intention in forming the details of the text. The limitations of human expression through language necessarily impose some such requirement; one cannot say or write everything one wishes to all at once in a single burst.[51] The same requirement then falls upon the spiritual sense if it is to serve as an application of a particular text. In order to be an extension rather than a creation of meaning, individual uses of the spiritual sense must share in the intended subject of the text even as they explore aspects of that subject going beyond the scope of authorial intention.

Qui venit in nomine Domini

With the "whence" of the spiritual sense established by the shaped intention of the text and the "whither" by the circumstances of interpreter and audience, the next question to arise is the "how." By what

50. "Old Distich," 122.

51. Cf. Plato's reservations about written communications (*Phaedrus* 275a–e), or even speech in general (*Letter VII* 341c–344d). The former find at least some echo within the Christian tradition, cf. Papias's preference for the *viva voce* (Eusebius, *Ecclesiastical History* III.39.3).

means does the transition from past meaning to present situation take place? An answer that provides some degree of concrete guidance is necessary, if references to the spiritual sense are to be more than a hand-waving cover for random improvisations. Once this answer is in hand, the fixed structure beneath the variation becomes apparent. As de Lubac recognized, despite the sheer number of readings, their impetus can be traced back to one dynamic movement of application. He consistently emphasized that fundamental unity-in-motion, even as it caused him a certain amount of difficulty, and a similar effort is required of us to ensure that neither the unity nor the dynamism is neglected. If the former dissolves, the spiritual sense becomes an accidental bundle of *ad hoc* connections; if the latter disappears, the spiritual sense degenerates into a mechanical exercise of deciphering hieroglyphs.

While metaphors drawn from physical movement may help to maintain a proper balance between stability and flexibility, inasmuch as common experience tends to offer a range of choices for making one and the same journey, that is little more than a happy coincidence of language, which can support an argument without being one in its own right. A more coherent account begins with the principle taken above as a basis for the material unity of the Bible. Just as a concern for understanding what God intended to communicate through Scripture leads to a substantive focus on Christ as the primary manifestation of God in the world, so also a concern for applying the biblical witness takes direction from the understood reality of Christ as it seeks to bring that reality to concrete expression in particular situations. An image that holds a central position is that of a triple Advent. As de Lubac put it, albeit for illustrative purposes:

> The first coming . . . achieves the work of redemption which is continued in the Church and its sacraments: it is the object of allegory properly speaking. The second coming . . . takes place in the soul of each disciple, and it is tropology which explains it. The third coming is reserved for the "consummation of the age," when Christ will appear in his glory and seek out his own to be with him: this is the object of anagogy.[52]

52. *Exégèse médiévale* II.621. Susan Wood's tracing of the linkage between

For us the idea can play a more significant role. Deriving the facets of the spiritual sense from the different modes whereby we can speak of Jesus becoming present and active in the world provides a framework for application that is both structured and open. Structured, since there is in the notion of Advent a genuine threefold aspect that is stable and bound to core elements of Christian teaching.[53] And yet open, since its character as a process does not predetermine which part of the complex reality of Christ is to be drawn out in particular cases. That can be left to the mutual interaction of intended subject and interpretive situation without losing any of their detail.

An additional benefit in adoption of this guiding metaphor of Advent is foreshadowed by the discussion of Origen above. One of the Alexandrian's hallmarks was an insistence on the applicability of the Bible in whatever circumstances may be at hand. The task of realizing this potential in particular cases could be entrusted to the individual Christian interpreter, with confidence that the Spirit at work in the genesis of Scripture would also be active in its ongoing use. While the Spirit's role will be brought up below, the point itself can be made in terms of the present argument. It is possible to ground the affirmation of Scripture's universal applicability in the same divine purpose that establishes the biblical canon as a meaningful whole with a Christocentric focus. Because the Bible is intended by God as an instrument of communication, and so necessarily implies a receiver or audience, God's intention takes that audience into account. More accurately, it takes *those* audiences into account, for though human authors are not aware of the full and actual range of their potential audiences, God is.[54] While this awareness does not overcome the limitations that "the circumstances of the letter" impose upon human

---

de Lubac's approach to the spiritual sense and his ecclesiology also picks up on the modes and theme of presence; see *Spiritual Exegesis and the Church*, 59–63.

53. The current Roman Rite offers a pleasing echo in one of its eucharistic acclamations: "Christ has died, Christ is risen, Christ will come again."

54. This is the principal grain of truth in Thomas's acceptance of multiple literal senses as a consequence of God's infinite understanding. The difference for us is that it falls on the side of application, rather than generating an indefinite multitude of literal understandings.

language, it can expand the scope of application by providing a linkage between authorial purpose and contingent application that is uniquely biblical. So long as one begins from meaning as expressed in a text, in the attempt to pursue further dimensions of that meaning suited to the particular needs of one's situation, we may say in the case of Scripture that such applications not only agree with but are somehow included in God's intention.

Use of the threefold Advent as an architectonic tool in forming applications strengthens their link with textual intent by rendering it more specific. This is a valuable service, for there would be a flawed element in the argument if it were based solely on God's grasp of the differing receptions given to the biblical text. That point does set up a firmer connection between intention and application with respect to the Bible, but the contribution is almost entirely formal, and one finds in it little assistance as to the substance of potential connections. Starting with the infinite divine knowledge can guarantee possibility, yet finite intellects need something more to reduce possibility to act in particular cases. Focus on the ways in which Christ becomes present in the world provides that necessary supplement, and does so as a consequence of God's purpose at work in Scripture. To the extent that the general *skopos* governing the canon finds its substance in the Christ-event, contingent applications of particular texts may with some confidence set their own goal as bringing the significance of that event to a present situation. While parallelism of purpose by itself is perhaps not an adequate foundation for confidence, or for speaking of such applications as genuine senses of the text, it can prove sufficient when joined with an explicit recognition that no interpretive audience or situation escapes the divine author's concern.

The balance of this section traces out some further consequences of this shared concern and purpose. De Lubac drew the image of Advent into a correspondence with the three classical levels of the spiritual sense, and what is said presupposes his explanation of them. Yet the anchors of intention and application require here, as they did above, adjustment in the traditional framework. The most striking concerns the role of allegory, and represents a significant nod toward a position taken by Childs: there may after all be a relevant difference between the apostolic and the post-apostolic situation.

The standard practice of allegory depended on reading biblical realities in light of the act of Christ, understood in the broadest fashion, in order to see that action foreshadowed or illuminated in what had gone before. Its initial impetus came from the New Testament in general, and Paul in particular, as they reflected the sustained reexamination of Israel's Bible taking place among the first Christian generations. There the paschal kerygma upheld by the Spirit had provided the lens through which the entire body of Scripture was viewed; notwithstanding its importance, the biblical witness was ultimately and clearly subordinate to the living Christian experience.[55] (In terms of the present argument, all or nearly all interpretation in this environment was application.) When de Lubac took this apostolic or immediate sub-apostolic period and its procedures as a direct model for the use of allegory, though, he neglected to consider the impact made by the addition of the written New Testament to the canon. Correction of this oversight leads to an understanding of allegory that differs from its exemplar without being unfaithful to it.

The position of the apostolic community in the face of the only scripture known to them can be seen in a remark of Paul's (2 Cor 3.15–16): "To this day, in fact, whenever Moses is read, a veil lies over their hearts, but whenever a person turns to the Lord the veil is removed." It is not that the reading itself changes but that an impediment to understanding is lifted from the hearer. The new perception that follows depends on that change in the subject if it is to elevate itself beyond fantasy. The change is not entirely "subjective" in the pejorative sense, since it does have a cognitive component in the kerygmatic message, which reveals the significance of God's actions in Christ. However, despite its consequences for understanding the scriptures of Israel, this new perception is not strictly speaking the re-

55. Cf. de Lubac above; and also Hays, *Echoes of Scripture*, 154: "Entering into 'the knowledge of the glory of God in the face of Jesus Christ' (2 Cor 4.6) liberates believers from bondage to a circumscribed reading of the old covenant and empowers them to read it with freedom—more precisely, to live it with freedom—as a witness to the righteousness of God in Jesus Christ."

sult of interpretation (as the term has been discussed here) inasmuch as it stems from lived experience and oral communication rather than encounter with written texts. The difference is similar to that between a new reading of *Les Misérables* based upon a comprehensive review of the book and one based upon family traditions about Victor Hugo's aims and purposes set out by a descendant living in a disadvantaged Parisian neighborhood. As interesting and thought-provoking as the latter might be, one could rightfully question its adequacy as an interpretation of the text. As the discussion of authorial intent has already noted, casting a communicative intention into writing lends it a stability that resembles the fixed form imposed upon clay by the kiln; the work itself is the measure of the writer's intention and skill just as the pottery is of the potter's. Other sources of knowledge will certainly be relevant to a better understanding, be they biographical, historical, linguistic, or literary, but the degree of relevance is measured by their ability to shed light on what is written. Every text thus becomes in a sense a *norma non normata* for its own interpretation. Recognition that the first Christian writings take a different approach that renders the older scriptures quite *normata* accounts for much of the modern reserve shown toward their practice.[56]

When these writings come to be received as Scripture in their own right, though, the situation assumes a different aspect. Their interpretive moves are not invalidated, but instead reshaped and stabilized. As Rahner noted, this is a general result of the canonization process: "the church objectifies its faith and its life in written documents, and it recognizes these objectifications as so pure and so successful that they are able to hand on the apostolic church as a norm for future ages."[57] With respect to the Bible, the experience that generates a rereading of the OT in terms of Christ achieves a fixed ex-

56. As most clearly illustrated in this investigation by Childs. Others show an equal reserve toward a focus on intention; however, for reasons discussed earlier in this chapter, that is not a viable response.

57. Rahner, *Foundations,* 373; cf. 374–75 for the constitutive role of the Spirit, which distinguishes this recognition from a secular organization's formulation of a "mission statement."

pression in the NT. While this ensures its continued accessibility, it also means that for the future this experience is mediated by and dependent upon the texts comprising the NT witness. That is the essential shift, for with it the Christian use of Scripture becomes not only a rereading but also a reading. There is a directness in the NT presentation of the apostolic preaching and teaching, revealing "the plan of the mystery hidden from ages past in God" (Eph 3.9), which no longer requires a veil to be lifted from the hearts of the audience. It could be understood on the level of ordinary interpretation, from the sense of the words as they conveyed the meaning of their authors.[58] A Christocentric approach to the OT then appears as a way of using the clear and distinct to shed light on what is less evident, guaranteed by the knowledge that "long ago God spoke to our ancestors in many and various ways by the prophets, but in these last days he has spoken to us by a Son" (Heb 1.1–2), and taking models for imitation from particular instances found in the apostolic writings.[59]

The consequence of this is to narrow the scope of the spiritual sense by transferring part of its subject into the realm of understanding. For de Lubac, the special concern of allegory within the larger framework is "the work of redemption which is continued in the Church and its sacraments," and its task is to trace the significance of prior figures and events in relation to the accomplishment of that initial Advent.[60] But where this was a matter of application for the ini-

58. Affirmation of the biblical writings as truly revealing "the plan of the mystery" may still be seen as a result of the active presence of the Spirit, or encounters with Scripture as also opening a door for the Spirit's work, but not necessarily the work of understanding per se.

59. Hays's *Echoes of Scripture* being a signal example of this, along with the classical paths outlined by de Lubac; a fruitful conversation could be had, and is already underway to an extent, regarding the specific lessons to be learned from the history of interpretation, and their programmatic implications for the present, so long as a slavish and antiquarian repetition is avoided. Remarks such as Thomas Oden's that "there is precious little of enduring value in exegesis that was not known by the fifth century" (quoted in Michael Cahill, "The History of Exegesis and Our Theological Future," *Theological Studies* 61 [2000]: 341 n. 27) demonstrate that some fail to avoid it. Cahill's article itself is a useful review of the present scene, as is the slightly varying perspective of Marie Anne Mayeski, "Quaestio Disputata: Catholic Theology and the History of Exegesis," *Theological Studies* 62 (2001): 140–53.

60. *Exégèse médiévale* II.621.

tial Christian generations, for the later community, which possesses both OT and NT in tandem, that is not the case. Inclusion of the NT in the body of authoritative Scripture provides a stable if many-sided narrative and explanatory center to God's action. Drawing what had gone before into more explicit connection with that center then becomes a matter of discerning purpose and meaning operative at the level of the canonical whole. There is almost nothing of application in reading Isaiah's Servant Songs and the Akedah as echoes or illuminations of Christ, for example, nor in bringing the Red Sea and baptism together. Connections of that sort take place among the *gesta Dei* found in the biblical witness, between the preparatory and the decisive stages of redemption, and not between past intention and present situation. This need not alter the ways of articulating such connections, leaving many of the traditional procedures open to further use, but it does alter their position. The kinds of readings associated with allegory in the narrow meaning of the term—for example, portraying the Song of Songs in light of the relationship between Christ and the Church—cease to be instances of the spiritual sense in action. Instead, they form part of the dual authorial meaning as discussed in the first half of this chapter.

Shifting allegory itself away from the spiritual sense may seem odd, but it follows closely and perhaps necessarily from a recognition of the unique human and divine agency in the Bible. The larger framework may even benefit, inasmuch as allegory serves as a basis for additional readings. To return to an image, the first Advent draws the full array of biblical realities into formation around itself and so makes it possible to speak of a second and third Advent, where the effects of the first come to fruition in varying ways. The treatment here leaves the substance of that initial stage unaltered, but it does provide a more solid account of the interrelated intentions embodied in Scripture. This increases the epistemic stability of traditional allegory by linking it with biblical meaning in a way that respects both human and divine authors. Other components of the classic spiritual sense can then function as more or less pure instances of application, subject only to a correct understanding of the text or texts in question; with that qualification, the explanation of the moral and anagogical levels given above during our consideration of de Lubac may be taken as a model.[61]

"Moved by the Holy Spirit"

Our initial discussion of authors and their intentions recognized the range of contending opinions without making a direct attempt to settle the matter, because of the complexity of the hermeneutic issues involved. It was sufficient for present purposes, given the plurality of philosophical opinion, that at least some of those opinions justified the reading of texts as intentional communications shaped by their writers. Theological concerns for continuity with the witness of Israel and the apostolic church could then generate a sufficient predisposition toward such approaches to effect a practical resolution of the question. A roughly similar pattern comes into play here as the treatment of application draws to a close, for there are also a number of different ways for bringing a text to bear on a given interpretive situation. One was traced with some detail in the examination of Segundo, and others could have been chosen.[62] Yet while hermeneutical considerations need not necessarily grant precedence to the modified account of the spiritual sense given in this section, theological factors may.

Among the evaluative criteria recalled at the beginning of this chapter was consonance with tradition, understood in this case as the interpretive practices found in the NT. Fidelity to the witness of the NT can be said to require this, inasmuch as a certain approach to the Bible plays a constitutive role in the kerygma itself, and to do otherwise represents a failure to attend to the conditions of possibility for Christian faith that is closely akin to sawing off the branch one

61. William F. Murphy, "Henri de Lubac's Mystical Tropology," *Communio* 27 (2000): 171–201, provides a recent example of reconsidering the present situation, especially with respect to the linkage between Scripture and ethics.

62. Although laid out in terms of general approaches to the Bible rather than the specific topic of application, the wide range of contemporary options can be seen in John Barton, ed., *The Cambridge Companion to Biblical Interpretation* (Cambridge: Cambridge University Press, 1998), 9–180.

is sitting on. Some of this has already figured in the discussion, but our present concern is with the role allotted to the Holy Spirit. As has been mentioned, the NT writers in their various ways all emphasized the fulfillment of God's saving promises in Christ. This provided the standpoint from which they read the Scripture they knew, and it would appear to constitute an invariant element of subsequent Christian faith. There is an almost equally consistent emphasis on the involvement of the Spirit. In Paul it is the gift of the Spirit that effects turning to the Lord or participating in the mind of Christ and makes it possible for the Christian reader to discern the underlying significance of the biblical text, "written down to instruct us" (1 Cor 10.11). With John the truth into which the Paraclete will lead the disciples includes among other things the recognition that the scriptures of Israel bear witness to Jesus (5.39). Other examples could be drawn from the remainder of the NT without going beyond translation of a common insight into the theological vernacular of individual writings.[63] A glance at the classic *loci* in the NT for what would become the notion of biblical inspiration, 2 Timothy 3.15–16 and 2 Peter 20–21, further shows the connection with the immediate use of Scripture in the life of the community; the past agency of the Spirit with respect to the text serves for the most part as a form of quality assurance for the reliability of its current function. The point is made explicitly in 2 Timothy with a view to the rising generation of leadership, and in a more implicit but no less real fashion in 2 Peter. There the direct reference is to the prophets who were "moved by the Holy Spirit" rather than the Bible, but the rhetorical purpose is to confirm for the readers that the same Spirit is behind the kerygma presented to them (in contrast to the false teachings supplied by private inter-

63. This is of course one element within the Spirit's general task of empowering and mediating the reconciled *koinonia* between God and humans in light of Jesus' resurrection and ascension. See Yves Congar, *I Believe in the Holy Spirit,* trans. David Smith (New York: Crossroad, 1997), 3–64, for a classic summary of the biblical material within the context of a comprehensive review of pneumatology. With respect to Paul, see Hays's *Echoes of Scripture,* as well as the massive work of Gordon Fee, *God's Empowering Presence: The Holy Spirit in the Letters of Paul* (Peabody, Mass.: Hendrickson, 1994). For John, the point was made above via a criticism of Segundo.

pretation and condemned in the second chapter of the letter).[64] The matter can perhaps be summarized by saying that an active presence of the Spirit, on the side both of the interpreter and of the text, forms an integral aspect of engagement with the Bible.

Together with a Christocentric focus for biblical meaning, such a recognition of the Spirit at work helps to provide a substantive baseline for what it means to be consonant with the NT approach to Scripture. Although the two principles are not of themselves sufficient for a complete way of reading, an interpretive framework should take them into account in order to be fully successful as an instrument of Christian theology. Adoption of the spiritual sense as outlined here goes far toward achieving this, for its acknowledgment of an active component derived from faith and borne by the Spirit not only fits the portrait of interaction with Scripture given by the NT but also helps to ensure that the role of explicit faith is neither relegated to an extrinsic motivation nor absorbed by some general theory of the religious classic. When the weight of the spiritual sense is seen to fall mainly on the side of application, with the Spirit's influence upon text and interpreter combining to bring out the significance of Christ for a particular environment and situation, pressure is reduced and a space opened where understanding of the communicative intentions that shaped the text for specific historical and canonical contexts can be pursued.

CONCLUSION

The strategy adopted at the outset of this project was indirect. Rather than address the points of friction between classical and modern approaches to the Bible head-on, the focus turned toward a series of figures committed personally and professionally to historical scholarship as well as the community of faith. That alone was not a

64. See Raymond Collins, "Inspiration," 1024–27. The article reveals a relative lack of engagement with the topic in recent years, due perhaps to weariness but more positively to a recovery of the NT's essentially functional account of inspiration. Gerald O'Collins and Daniel Kendall, *The Bible for Theology: Ten Principles for the Theological Use of Scripture* (Mahwah: Paulist Press, 1997), ends with a brief appendix (163–70) that also insists on the active and explicit role of the Spirit.

unique factor, given the number of scholars with similar commitment, and neither was sheer stature as theologians. Their main value as examples stemmed instead from the efforts each made to develop an account of Scripture and its use that was adequate to the demands of both faith and historical criticism, without abandoning one or the other. Analysis and critique of the varying attempts then provided a set of resources for bringing together an essay in aid of a synthesis. The reasons for adopting this procedure were both pragmatic and substantive. To say nothing else, confining the range of investigation to a given set of thinkers made it possible to set reasonable bounds to the scope of the project. The more substantive concern came from the long history of conflict between theological and historical perspectives on the Bible, which fostered significant doubts as to the possibility, let alone the success, of any rapprochement between them. To begin with real individuals whose existential adherence to both perspectives was clear, if perhaps not always explicitly reasoned out, was a way of affirming their fundamental compatibility.

Now that the project has been completed, such as it is, it will be worthwhile to consider how far the compatibility extends. True compatibility is more than the absence of conflict and has to include a genuine mutuality or shared experience; the etymological roots of the word imply as much. In this case effective compatibility requires that there be tasks and functions of mutual value on each side. Historical-critical perspectives need to be of service to the community of faith, and similarly, theological approaches ought to be of some use in the historical enterprise. Without claiming to exhaust the range of potential options, the particular account given here does offer something to satisfy these concerns.

The advantages that accrue to theological use of the Bible from modern historical scholarship have to do with preserving continuity and maintaining distance. As noted earlier, there is an intrinsic need for Christian reflection to remain in contact with the experience of biblical Israel and the apostolic Church. Inasmuch as the main avenue of access to that experience consists in the written communicative intentions shaped by the biblical writers and preserved in Scripture, the skills and knowledge derived from the full use of historical-critical tools have an essential role. Formal acknowledgment of this was a major achievement of Catholic theology in the past century (even as the process of integrating all its material implications continues).[65] The same skills and knowledge are also necessary with respect to God's communicative intention, which becomes accessible only through the ensemble of human intentions gathered into the biblical canon. There can be no real grasp of the former that does not run through the latter. Important as the continuity is, however, the maintenance of discontinuity is equally important and perhaps a more uniquely modern contribution. Clear recognition of historicity as a conditioning factor in human existence generates an increased sensitivity to the features that distinguish one historical setting from another. This helps balance the stress on continuity, which sometimes can blur or erase those differences in much the same way as Renaissance painters clothing ancient Romans in the dress of fifteenth-century Italians. A striking example of the service rendered by a grasp of discontinuity is the contemporary appreciation of the diversity within late Second Temple Judaism. Reading the Reformation debates over law and gospel back into that situation not only was mistaken, but also contributed to radical distortions of the relationship between Christianity and later Judaism.[66]

The value of theological perspective to historical engagement with the biblical text is perhaps less apparent, and more particular to certain concerns and situations, but no less real. Part of the reason that Troeltsch represented classic historical criticism in the first chapter was the lack of influence from the doubts expressed in Nietzsche's *On the Advantage and Disadvantage of History for Life* (1874). Horizons and the role of historical knowledge in the present have been an issue ever since Nietzsche began to be taken seriously, and a

65. Recent articles from Joseph Fitzmyer and Roland Murphy (see bibliography) also raise the issue, sharing Brown's concern that the integration of history may fail to take root.

66. E. P. Sanders, *Paul and Palestinian Judaism*, 33–238, especially 33–59; a similar example without such harmful consequences is drawn out by Pesch, "Paul as Professor of Theology."

hermeneutics of authorial intention does not extinguish the topic. Segundo's focus on the effective consequences of biblical study, dissatisfaction with monadic and exclusive uses of historical tools, and an increasing emphasis on actualization: all these go to show the need for some principled way of bringing the historically understood Bible into vital connection with contemporary existence. While there are a number of ways this could be done, choosing an option explicitly grounded in theology offers significant benefits. Varied as individual backgrounds and traditions may be, little sociology of knowledge is required to recognize that the greater share of active biblical researchers, together with their audience, operate within the community of Christian belief.[67] A productive and positive place for theological application and use of Scripture helps to prevent this basic circumstance from degenerating into a form of multiple personality disorder, as though individuals could be of one mind in the classroom and another in the church. The tasks of those venues are different, but one and the same subject should be able to perform them without fear of working at cross-purposes.[68]

It is the absence of an understanding such as the one proposed here that endangers the integrity of the historical-critical task, by fostering an impression of disengagement or conflict between faith and history that a discipline concerned for its own conditions of possibility would do well to avoid. One already sees the (hesitant or perhaps resigned) suggestion that

> the academic establishment allow two branches of Biblical studies to emerge, of parallel authority in the "guild": a secular approach to Scriptural interpretation, open to non-believer and former believers, as well as to believers who prefer to approach the Bible simply on historical terms;

67. Although derived from anecdotal evidence and personal experience, the point does not seem a difficult one. Even on the most pragmatic level, the bar for professional competence in biblical studies is set high enough to demand religious commitment or another equally strong motive in order to reach it.

68. It is surely troubling when the head of a popular diocesan biblical program can say that teachers with training in Bible beyond an M.A. are not normally brought in, because "for many who get their doctorates, it's hard to come back" to helping contemporary people engage Scripture (Peter S. Williamson, "Actualization: A New Emphasis in Catholic Scripture Study," *America* [May 20, 1995]: 19).

and an explicitly theological approach, which asks not simply textual and historical questions, but questions of how Christians might hear and use Biblical texts today, in the context of the whole tradition of a Biblically grounded Christian faith.[69]

If such a division between historical and theological tasks were ever woven into the structure of advanced studies, it would mean that a distinction of stages within one single process of exegesis had broken down into separate enterprises. The past record indicates that with history held apart from the actual use of Scripture in the life of Christian communities, the practice of history tends to fade into irrelevance or undergo actual suppression.[70]

Attention to these potential difficulties, emphasizing the biblical canon as an ensemble of voices given an intentional *skopos* by the action of God in Christ, which establishes open guidelines for application across a range of situations, makes it possible to avoid conflict and forestall disengagement. On the one hand, entirely theological concerns in conjunction with historicity as a core component of human existence provide a free space for the full employment of critical resources upon the biblical text. On the other hand, acknowledgment of divine intentionality constituting Scripture as a canonical unity creates avenues for theological reflection and application. This rests in clear dependence on faith, but in a way that requires attention to the human goals and circumstances of individual texts in order to discern what God may mean by them. Applications of the biblical witness to a particular situation can then build upon that foundation, even as the freedom and confidence of the Spirit allows for adjustment to the needs and circumstances at hand. If the overall prospect of such an approach portrays a complex interaction of historical and theological components, it is no more than could be expected. The lesser words parallel and reflect the greater Word; the de-

69. Daley, "Patristic Exegesis," 215; it should be clear that Daley does not see this as a desirable outcome, but perhaps the only way to clear space today for an openly theological reading and application of the Bible.

70. Irrelevance with respect to Jerome and the Victorines, active rejection of historical studies with the Modernist crisis, and perhaps a mixture with Richard Simon.

rivative *communicatio idiomatum* involved in saying that "the words of God, expressed in the words of men, are in every way like human language, just as the Word of the eternal Father, when he took on himself the flesh of human weakness, became like men" cannot be a one-way street.[71]

71. *Dei Verbum* 13; the argument of Lewis Ayres and Stephen E. Fowl, "Misreading the Face of God: *The Interpretation of the Bible in the Church*," *Theological Studies* 60 (1999): 513–28, that *DV* 13's Christological parallel does not necessarily require attention to the human and historical intention of biblical writers as a foundation is without merit as an interpretation of the conciliar document, and derived from a postmodern allergy to the notion of authorial meaning.

BIBLIOGRAPHY

Aageson, James W. *Written Also for Our Sake: Paul and the Art of Biblical Interpretation.* Louisville: John Knox, 1993.

Achtemeier, Paul J. *The Inspiration of Scripture.* Philadelphia: Fortress Press, 1980.

Aillet, Marc. *Lire la Bible avec S. Thomas.* Fribourg Suisse: Editions Universitaires, 1993.

Akkerman, Fokke. "Le caractère rhétorique du Traité théologico-politique." In *Spinoza entre lumière et romantisme.* Fontenay-aux-Roses: E.N.S., 1985.

Alonso Schokel, Luis. *The Inspired Word.* Translated by Francis Martin. New York: Herder and Herder, 1965.

Alter, Robert. *The World of Biblical Literature.* New York: Basic Books, 1992.

Anatolios, Khaled. "Christ, Scripture, and the Christian Story of Meaning in Origen." *Gregorianum* 78 (1997): 55–77.

Attridge, Harold W. *The Epistle to the Hebrews: A Commentary on the Epistle to the Hebrews.* Minneapolis: Fortress Press, 1989.

Ayres, Lewis, and Stephen E. Fowl. "Misreading the Face of God: *The Interpretation of the Bible in the Church.*" *Theological Studies* 60 (1999): 513–28.

Bagley, Paul J. "Harris, Strauss, and Esotericism in Spinoza's *Tractatus theologico-politicus.*" *Interpretation* 23 (1996): 387–415.

Baker, David L. *Two Testaments, One Bible: A Study of Some Modern Solutions to the Theological Problem of the Relationship between the Old and New Testaments.* Downers Grove: InterVarsity, 1976.

——. "Typology and the Christian Use of the Old Testament." *Scottish Journal of Theology* 29 (1976): 137–57.

Barker, Patrick G. "Allegory and Typology in Galatians 4:21–31." *St. Vladimir's Theological Quarterly* 38 (1994): 193–209.

Barr, James. *The Bible in the Modern World.* New York: Harper and Row, 1973.

——. *Holy Scripture: Canon, Authority, Criticism.* Philadelphia: Westminster, 1983.

——. "Jowett and the 'Original Meaning' of Scripture." *Religious Studies* 18 (1982): 433–37.

——. "Jowett and the Reading of the Bible 'Like Any Other Book.'" *Horizons in Biblical Theology* 5 (1982–83): 1–44.

——. "The Literal, the Allegorical, and Modern Biblical Scholarship." *Journal for the Study of the Old Testament* 44 (1989): 3–17.

——. *Old and New in Interpretation.* New York: Harper and Row, 1966.

——. "Paul and the LXX: A Note on Some Recent Work." *Journal of Theological Studies* 45 (1994): 593–601.

Barstad, Hans M. "Le canon comme principe exégétique. Autour de la contribution de Brevard S. Childs à une 'herméneutique' de l'Ancien Testament." *Studia theologica* 38 (1984): 85–87.

Barth, Karl. *The Epistle to the Romans*. Translated by Edwyn C. Hoskyns. New York: Oxford University Press, 1968.

Bartlett, D. L. "The Historical Jesus and the Life of Faith." *Christian Century* 109 (6 May 1993): 489–93.

Barton, John. *Reading the Old Testament*. Philadelphia: Westminster, 1984.

——, ed. *The Cambridge Companion to Biblical Interpretation*. Cambridge: Cambridge University Press, 1998.

Bauckham, Richard. "The Brothers and Sisters of Jesus: An Epiphanian Response to John P. Meier." *Catholic Biblical Quarterly* 56 (1994): 686–700.

——. Review of *Biblical Theology of the Old and New Testaments* by Brevard S. Childs. *Biblical Interpretation* 2 (1994): 246–50.

Beauchamp, Paul. "L'interprétation figurative et ses présupposés." *Recherches de science religieuse* 63 (1975): 299–311.

Becker, Jurgen. *Paul: Apostle to the Gentiles*. Translated by O. C. Dean, Jr. Louisville: Westminster/John Knox, 1993.

Beker, J. Christiaan. *Paul the Apostle*. Philadelphia: Fortress Press, 1980.

——. "Paul's Theology: Consistent or Inconsistent?" *New Testament Studies* 34 (1988): 364–77.

Benoit, Pierre. "La plénitude de sens des livres saints." *Revue biblique* 67 (1960): 161–96.

Benoit, Pierre, and Paul Synave. *Prophecy and Inspiration*. Translated by Avery R. Dulles and Thomas L. Sheridan. New York: Descleé, 1961.

Bertoldi, F. "Henri de Lubac on *Dei Verbum*." *Communio* 17 (1990): 88–94.

Bianchi, Enzo. "The Centrality of the Word of God." In *The Reception of Vatican II*, edited by Giuseppe Alberigo, Jean-Pierre Jossua, and Joseph A. Komonchak. Translated by Matthew J. O'Connell. Washington, D.C.: Catholic University of America Press, 1987.

Blanche, A. "Le sens littéral des Écritures d'après S. Thomas d'Aquin." *Revue Thomiste* 14 (1906): 192–212.

Bostock, Gerald. "Allegory and the Interpretation of the Bible in Origen." *Literature and Theology* 1 (1987): 39–53.

Bouyer, Louis. "Point de vue du théologien: théologie catholique et exégèse biblique." In *Qu'est-ce qu'un texte: éléments pour une herméneutique*, edited by Edmond Barbotin. Paris: J. Corti, 1975.

Boyle, John F. "St. Thomas Aquinas and Sacred Scripture." *Pro ecclesia* 4 (1995): 92–104.

Braaten, Carl. "The Problem of the Absoluteness of Christianity." *Interpretation* 40 (1986): 341–53.

Braun, F.-M. *The Work of Père Lagrange*. Edited and translated by Richard T. A. Murphy. Milwaukee: Bruce Publishing, 1963.

Brett, Mark G. "Against the Grain: Brevard Childs' *Biblical Theology of the Old and New Testaments: Theological Reflections on the Christian Bible*." *Modern Theology* 10 (1994): 281–87.

——. *Biblical Criticism in Crisis?: The Impact of the Canonical Approach on Old Testament Studies*. Cambridge: Cambridge University Press, 1991.

Brewer, David Instone. "1 Corinthians 9:9–11: A Literal Interpretation of 'Do not Muzzle the Ox.'" *New Testament Studies* 38 (1992): 554–65.

Brown, Raymond E. "All Gaul Is Divided: A Review Essay." *Union Seminary Quarterly Review* 40 (1985): 99–103.

——. *Biblical Exegesis and Church Doctrine.* New York: Paulist Press, 1985.

——. *The Birth of the Messiah.* Revised edition. New York: Doubleday, 1993.

——. *The Churches the Apostles Left Behind.* New York: Paulist Press, 1984.

——. *The Critical Meaning of the Bible.* New York: Paulist Press, 1981.

——. *The Death of the Messiah.* New York: Doubleday, 1994.

——. *The Epistles of John.* Garden City: Doubleday, 1982.

——. *The Gospel according to John.* Garden City: Doubleday, 1966–70.

——. "The *Gospel of Peter* and Canonical Gospel Priority." *New Testament Studies* 33 (1987): 321–43.

——. *An Introduction to New Testament Christology.* New York: Paulist Press, 1994.

——. *An Introduction to the New Testament.* New York: Doubleday, 1997.

——. *Priest and Bishop: Biblical Reflections.* Paramus: Paulist Press, 1970.

——. *The* Sensus Plenior *of Sacred Scripture.* Baltimore: St. Mary's University, 1955.

Brown, Raymond E., and Raymond F. Collins. "Canonicity." In *The New Jerome Biblical Commentary,* edited by Raymond E. Brown, Joseph A. Fitzmyer, and Roland E. Murphy. Englewood Cliffs: Prentice Hall, 1990.

Brown, Raymond E., with John P. Meier. *Antioch and Rome.* New York: Paulist Press, 1983.

Brown, Raymond E., and Sandra M. Schneiders. "Hermeneutics." In *The New Jerome Biblical Commentary,* edited by Raymond E. Brown, Joseph A. Fitzmyer, and Roland E. Murphy. Englewood Cliffs: Prentice Hall, 1990.

Brown, Raymond E., Joseph A. Fitzmyer, and Roland E. Murphy, eds. *The New Jerome Biblical Commentary.* Englewood Cliffs: Prentice Hall, 1990.

Brown, Raymond E., and Gustav Thils, eds. *Exégèse et théologie: Les Saintes Écritures et leur interprétation théologique.* Gembloux: J. Duculot, 1968.

Brueggeman, D. A. "Brevard Childs's Canon Criticism: An Example of Post-critical Naïveté." *Journal of the Evangelical Theological Society* 32 (1989): 311–26.

Brueggeman, Walter. "Against the Stream: Brevard Childs's Biblical Theology." *Theology Today* 50 (1993): 279–84.

——. *Interpretation and Obedience.* Minneapolis: Fortress Press, 1991.

Bultmann, Rudolf. *New Testament and Mythology and Other Basic Writings.* Edited and translated by Schubert M. Ogden. Philadelphia: Fortress Press, 1984.

Burghardt, Walter J. "On Early Christian Exegesis." *Theological Studies* 11 (1950): 78–116.

Burtchaell, James Tunstead. *Catholic Theories of Biblical Inspiration since 1810.* Cambridge: Cambridge University Press, 1969.

Cahill, Michael. "The History of Exegesis and Our Theological Future." *Theological Studies* 61 (2000): 332–47.

——. "Reader-Response Criticism and the Allegorizing Reader." *Theological Studies* 57 (1996): 89–96.

Carson, D. A., and G. M. Williamson, eds. *"It Is Written": Scripture Citing Scripture: Essays in Honor of Barnabas Lindars SSF.* Cambridge: Cambridge University Press, 1988.

Certeau, Michel de. "Exégèse, théologie, et spiritualité." *Revue d'ascétique et de mystique* 36 (1960): 357–71.

Ceuppens, F. "Quid S. Thomas de multiplici sensu litterali in Scriptura senserit?" *Divus Thomas* 33 (1930): 164–75.

Charlier, Celestin. "Exégèse patristique et exégèse scientifique." *Esprit et Vie* 2 (1949): 52–69.

——. *La lecture chrétienne de la Bible.* Paris: Editions de Maredsous, 1957.

——. "Typologie ou évolution, problèmes d'exégèse spirituelle." *Esprit et Vie* 2 (1949): 578–97.

Chenu, M.-D. *La théologie comme science au XIII siècle.* Paris: J. Vrin, 1957.

——. *Toward Understanding St. Thomas.* Translated by A. M. Landry and D. Hughes. Chicago: Regnery, 1964.

Childs, Brevard S. *Biblical Theology in Crisis.* Philadelphia: Westminster, 1970.

——. *Biblical Theology of the Old and New Testaments.* Minneapolis: Fortress Press, 1993.

——. *The Book of Exodus: A Critical, Theological Commentary.* Philadelphia: Westminster, 1974.

——. "Critical Reflections on James Barr's Understanding of the Literal and the Allegorical." *Journal for the Study of the Old Testament* 46 (1990): 3–9.

——. *Introduction to the Old Testament as Scripture.* Philadelphia: Fortress Press, 1979.

——. *Isaiah: A Commentary.* Louisville: Westminster John Knox, 2001.

——. *The New Testament as Canon: An Introduction.* Philadelphia: Fortress Press, 1985.

——. *Old Testament Theology in a Canonical Context.* Philadelphia: Fortress Press, 1985.

——. "Response to Reviewers of *Introduction to the Old Testament as Scripture.*" *Journal for the Study of the Old Testament* 16 (1980): 52–60.

——. "Some Reflections on the Search for a Biblical Theology." *Horizons in Biblical Theology* 4 (1982): 1–12.

Chilton, Bruce, and Craig A. Evans, eds. *Studying the Historical Jesus: Evaluations of the State of Current Research.* Leiden: E. J. Brill, 1994.

Clavier, H. "Remarques sur la méthode en théologie biblique." *Novum Testamentum* 14 (1972): 161–90.

Clifford, Richard J. Review of *Biblical Theology of the Old and New Testaments* by Brevard S. Childs. *Theological Studies* 54 (1993): 728–30.

Coakley, Sarah. *Christ without Absolutes: A Study of the Christology of Ernst Troeltsch.* New York: Oxford University Press, 1988.

Cohen, Shaye J. D. *From the Maccabees to the Mishnah.* Philadelphia: Westminster, 1987.

Cohn-Sherbok, Daniel. "Paul and Rabbinic Exegesis." *Scottish Journal of Theology* 35 (1982): 117–32.

Collingwood, R. G. *An Autobiography.* Oxford: Clarendon, 1978.

——. *The Idea of History.* Revised edition. Edited by Jan van der Dussen. Oxford: Oxford University Press, 1994.

Collins, J. J. "Historical Criticism and the State of Biblical Theology." *Christian Century* 110 (28 July 1993): 743–47.

Collins, Raymond F. "Augustine of Hippo, Precursor of Modern Biblical Scholarship." *Louvain Studies* 12 (1987): 131–51.

———. "Inspiration." In *The New Jerome Biblical Commentary,* edited by Raymond E. Brown, Joseph A. Fitzmyer, and Roland E. Murphy. Englewood Cliffs: Prentice Hall, 1990.

Congar, Yves. *I Believe in the Holy Spirit.* Translated by David Smith. New York: Crossroad, 1997.

Coppens, Joseph. "Nouvelles réflexions sur les divers sens des saintes Écritures." *Nouvelle revue theologique* 74 (1952): 3–20.

Croatto, J. Severino. *Biblical Hermeneutics: Toward a Theory of Reading as the Production of Meaning.* Translated by R. R. Barr. Maryknoll: Orbis, 1987.

———. "L'Herméneutique biblique en face des méthodes critiques: défi et perspectives." *Vetus Testamentum supplementum* 36 (1985): 67–80.

Crouzel, Henri. "La distinction de la 'typologie' et de l'"allégorie.'" *Bulletin de littérature ecclesiastique* 65 (1964): 161–74.

———. *Origen.* Translated by A. S. Worrall. San Francisco: Harper and Row, 1989.

———. "Origène et le sens littéral dans ses homélies sur l'Hexateuque." *Bulletin de littérature ecclesiastique* 70 (1969): 241–63.

Daley, Brian E. "Is Patristic Exegesis Still Usable?: Reflections on Early Christian Interpretation of the Psalms." *Communio* 29 (2002): 184–216.

Daly, Gabriel. *Transcendence and Immanence: A Study in Catholic Modernism and Integrism.* Oxford: Clarendon, 1980.

D'Ambrosio, Marcellino G. "Henri de Lubac and the Recovery of the Traditional Hermeneutic." Ph.D diss., The Catholic University of America, 1991.

Daniélou, Jean. "Les divers sens de l'Écriture dans la tradition chrétienne primitive." *Ephemerides theologicae Lovaniensis* 24 (1948): 199–226.

———."Exégèse et typologie patristiques." In *Dictionnaire de spiritualite: Ascetique et mystique, doctrine et histoire,* s.v. "Écriture Sainte et vie spirituelle." Paris: Beauchesne, 1960.

———. *Origen.* Translated by W. Mitchell. New York: Sheed and Ward, 1955.

Davis, C. "The Theological Career of Historical Criticism on the Bible." *Cross Currents* 32 (1982): 267–84.

Dawson, David. *Allegorical Readers and Cultural Revision in Ancient Alexandria.* Berkeley: University of California Press, 1992.

de la Potterie, Ignace. "Interpretation of Holy Scripture in the Spirit in Which It Was Written (*Dei Verbum* 12c)." In *Vatican II: Assessment and Perspectives: Twenty-Five Years After.* 3 vols. Edited by René Latourelle. Mahwah: Paulist Press, 1988.

———. "Reading Holy Scripture 'in the Spirit': Is the Patristic Way of Reading the Bible Still Possible Today?" *Communio* 14 (1986): 308–25.

———. "The Spiritual Sense of Scripture." *Communio* 23 (1996): 738–56.

———. "La vérité de l'Écriture et l'herméneutique biblique." *Revue theologique de Louvain* 18 (1987): 171–86.

de Lubac, Henri. *At the Service of the Church: Henri de Lubac Reflects on the Circumstances That Occasioned His Writings.* Translated by Anne Elizabeth Englund. San Francisco: Ignatius, 1993. Originally published as *Mémoire sur l'occasion de mes écrits* (Namur: Culture et vérité, 1989).

——. *Catholicism: Christ and the Common Destiny of Man.* Translated by Lancelot C. Sheppard and Elizabeth Englund. San Francisco: Ignatius, 1988. Originally published as *Catholicisme: Les aspects sociaux du dogme chrétien,* 4th ed. (Paris: Cerf, 1947).

——. *Corpus Mysticum: l'Eucharistie et l'Église au moyen age.* Paris: Aubier, 1944.

——. *L'Église dans la crise actuelle.* Paris: Cerf, 1969.

——. *Entretien autour de Vatican II: Souvenirs et réflexions.* Paris: Cerf, 1985.

——. *Exégèse Médiévale: Les quatre sens de l'Écriture.* 4 vols. Paris: Éditions Montaigne, 1959–64. Vols. 1 and 2 translated under the title *Medieval Exegesis: The Four Senses of Scripture.* 2 vols. Grand Rapids: Eerdmans, 1998–2000. Vol. 1 translated by Mark Sebanc. Vol. 2 translated by E. M. Macierowski.

——. "Hellenistic and Christian Allegory." In *Theological Fragments.* Translated by Rebecca Howell Balinski. San Francisco: Ignatius, 1989. Originally published as *Théologies d'occasion* (Paris: Desclée de Brouwer, 1984).

——. *Histoire et Esprit: l'Intelligence de l'Écriture d'après Origène.* Paris: Aubier, 1950.

——. *Meditation sur l'Église.* Paris: Aubier, 1955.

——. "On an Old Distich: The Doctrine of the 'Fourfold Sense' in Scripture." In *Theological Fragments.* Translated by Rebecca Howell Balinski. San Francisco: Ignatius, 1989. Originally published as *Théologies d'occasion* (Paris: Desclée de Brouwer, 1984).

——. "Le problème du développment du dogme." *Recherches de science religieuse* 35 (1948): 130–60.

——. "Pour le Christ et la Bible." *Vie spirituelle* 66 (June 1942): 542–50; 67 (1942): 200–212.

——. "Sens Spirituel." *Recherches de science religieuse* 36 (1949): 542–76.

——. *The Sources of Revelation.* Translated by Luke O'Neill. New York: Herder and Herder, 1968. Originally published as *L'Écriture dans la tradition* (Paris: Aubier, 1967).

——. *Surnaturel: Études historiques.* Paris: Aubier, 1946.

——. *Theological Fragments.* Translated by Rebecca Howell Balinski. San Francisco: Ignatius, 1989. Originally published as *Théologies d'occasion* (Paris: Desclée de Brouwer, 1984).

——. "Typology and Allegorization." In *Theological Fragments.* Translated by Rebecca Howell Balinski. San Francisco: Ignatius, 1989. Originally published as *Théologies d'occasion* (Paris: Desclée de Brouwer, 1984).

de Margerie, Bertrand. *Introduction a l'histoire de l'exégèse.* Paris: Cerf, 1980.

Devenish, Peter. "Can a Roman Catholic Be an Historian?" *Journal of Ecumenical Studies* 20 (1983): 67–85.

Dodd, C. H. *According to the Scriptures: The Sub-structure of New Testament Theology.* London: Nisbet, 1952.

Drescher, Hans-Georg. *Ernst Troeltsch: His Life and Work.* Translated by John Bowden. Minneapolis: Fortress Press, 1994.

Dreyfus, François. "L'actualisation de l'écriture." *Revue biblique* 86 (1979): 5–58, 161–93, 321–84.

——. "L'actualisation a l'intérieur de la Bible." *Revue biblique* 83 (1976): 161–202.

——. "Exégèse en Sorbonne, exégèse en Église." *Revue biblique* 82 (1975): 321–59.

Dubarle, A. M. "Le sens spirituel de l'Écriture." *Revue des science philosophiques et théologiques* 31 (1947): 41–72.
Duffy, Kevin. "The Ecclesial Hermeneutic of Raymond E. Brown." *Heythrop Journal of Theology* 39 (1998): 37–56.
Dulles, Avery. *Models of Revelation.* Maryknoll: Orbis, 1992.
——. Review of *Spiritual Exegesis and the Church in the Theology of Henri de Lubac* by Susan K. Wood. *Modern Theology* 16 (2000): 269–71.
Dumais, Marcel. "Sens de l'Écriture. Réexamen à la lumière de l'herméneutique philosophique et des approches littéraires récentes." *New Testament Studies* 45 (1999): 310–31.
Dunn, James D. G. "2 Corinthians III.17B 'The Lord is the Spirit.'" *Journal of Theological Studies* 21 (1970): 309–20.
——. *A Commentary on the Epistle to the Galatians.* London: A. C. Black, 1993.
——. *The Parting of the Ways.* London: SCM, 1991.
Edwards, O. C., Jr. "The Historical-Critical Method's Failure of Nerve and a Prescription for a Tonic: A Review of Some Recent Literature." *Ex auditu* 1 (1985): 92–105. First published in *Anglican Theological Review* 59 (1977): 115–34.
Ellis, E. Earle. *Paul's Use of the Old Testament.* Edinburgh: T and T Clark, 1957.
——. *Prophecy and Hermeneutic in Early Christianity.* Tubingen: J. C. B. Mohr, 1978.
Evans, Craig A., and James A. Sanders, eds. *Paul and the Scriptures of Israel.* Sheffield: Sheffield Academic Press, 1993.
Evans, Gillian R. *The Language and Logic of the Bible: The Earlier Middle Ages.* Cambridge: Cambridge University Press, 1984.
——. *The Language and Logic of the Bible: The Road to Reformation.* Cambridge: Cambridge University Press, 1985.
Farkasfalvy, Denis. "The Case for Spiritual Exegesis." *Communio* 10 (1983): 332–50.
——. "A Heritage in Search of Heirs: The Future of Ancient Christian Exegesis." *Communio* 25 (1998): 505–19.
——. "In Search of a 'Post-critical' Method of Biblical Interpretation for Catholic Theology." *Communio* 13 (1986): 287–307.
Fee, Gordon. *The First Epistle to the Corinthians.* Grand Rapids: Eerdmans, 1987.
——. *God's Empowering Presence: The Holy Spirit in the Letters of Paul.* Peabody, Mass.: Hendrickson Publishers, 1994.
Ferguson, D. S. *Biblical Hermeneutics: An Introduction.* Atlanta: John Knox, 1986.
Fernandez, A. "Sentido plenior, literal, típico, espiritual." *Biblica* 32 (1953): 299–326.
Fitzmyer, Joseph A. "The Biblical Commission and Christology." *Theological Studies* 46 (1985): 407–79.
——. *The Biblical Commission's Document "The Interpretation of the Bible in the Church": Text and Commentary.* Rome: Editrice Pontificio Istituto Biblico, 1995.
——. "Concerning the Interpretation of the Bible in the Church." *Josephinum Journal of Theology* 6 (1999): 5–20.
——. "Historical Criticism: Its Role in Biblical Interpretation and Church Life." *Theological Studies* 50 (1989): 244–59.

——. "The Interpretation of the Bible in the Church Today." *Irish Theological Quarterly* 62 (1996): 84–100.

——. "Problems of the Literal and Spiritual Senses of Scripture." *Louvain Studies* 20 (1995): 134–46.

——. *Romans.* New York: Doubleday, 1993.

——. *Scripture, the Soul of Theology.* New York: Paulist Press, 1994.

——. "The Senses of Scripture Today." *Irish Theological Quarterly* 62 (1996): 101–17.

Fitzmyer, Joseph A., and J. H. P. Reumann. "Scripture as Norm for Our Common Faith." *Journal of Ecumenical Studies* 30 (1993): 81–107.

Fogarty, Gerald P. *American Catholic Biblical Scholarship: A History from the Early Republic to Vatican II.* San Francisco: Harper and Row, 1989.

Fowl, Stephen E. "The Canonical Approach of Brevard Childs." *Expository Times* 96 (1985): 173–76.

——. *Engaging Scripture: A Model for Theological Interpretation.* Oxford: Blackwell, 1998.

——. "The Role of Authorial Intention in the Theological Interpretation of Scripture." In *Between Two Horizons: Spanning New Testament Studies and Systematic Theology,* edited by Joel B. Green and Max Turner. Grand Rapids: Eerdmans, 2000.

——. Review of *Is There a Meaning in This Text?* by Kevin J. Vanhoozer. *Modern Theology* 16 (2000): 260–62.

Friedman, R. E., and H. G. M. Williamson, eds. *The Future of Biblical Studies.* Atlanta: Scholars Press, 1987.

Froehlich, Karlfried. *Biblical Interpretation in the Early Church.* Philadelphia: Fortress Press, 1985.

Frye, Northrop. *The Great Code: The Bible and Literature.* New York: Harcourt Brace Jovanovich, 1982.

Funk, Robert W. *Honest to Jesus.* San Francisco: Harper Collins, 1996.

Furnish, Victor Paul. *II Corinthians.* New York: Doubleday, 1984.

Galvin, John P. "Jesus Christ." In *Systematic Theology: Roman Catholic Perspectives,* vol. 1, edited by Francis Schüssler Fiorenza and John P. Galvin. Minneapolis: Fortress Press, 1991.

——. Review of *The Humanist Christology of Paul* by Juan Luis Segundo. *Heythrop Journal of Theology* 30 (1989): 256–258.

Gamble, Harry. Review of *The New Testament as Canon* by Brevard S. Childs. *Journal of Biblical Literature* 106 (1987): 330–33.

Gaventa, Beverly Roberts. Review of *Engaging Scripture: A Model for Theological Interpretation* by Stephen E. Fowl. *Modern Theology* 16 (2000): 271–72.

Gifford, Paul. "The Critical Understanding of the Bible." *Downside Review* 105 (April 1987): 75–97.

Goppelt, Leonhard. *Typos: The Typological Interpretation of the Old Testament in the New.* Translated by Donald H. Madvig. Grand Rapids: Eerdmans, 1982.

Gottwald, Norman K., and R. A. Horsley, eds. *The Bible and Liberation.* Revised edition. Maryknoll: Orbis, 1993.

Gracia, Jorge J. E. *How Can We Know What God Means?: The Interpretation of Revelation.* New York: Palgrave Macmillan, 2001.

Grant, Robert M. *The Letter and the Spirit.* London: SPCK, 1957.

Grant, Robert M., with David Tracy. *A Short History of the Interpretation of the Bible*. Philadelphia: Fortress: 1984.

Green, Joel B., and Max Turner. "New Testament Commentary and Systematic Theology: Strangers or Friends?" In *Between Two Horizons: Spanning New Testament Studies and Systematic Theology*, edited by Joel B. Green and Max Turner. Grand Rapids: Eerdmans, 2000.

———. "Scripture and Theology: Uniting the Two So Long Divided." In *Between Two Horizons: Spanning New Testament Studies and Systematic Theology*, edited by Joel B. Green and Max Turner. Grand Rapids: Eerdmans, 2000.

Greene-McCreight, Kathryn. "'We Are Companions of the Patriarchs' or Scripture Absorbs Calvin's World." *Modern Theology* 14 (1998): 211–24.

Greenspahn, Frederick E. *Scripture in the Jewish and Christian Traditions: Authority, Interpretation, Relevance*. Nashville: Abingdon, 1982.

Greer, Rowan. "The Good Shepherd: Canonical Interpretations in the Early Church?" In *Theological Exegesis: Essays in Honor of Brevard S. Childs*, edited by Christopher Seitz and Kathryn Greene-McCreight. Grand Rapids: Eerdmans, 1999.

Gregory, Brad S. Introduction to *Tractatus Theologico-Politicus*, by Baruch Spinoza, translated by Samuel Shirley. Leiden: E. J. Brill, 1989.

Grelot, Pierre. *Bible et théologie: l'Ancienne Alliance et l'Écriture Sainte*. Paris: Desclée, 1965.

———. "L'exégèse biblique au carrefour." *Nouvelle revue théologique* 98 (1976): 416–34, 481–511.

———. *Sens chrétien de l'Ancien Testament*. Tournai: Desclée, 1962.

Gribomont, Jean. "Le lien des deux testaments selon la théologie de S. Thomas." *Ephemerides theologicae Lovaniensis* 22 (1946): 70–89.

———. "Sens plenier, sens typique et sens litteral." *Ephemerides theologicae Lovaniensis* 25 (1949): 577–87.

Grillmeier, Alois. "*Dei Verbum:* Chapter III." In *Commentary on the Documents of Vatican II*. Vol. 3. Edited by Herbert Vorgrimler. New York: Herder, 1969.

Guibal, Francis. "Existence, sens, Écriture(s): La théologie fondamentale d'un théologien de la libération (J.-L. Segundo)." *Études théologiques et religieuses* 74 (1999): 505–22.

Guillet, Jacques. "Les exégèses d'Alexandrie et d'Antioche: Conflit ou malentendu?" *Recherches de science religieuse* 34 (1947): 257–302.

Hafemann, Scott. "The Glory and Veil of Moses in 2 Cor. 3:7–14." *Horizons in Biblical Theology* 14 (1992): 31–49.

Hanson, A. T. *The Living Utterances of God: The New Testament Exegesis of the Old*. London: Darton, Longman and Todd, 1983.

———. "The Midrash in II Corinthians 3: A Reconsideration." *Journal for the Study of the New Testament* 9 (1980): 2–28.

———. *Studies in Paul's Technique and Theology*. London: SPCK, 1974.

Hanson, R. P. C. *Allegory and Event*. London: SCM, 1959.

———. *Origen's Doctrine of Tradition*. London: SPCK, 1954.

Harl, Marguerite. "Origène et les interpretations patristiques grecques de l''obscurité' biblique." *Vigiliae Christianae* 36 (1982): 334–71.

Harnack, Adolf. *What is Christianity?* Translated by T. B. Saunders. Philadelphia: Fortress Press, 1986.

Harrington, Wilfrid. *Revelation.* Collegeville, Minn.: Liturgical Press, 1993.

Harrisville, Roy A., and Walter Sundberg. *The Bible in Modern Culture: Baruch Spinoza to Brevard Childs.* 2nd edition. Grand Rapids: Eerdmans, 2002.

Hauck, Robert J. *The More Divine Proof: Prophecy and Inspiration in Celsus and Origen.* Atlanta: Scholars Press, 1989.

Hawthorne, Gerald F., with Otto Betz, eds. *Tradition and Interpretation in the New Testament.* Grand Rapids: Eerdmans, 1987.

Hays, Richard B. *Echoes of Scripture in the Letters of Paul.* New Haven: Yale University Press, 1989.

———. "Response to Robert Wilken, 'In Dominico Eloquio.'" *Communio* 25 (1998): 520–31.

Heine, R. E. "Gregory of Nyssa's Apology for Allegory." *Vigiliae Christianae* 38 (1984): 360–70.

Hengel, Martin. *Judaism and Hellenism.* 2nd edition. Translated by John Bowden. Minneapolis: Fortress Press, 1991.

Hengel, Martin, and Roland Deines. *The Pre-Christian Paul.* Translated by John Bowden. London: SCM, 1991.

Hennelly, Alfred T. "The Biblical Hermeneutics of Juan Luis Segundo." In *The Use of Scripture in Moral Theology,* edited by Charles Curran and Richard McCormick. New York: Paulist Press, 1984.

———. *Theologies in Conflict: the Challenge of Juan Luis Segundo.* Maryknoll: Orbis Books, 1979.

Henry, Carl F. H. "Canonical Theology: An Evangelical Appraisal." *Scottish Bulletin of Evangelical Theology* 8 (1990): 76–108.

Hooker, Morna D. "Beyond the Things That Are Written? St. Paul's Use of Scripture." *New Testament Studies* 27 (1980–81): 295–309.

Jewett, P. K. "Concerning the Allegorical Interpretation of Scripture." *Westminster Theological Journal* 17 (1954): 1–20.

Johnson, Luke Timothy. "The glass is Half Full/Empty." *Commonweal* (27 March 1998): 30.

———. "Imagining the World Scripture Imagines." *Modern Theology* 14 (1998): 165–80.

———. *The Real Jesus.* San Francisco: HarperCollins, 1996.

———. "So What's Catholic about It? The State of Catholic Biblical Scholarship." *Commonweal* (12 Jan. 1998): 12–16.

Johnson, Luke Timothy, and William S. Kurz. *The Future of Catholic Biblical Scholarship.* Grand Rapids: Eerdmans, 2002.

Johnson, Mark F. "Another Look at the Plurality of the Literal Sense." *Medieval Philosophy and Theology* 2 (1992): 117–41.

Journet, Charles. *Le Message révélé. Sa transmission, son développment, ses dépendences.* Paris: Desclée, 1964.

Jowett, Benjamin. "On the Quotations from the Old Testament in the Writings of St. Paul." In *The Epistles of St. Paul to the Thessalonians, Galatians, Romans, with Critical Notes and Dissertation.* London: J. Murray, 1859.

Juel, Donald. *Messianic Exegesis: Christological Interpretation of the Old Testament in Early Christianity.* Philadelpia: Fortress Press, 1988.

Kaiser, Walter C. *The Uses of the Old Testament in the New.* Chicago: University of Chicago Press, 1985.

Kannengiesser, Charles. *Holy Scripture and Hellenistic Hermeneutics in Alexandrian Christology: The Arian Chrisis.* Berkeley: University of California Press, 1982.

———. "Listening to the Fathers." *Communio* 16 (1989): 413–18.

Kannengiesser, Charles, and W. L. Petersen, eds. *Origen of Alexandria: His World and His Legacy.* Notre Dame: Notre Dame University Press, 1988.

Käsemann, Ernst. "The Spirit and the Letter." In *Perspectives on Paul.* Translated by Margaret Kohl. Philadelphia: Fortress Press, 1971.

Keegan, Terence. *Interpreting the Bible: A Popular Introduction to Biblical Hermeneutics.* New York: Paulist Press, 1985.

Kelly, George A. *The New Biblical Theorists: Raymond E. Brown and Beyond.* Ann Arbor: Servant Books, 1983.

Kelly, J. N. D. *Golden Mouth: The Story of John Chrysostom.* Ithaca: Cornell University Press, 1995.

———. *Jerome.* New York: Harper and Row, 1975.

Kelsey, David H. *The Uses of Scripture in Recent Theology.* Philadelphia: Fortress Press, 1975.

Kereszty, Roc. "Historical Research, Theological Inquiry, and the Reality of Jesus: Reflections on the Method of J. Meier." *Communio* 19 (1992): 576–600.

Komonchak, Joseph A. "Theology and Culture at Mid-Century: The Example of Henri de Lubac." *Theological Studies* 51 (1990): 579–602.

Krenz, Edgar. *The Historical-Critical Method.* Philadelphia: Fortress Press, 1975.

Kugel, James, and Rowan A. Greer, eds. *Early Biblical Interpretation.* Philadelphia: Fortress Press, 1988.

Kung, Hans, and Jurgen Moltmann, eds. *Conflicting Ways of Interpreting the Bible.* New York: Crossroad, 1980.

Kurz, William S., and Miller, Kevin E. "The Use of Scripture in the *Catechism of the Catholic Church.*" *Communio* 23 (1996): 480–507.

L'Homme devant Dieu: Mélanges offerts au Père de Lubac. Paris: Aubier, 1964.

L'Hour, Jean. "Pour une lecture 'catholique' de la Bible." *Biblical Interpretation* 5 (1998): 113–32.

Lagrange, M.-J. *Au service de la Bible.* Paris: Cerf, 1967.

———. "L'inspiration et les exigences de la critique." *Revue biblique* 5 (1896): 496–518.

Lampe, G. W. H., and K. J. Woolcombe, eds. *Essays on Typology.* Naperville, IL: A. R. Allenson, 1957.

Lang, Berel. "The Politics of Interpretation: Spinoza's Modernist Turn." *Review of Metaphysics* 43 (1989): 327–56.

Laurentin, René. *Comment reconciliet l'exégèse et la foi.* Paris: O.E.I.L., 1984.

Letellier, D. J. "La thème du voilé de Moïse, chez Origène: Exode 32:33–35 et 2 Corinthiens 3:12–18." *Recherches de sciences religieuses* 62 (1988): 14–26.

Letis, T. "Brevard Childs and the Protestant Dogmaticians: A Window to a New Paradigm of Biblical Interpretation." *Churchman* 105 (1991): 261–77.

Levenson, Jon. *The Hebrew Bible, the Old Testament, and Historical Criticism.* Louisville: Westminster/John Knox, 1993.

Levie, Jean. *La Bible, parole humaine et message de Dieu.* Paris: Desclée, 1958.

Lindbeck, George A. *The Nature of Doctrine: Religion and Theology in a Postliberal Age.* Philadelphia: Fortress Press, 1984.

———. "Postcritical Canonical Interpretation: Three Modes of Retrieval." In *Theological Exegesis: Essays in Honor of Brevard S. Childs,* edited by Christopher Seitz and Kathryn Greene-McCreight. Grand Rapids: Eerdmans, 1999.

Llanes Maestre, J. L. "La teología como saber de totalidad: En torno al proyecto teológico de Henri de Lubac." *Revista española de teologia* 48 (1988): 149–92.

Loewe, William. "From the Humanity of Christ to the Historical Jesus." *Theological Studies* 61 (2000): 314–31.

Lonergan, Bernard. *Method in Theology.* Toronto: University of Toronto Press, 1990.

Longenecker, Richard N. *Biblical Exegesis in the Apostolic Period.* Grand Rapids: Eerdmans, 1975.

Louth, Andrew. *Discerning the Mystery: An Essay on the Nature of Theology.* Oxford: Oxford University Press, 1983.

Lull, Timothy F. "Why Does Childs Matter?" *Dialog* 33 (1994): 85–98.

Maier, Gerhard. *The End of the Historical-Critical Method.* Translated by Edwin W. Leverenz and Rudolf F. Norden. St. Louis: Concordia, 1977.

Mailhiot, M. D. "La pensée de S. Thomas sur le sens spirituel." *Revue Thomiste* 59 (1959): 613–63.

Malet, A. *La traité théologico-politique de Spinoza et la pensée biblique.* Paris: Société Les Belles Lettres, 1966.

Marks, Herbert. "Pauline Typology and Revisionary Criticism." *Journal of the American Academy of Religion* 52 (1984): 71–92.

Markus, R. A. "Presuppositions of the Typological Approach to Scripture." *Church Quarterly Review* 158 (1957): 442–51.

Marlé, René. "Foi, idéologie, religion chez J.-L. Segundo." *Recherches de sciences religieuses* 76 (1988): 267–82.

Martin, Francis. "Literary Theory, Philosophy of History, and Exegesis." *Thomist* 52 (1988): 575–604.

———. "St. Matthew's Spiritual Understanding of the Healing of the Centurion's Boy." *Communio* 25 (1998): 160–77.

Martyn, J. L. "Listening to John and Paul on the Subject of Gospel and Scripture." *Word and World* 12 (1992): 68–81.

Mayeski, Marie Anne. "Quaestio Disputata: Catholic Theology and the History of Exegesis." *Theological Studies* 62 (2001): 140–53.

McCartney, Dan G. "Literal and Allegorical Interpretation in Origen's *Contra Celsum.*" *Westminster Theological Journal* 48 (1986): 281–301.

McEvenue, Sean E. *Interpretation and Bible: Essays on Truth in Literature.* Collegeville, Minn.: Liturgical Press, 1994.

McFarland, Ian A. "Who Is my Neighbor?: The Good Samaritan as a Source for Theological Anthropology." *Modern Theology* 17 (2001): 57–66.

McGovern, Arthur F. *Liberation Theology and Its Critics.* Maryknoll: Orbis Books, 1989.

McGuckin, Terence. "Saint Thomas Aquinas and Theological Exegesis of Sacred Scripture." *Louvain Studies* 16 (1991): 99–120.

McKenzie, John L. "A Chapter in the History of Spiritual Exegesis: De Lubac's *Histoire et Esprit.*" *Theological Studies* 12 (1951): 365–81.

——. "Problems of Hermeneutics in Roman Catholic Exegesis." *Journal of Biblical Literature* 77 (1958): 197–204.

——. "The Significance of the Old Testament for Christian Faith in Roman Catholicism." In *The Old Testament and Christian Faith,* edited by Bernhard Anderson. New York: Herder and Herder, 1969.

McKim, Donald K., ed. *A Guide to Contemporary Hermeneutics: Major Trends in Biblical Interpretation.* Grand Rapids: Eerdmans, 1986.

McNally, R. E. "Medieval Exegesis." *Theological Studies* 22 (1961): 445–54.

Meier, John P. "The Bible as a Source for Theology." *Proceedings of the Catholic Theological Society of America* 43 (1988): 1–14.

——. "The Brothers and Sisters of Jesus in Ecumenical Perspective." *Catholic Biblical Quarterly* 54 (1992): 1–28.

——. "Jesus among the Theologians." In *The Mission of Christ and His Church.* Wilmington, Del.: Michael Glazier, 1990.

——. *A Marginal Jew.* Vol. 1, *The Roots of the Problem and the Person.* New York: Doubleday, 1991.

——. *A Marginal Jew.* Vol. 2, *Mentor, Message, and Miracles.* New York: Doubleday, 1994.

——. *The Mission of Christ and His Church.* Wilmington, Del.: Michael Glazier, 1990.

——. "On the Veiling of Hermeneutics (1 Cor 11:2–16)." *Catholic Biblical Quarterly* 40 (1978): 212–26.

Metzger, Bruce M. *The Canon of the New Testament: Its Origin, Development, and Significance.* Oxford: Oxford University Press, 1987.

Meyer, Ben F. *The Aims of Jesus.* London: SCM, 1979.

——. "Conversion and the Hermeneutics of Consent." *Ex auditu* 1 (1985): 36–46.

——. "Jesus' Ministry and Self-understanding." In *Studying the Historical Jesus: Evaluations of the State of Current Research,* edited by Bruce Chilton and C. A. Evans. Leiden: E. J. Brill, 1994.

——. "The Primacy of the Intended Sense of Texts." In *Lonergan's Hermeneutics,* edited by Ben F. Meyer and Sean E. McEvenue. Washington, D.C.: Catholic University of America Press, 1989.

——. *Reality and Illusion in New Testament Scholarship.* Collegeville, Minn.: Liturgical Press, 1994.

——. "The Relevance of 'Horizon.'" *Downside Review* 112 (1994): 1–14.

Meyer, Ben F., and Sean E. McEvenue, eds. *Lonergan's Hermeneutics.* Washington, D.C.: Catholic University Press, 1989.

Meynell, Hugo. "The Great Code and the Christian Faith." In Ben F. Meyer and Sean E. McEvenue, eds. *Lonergan's Hermeneutics.* Washington, D.C.: Catholic University of America Press, 1989.

Miguens, Manuel. "The Infancy Narratives and Critical Biblical Method." *Communio* 7 (1980): 23–54.

Moberly, R. W. L. "The Church's Use of the Bible: The Work of Brevard Childs." *Expository Times* 99 (1988): 104–9.

Molina, Mario A. "La revoción del velo o el acceso a la libertad: Ensayo hermeneutico." *Estudios biblicos* 41 (1983): 285–324.

Morgan, Robert, with John Barton. *Biblical Interpretation.* Oxford: Oxford University Press, 1988.

Munitiz, Joseph A. Review of *The Christ of the Ignatian Exercises* by Juan Luis Segundo. *Heythrop Journal of Theology* 30 (1989): 257–60.

Murphy, Roland. "Quaestio Disputata: Is the Paschal Mystery Really the Primary Hermeneutical Principle?" *Theological Studies* 61 (2000): 139–46.

———. "What Is Catholic about Catholic Biblical Scholarship?—Revisited." *Biblical Theology Bulletin* (1998): 112–19.

Murphy, William F. "Henri de Lubac's Mystical Tropology." *Communio* 27 (2000): 171–201.

Murphy-O'Connor, Jerome. "The First Letter to the Corinthians." In *The New Jerome Biblical Commentary,* edited by Raymond E. Brown, Joseph A. Fitzmyer, and Roland E. Murphy. Englewood Cliffs: Prentice Hall, 1990.

Nardoni, Enrique. "Origen's Concept of Biblical Inspiration." *Second Century* 4 (1984): 9–23.

Nations, Archie L. "Historical Criticism and the Current Methodological Crisis." *Ex auditu* 1 (1985): 125–32. First published in *Scottish Journal of Theology* 36 (1983): 59–72.

Nautin, Pierre. *Origène: Sa vie et son oeuvre.* Paris: Beauchesne, 1977.

Neill, Stephen, and N. T. Wright. *The Interpretation of the New Testament 1861–1986.* Oxford: Oxford University Press, 1988.

Neuhaus, Richard John, ed. *Biblical Interpretation in Crisis.* Grand Rapids: Eerdmans, 1989.

———. "The Historically Verifiable Jesus." *First Things* 51 (March 1995): 70–71.

Newman, John Henry. *An Essay on the Development of Christian Doctrine.* Notre Dame: University of Notre Dame Press, 1989.

Nickle, K. F. "More about Jesus Would I Know." *Theology Today* 49 (1992): 398–407.

Nietzsche, Friedrich. *On the Advantage and Disadvantage of History for Life.* Translated by Peter Preuss. Indianapolis: Hackett, 1980.

Nilson, Jon. "A Response to John Meier." *Proceedings of the Catholic Theological Society of America* 43 (1988): 15–18.

Noble, Paul R. *The Canonical Approach: A Critical Reconstruction of the Hermeneutics of Brevard S. Childs.* Leiden: E. J. Brill, 1995.

———. "The *sensus literalis:* Jowett, Childs, and Barr." *Journal of Theological Studies* 44 (1993): 1–23.

Ocker, Christopher. "Medieval Exegesis and the Origin of Hermeneutics." *Scottish Journal of Theology* 52 (1999): 328–45.

O'Collins, Gerald, and Daniel Kendall. *The Bible for Theology: Ten Principles for the Theological Use of Scripture.* Mahwah: Paulist Press, 1997.

O'Connor, M. "How the Text Is Heard: The Biblical Theology of Brevard Childs." *Religious Studies Review* 21 (1995): 91–95.

Okure, Teresa. "'I Will Open My Mouth in Parables' (Matt. 13.35): A Case for a Gospel-Based Biblical Hermeneutics." *New Testament Studies* 46 (2000): 445–63.

Olsen, Glenn W. "Allegory, Typology, and Symbol: the *Sensus Spiritualis.*" *Communio* 4 (1977): 161–79.

Pépin, Jean. *Mythe et Allégorie: Les origines grecques et les contestations judeo-chrétiennes.* Paris: Éditions Montaigne, 1958.

——. *La tradition de l'allégorie de Philon d'Alexandrie à Dante.* Paris: Études Augustiniennes, 1987.

Perkins, Pheme. "The Gospel according to John." In *The New Jerome Biblical Commentary,* edited by Raymond E. Brown, Joseph A. Fitzmyer, and Roland E. Murphy. Englewood Cliffs: Prentice Hall, 1990.

Persson, Per Erik. *Sacra Doctrina: Reason and Revelation in Aquinas.* Oxford: Oxford University Press, 1970.

Pesch, Otto Hermann. "Paul as Professor of Theology: The Image of the Apostle in St. Thomas's Theology." *Thomist* 38 (1974): 584–605.

Phan, Peter. "Method in Liberation Theologies." *Theological Studies* 61 (2000): 40–63.

Plantinga, Alvin. "Two (or More) Kinds of Scripture Scholarship." *Modern Theology* 14 (1998): 243–78.

Pontifical Biblical Commission. *The Interpretation of the Bible in the Church.* Boston: St. Paul Books and Media, 1993.

——. *The Jewish People and Their Sacred Scriptures in the Christian Bible.* Boston: St. Paul Books and Media, 2001.

Pope-Levison, P., and J. R. Levison. *Jesus in Global Contexts.* Louisville: Westminster/John Knox, 1993.

Popkin, Richard H. "Spinoza and Bible Scholarship." In *The Cambridge Companion to Spinoza,* edited by Don Garrett. Cambridge: Cambridge University Press, 1996.

Poythress, V. S. "Divine Meaning of Scripture." *Westminster Theological Journal* 48 (1986): 241–79.

Preus, J. Samuel. *Spinoza and the Irrelevance of Biblical Authority.* Cambridge: Cambridge University Press, 2001.

Provan, Iain. "Canons to the Left of Him: Brevard Childs, His Critics, and the Future of Old Testament Theology." *Scottish Journal of Theology* 50 (1997): 1–38.

Quesnell, Quentin. "Mutual Misunderstanding: The Dialectic of Contemporary Hermeneutics." In *Lonergan's Hermeneutics,* edited by Ben F. Meyer and Sean E. McEvenue. Washington, D.C.: Catholic University of America Press, 1989.

Rahner, Karl. "Exegesis and Dogmatic Theology." In *Theological Investigations,* vol. 5. Baltimore: Helicon, 1966.

——. *Foundations of Christian Faith.* Translated by William V. Dych. New York: Crossroad, 1978.

——. *Inspiration in the Bible.* Translated by Charles H. Henkey. New York: Herder and Herder, 1961.

Ramlot, L. "Les sens de l'Écriture." *Bible et vie chrétienne* 73 (1967): 79–85.

Refoule, F. "L'Exégèse en question." *Le Supplement* 111 (1974): 391–423.

Reid, J. K. S. *The Authority of Scripture: A Study of the Reformation and Post-Reformation Understanding of the Bible.* New York: Methuen, 1957.

Rendtorff, Rolf. *Canon and Theology.* Translated and edited by Margaret Kohl. Minneapolis: Fortress Press, 1993.

Richard, Earl. "Polemics, Old Testament, and Theology: A Study of II Cor., III.1–IV.6." *Revue biblique* 88 (1981): 340–67.

Rist, John. *Augustine: Ancient Thought Baptized.* New York: Cambridge University Press, 1994.

Robinson, Robert Bruce. *Roman Catholic Exegesis since* Divino Afflante Spiritu: *Hermeneutical Implications.* Atlanta: Scholars Press, 1988.

Roques, René. Review of *Exégèse Médiévale* by Henri de Lubac. *Revue de l'histoire des religions* 158 (1960): 204–19.

Rowland, Christopher, and Mark Corner. *Liberating Exegesis.* Louisville: Westminster/John Knox, 1989.

Sakenfeld, Katharine D. Review of *The Book of Exodus* by Brevard S. Childs. *Theology Today* 31 (1975): 275–79.

Sanders, E. P. *Judaism: Practice and Belief, 63 BCE–66 CE.* London: SCM, 1992.

———. *Paul and Palestinian Judaism.* Philadelphia: Fortress Press, 1977.

Sanders, James A. "Canon, OT." In *Anchor Bible Dictionary,* s.v.

———. *From Sacred Story to Sacred Text.* Philadelphia: Fortress Press, 1987.

———. Review of *The Book of Exodus* by Brevard S. Childs. *Journal of Biblical Literature* 95 (1976): 285–90.

Sandmel, Samuel. *Judaism and Christian Beginnings.* New York: Oxford University Press, 1978.

Sawyer, John F. A. *The Fifth Gospel: Isaiah in the History of Christianity.* New York: Cambridge University Press, 1996.

Scalise, Charles J. "Allegorical Flights of Fancy: The Problem of Origen's Exegesis." *Greek Orthodox Theological Review* 32 (1987): 69–88.

———. "Canonical Hermeneutics: Childs and Barth." *Scottish Journal of Theology* 47 (1994): 61–88.

———. *Hermeneutics as Theological Prolegomena: A Canonical Approach.* Macon: Mercer University Press 1994.

———. "The 'Sensus Literalis': A Hermeneutical Key to Biblical Exegesis." *Scottish Journal of Theology* 42 (1989): 45–65.

Schneiders, Sandra. "Faith, Hermeneutics, and the Literal Sense of Scripture." *Theological Studies* 39 (1978): 719–36.

———. "From Exegesis to Hermeneutics: The Problem of the Contemporary Meaning of Scripture." *Horizons* 8 (1981): 23–39.

———. "The Paschal Imagination: Objectivity and Subjectivity in New Testament Interpretation." *Theological Studies* 43 (1982): 52–68.

———. *The Revelatory Text: Interpreting the New Testament as Sacred Scripture.* 2nd edition. Collegeville, Minn.: Liturgical Press, 1999.

Schottroff, Luise, and Wolfgang Stegemann. *Jesus and the Hope of the Poor.* Maryknoll: Orbis, 1986.

———, eds. *God of the Lowly: Socio-Historical Interpretation of the Bible.* Maryknoll: Orbis, 1984.

Schüssler Fiorenza, Francis, and John P. Galvin, eds. *Systematic Theology: Roman Catholic Perspectives.* Minneapolis: Fortress Press, 1991.

Segal, Alan F. *Paul the Convert.* New Haven: Yale University Press, 1990.

Segundo, Juan Luis. *Jesus of Nazareth Yesterday and Today.* Vol. 1, *Faith and Ideologies.* Translated and edited by John Drury. Maryknoll: Orbis, 1984. Originally published as *El hombre de hoy ante Jesus de Nazaret* (Madrid: Ediciones Cristiandad, 1982).

——. *Jesus of Nazareth Yesterday and Today.* Vol. 2, *The Historical Jesus of the Synoptics.* Translated and edited by John Drury. Maryknoll: Orbis, 1985. Originally published as *El hombre de hoy ante Jesus de Nazaret* (Madrid: Ediciones Cristiandad, 1982).

——. *Jesus of Nazareth Yesterday and Today.* Vol. 3, *The Humanist Christology of Paul.* Translated and edited by John Drury. Maryknoll: Orbis, 1986. Originally published as *El hombre de hoy ante Jesus de Nazaret* (Madrid: Ediciones Cristiandad, 1982).

——. *Jesus of Nazareth Yesterday and Today.* Vol. 4, *The Christ of the Ignatian Exercises.* Translated and edited by John Drury. Maryknoll: Orbis, 1987. Originally published as *El hombre de hoy ante Jesus de Nazaret* (Madrid: Ediciones Cristiandad, 1982).

——. *Jesus of Nazareth Yesterday and Today.* Vol. 5, *An Evolutionary Approach to Jesus of Nazareth.* Translated and edited by John Drury. Maryknoll: Orbis, 1988. Originally published as *El hombre de hoy ante Jesus de Nazaret* (Madrid: Ediciones Cristiandad, 1982).

——. *The Liberation of Dogma: Faith, Revelation, and Dogmatic Teaching Authority.* Translated by Phillip Berryman. Maryknoll: Orbis, 1992. Originally published as *El dogma que libera: Fe, revelación y magisterio dogmatico* (Santander: Editorial Sal Terrae, 1989).

——. *The Liberation of Theology.* Translated by John Drury. Maryknoll: Orbis, 1976. Originally published as *Liberación de la teología* (Buenos Aires: Ediciones C. Lohlé 1975).

——. *Teología abierta para el laico adulto.* 4 vols. Madrid: Ediciones Cristiandad, 1983.

——. *Theology and the Church: A Response to Cardinal Ratzinger and a Warning to the Whole Church.* Translated by John W. Diercksmeier. San Francisco: Harper and Row, 1987. Originally published as *Teología de la liberación: Respuesta al Cardenal Ratzinger* (Madrid: Ediciones Cristiandad, 1985).

Seitz, Christopher. "Old Testament or Hebrew Bible: Some Theological Considerations." *Pro ecclesia* 5 (1996): 292–303.

Shin, Daniel. "Some Light from Origen: Scripture as Sacrament." *Worship* 73 (1999): 399–425.

Simonetti, Manlio. *Biblical Interpretation in the Early Church.* Edited by Anders Bergquist and Markus Bockmuehl. Translated by John A. Hughes. Edinburgh: T and T Clark, 1994.

Smalley, Beryl. *The Study of the Bible in the Middle Ages.* Notre Dame: Notre Dame University Press, 1964.

Spicq, Ceslaus. *Esquisse d'une histoire de l'exégèse latine au moyen age.* Paris: J. Vrin, 1944.

Spinoza, Baruch. *Tractatus Theologico-Politicus.* Translated by Samuel Shirley. Leiden: E. J. Brill, 1989.

Steiner, George. Review of *The Literary Guide to the Bible* by Robert Alter and Frank Kermode. *New Yorker* (January 11, 1988): 94–98.

Steinmetz, David C. "The Superiority of Precritical Exegesis." In *The Theological Interpretation of Scripture,* edited by Stephen E. Fowl. Oxford: Blackwell, 1997. First published in *Theology Today* 37 (1980): 27–38.

Strauss, Leo. *Spinoza's Critique of Religion*. New York: Schocken, 1965.

Stuhlmacher, Peter. "The Hermeneutical Significance of 1 Cor. 2:6–16." In *Tradition and Interpretation in the New Testament,* edited by Gerald F. Hawthorne and Otto Betz. Grand Rapids: Eerdmans, 1987.

——. *Historical Criticism and Theological Interpretation of Scripture.* Translated by Roy A. Harrisville. Philadelphia: Fortress Press, 1977.

Stump, Eleonore. "Visits to the Sepulchre and Biblical Exegesis." *Faith and Philosophy* 6 (1989): 353–77.

Sullivan, Francis A. *From Apostles to Bishops: The Development of the Episcopacy in the Early Church.* New York: Paulist Press, 2001.

Swiezawski, Waclaw. "L'exégèse biblique et la théologie speculative de S. Thomas d'Aquin." *Divinitas* 18 (1974): 138–53.

Synave, P. "La doctrine de Saint Thomas d'Aquin sur le sens littéral des Écritures." *Revue biblique* 35 (1926): 40–65.

Tabet, M. A. "El uso de las ciencias humanas en la hermenéutica biblica según la doctrina de Santo Thomas." *Euntes docetes* 33 (1980): 427–55.

Tambasco, Anthony J. *The Bible for Ethics: Juan Luis Segundo and First-World Ethics.* College Park, Md.: University Press of America, 1981.

Tavard, George H. *Holy Writ or Holy Church?* New York: Harper, 1959.

——. Review of *L'Écriture dans la Tradition* by Henri de Lubac. *Theological Studies* 30 (1969): 332–34.

Thiselton, Anthony C. *New Horizons in Hermeneutics*. Grand Rapids: Eerdmans, 1992.

——. *The Two Horizons.* Grand Rapids: Eerdmans, 1980.

Toinet, P. "Permanence de la foi et exégèse historico-critique." *Revue Thomiste* 82 (1982): 40–78, 575–602.

Topping, R. R. "The Canon and the Truth: Brevard Childs and James Barr on the Canon and the Historical-Critical Method." *Toronto Journal of Theology* 8 (1992): 239–60.

Torjesen, Karen Jo. "'Body,' 'Soul,' and 'Spirit' in Origen's Theory of Exegesis." *Anglican Theological Review* 67 (1985): 17–30.

Torrance, T. F. "Scientific Hermeneutics according to St. Thomas Aquinas." *Journal of Theological Studies* 13 (1962): 259–89.

Torrell, Jean-Pierre. *Saint Thomas Aquinas: The Person and His Work.* Translated by Robert Royal. Washington, D.C.: Catholic University of America Press, 1996.

Tracy, David. "On Reading the Scriptures Theologically." In *Theology and Dialogue: Essays in Conversation with George Lindbeck,* edited by Bruce D. Marshall. Notre Dame: University of Notre Dame Press, 1990.

Trigg, Joseph W., ed. *Biblical Interpretation.* Wilmington, Del.: Michael Glazier, 1988.

——. "The Charismatic Intellectual: Origen's Understanding of Religious Leadership." *Church History* 50 (1981): 5–19.

——. *Origen.* Atlanta: Scholars Press, 1983.

Troeltsch, Ernst. *Religion in History.* Translated by James Luther Adams and Walter F. Bense. Minneapolis: Fortress Press, 1991.

Turner, Max. "Historical Criticism and Theological Hermeneutics of the New

Testament." In *Between Two Horizons: Spanning New Testament Studies and Systematic Theology,* edited by Joel B. Green and Max Turner. Grand Rapids: Eerdmans, 2000.

Uffenheimer, Benjamin, and Henning Graf von Reventlow, eds. *Creative Biblical Exegesis: Christian and Jewish Hermeneutics through the Centuries.* Sheffield: JSOT, 1988.

Vander Gucht, Robert, and Herbert Vorgrimler, eds. *Bilan de la théologie du XX*[e] siècle. Paris: Casterman, 1970.

Van der Ploeg, J. "The Place of Holy Scripture in the Theology of St. Thomas." *Thomist* 10 (1947): 398–422.

Vanhoozer, Kevin J. *Is There a Meaning in This Text?: The Bible, the Reader, and the Morality of Literary Knowledge.* Grand Rapids: Zondervan, 1998.

Vanni, Ugo. "Exegesis and Actualization in the Light of *Dei Verbum.*" In *Vatican II: Assessment and Perspectives: Twenty-Five Years After.* 3 vols. Edited by René Latourelle. Mahwah: Paulist Press, 1988.

Vatican II: The Conciliar and Post-Conciliar Documents. Edited by Austin Flannery OP. Northport, NY: Costello, 1987.

Vauchez, Andre. *The Spirituality of the Medieval West.* Kalamazoo: Cistercian Publications, 1993.

Verkamp, Bernard J. "On Doing the Truth: Orthopraxis and the Theologian." *Theological Studies* 49 (1988): 3–24.

Vogels, W. "Les limites de la méthode historico-critique." *Laval theologique philosophique* 36 (1980): 173–94.

von Balthasar, Hans Urs, and Georges Chantraine. *Le Cardinal Henri de Lubac: l'Homme et son oeuvre.* Paris: Editions Lethielleux, 1983.

von Campenhausen, Hans. *Formation of the Christian Bible.* Translated by J. A. Baker. Philadelphia: Fortress Press, 1972.

von Rad, Gerhard. "Typological Interpretation of the Old Testament." *Interpretation* 15 (1961): 174–92.

von Reventlow, Henning Graf. *Problems of Biblical Theology in the Twentieth Century.* Philadelphia: Fortress Press, 1986.

Vorgrimler, Herbert, ed. *Commentary on the Documents of Vatican II.* Translated by Lalit Adolphus et al. New York: Crossroad, 1969.

Ward, Graham. "Allegoria: Reading as a Spiritual Exercise." *Modern Theology* 15 (1999): 271–95.

Weisheipl, James. *Friar Thomas D'Aquino: His Life, Thought, and Works.* Washington, D.C.: Catholic University of America Press, 1983.

Wells, Harold. "The Question of Ideological Determination in Liberation Theology." *Toronto Journal of Theology* 3 (1987): 209–20.

Wicks, Jared. "Biblical Criticism Criticized." *Gregorianum* 72 (1991): 117–28.

Wilken, Robert Louis. "In Defense of Allegory." *Modern Theology* 14 (1998): 197–212.

———. "*In Dominico Eloquio:* Learning the Lord's Style of Language." *Communio* 24 (1997): 846–66.

———. "Interpreting Job Allegorically: The Moralia of Gregory the Great." *Pro ecclesia* 10 (2001): 213–26.

Williams, Rowan. "The Literal Sense of Scripture." *Modern Theology* 7 (1991): 121–34.

Williamson, Peter S. "Actualization: A New Emphasis in Catholic Scripture Study." *America* (May 20, 1995): 17–19.

———. "Catholicism and the Bible: An Interview with Albert Vanhoye." *First Things* (June/July 1997): 35–40.

———. *Catholic Principles for Interpreting Scripture: A Study of the Pontifical Biblical Commission's* The Interpretation of the Bible in the Church. Rome: Editrice Pontificio Istituto Biblico, 2001.

Witherington, Ben. *The Jesus Quest: The Third Search for the Jew of Nazareth.* Downers Grove: InterVarsity, 1995.

Wolterstorff, Nicholas. *Divine Discourse: Philosophical Reflections on the Claim That God Speaks.* Cambridge: Cambridge University Press, 1995.

Wood, Susan K. *Spiritual Exegesis and the Church in the Theology of Henri de Lubac.* Grand Rapids: Eerdmans, 1998.

Woodbridge, John D. "Richard Simon le 'père de la critique biblique.'" In *Le Grand Siècle et la Bible,* edited by J.-R. Armogathe. Paris: Beauchesne, 1989.

Wright, N. T. *Jesus and the Victory of God.* Minneapolis: Fortress Press, 1996.

———. *The New Testament and the People of God.* Minneapolis: Fortress Press, 1992.

———. "The New Unimproved Jesus." *Christianity Today* 37 (13 Sept. 1993): 22–26.

———. *The Resurrection of the Son of God.* Minneapolis: Fortress Press, 2003.

Young, Frances M. *Biblical Exegesis and the Formation of Christian Culture.* Cambridge: Cambridge University Press, 1997.

Young, Robin Darling. "Ancient Culture and the Shape of Early Christian Discipleship." *Communio* 25 (1998): 150–59.

———. "*Theologia* in the Early Church." *Communio* 24 (1997): 681–90.

Yovel, Yirmiyahu. *The Marrano of Reason.* Vol. 1 of *Spinoza and Other Heretics.* Princeton: Princeton University Press, 1989.

Zarb, S. M. "Unité ou multiplicité des sens littéraux dans la Bible?" *Revue Thomiste* 37 (1932): 251–300.

INDEX

Receiving the Bible in Faith: Historical and Theological Exegesis was designed and composed in Galliard by Kachergis Book Design, Pittsboro, North Carolina; and printed on 60-pound Dexter Offset Natural and bound by Thomson-Shore, Inc., Dexter, Michigan.

www.ingramcontent.com/pod-product-compliance
Lightning Source LLC
LaVergne TN
LVHW041113090826
844660LV00062B/890/J

* 9 7 8 0 8 1 3 2 1 3 7 5 0 *